CONFESSING
THE CHURCH

PROCEEDINGS OF THE LOS ANGELES THEOLOGY CONFERENCE

This is the ninth volume in a series published by Zondervan Academic. It is the proceedings of the Los Angeles Theology Conference held under the auspices of Biola University in March 2023. The conference is an attempt to do several things. First, it provides a regional forum in which scholars, students, and clergy can come together to discuss and reflect upon central doctrinal claims of the Christian faith. It is also an ecumenical endeavor. Bringing together theologians from a number of different schools and confessions, the LATC seeks to foster serious engagement with Scripture and tradition in a spirit of collegial dialogue (and disagreement), looking to retrieve the best of the Christian past in order to forge theology for the future. Finally, each volume in the series focuses on a central topic in dogmatic theology. It is hoped that this endeavor will continue to fructify contemporary systematic theology and foster a greater understanding of the historic Christian faith amongst the members of its different communions.

LOS ANGELES
THEOLOGY
CONFERENCE

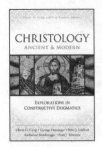

CHRISTOLOGY,
ANCIENT AND MODERN:
Explorations in Constructive
Dogmatics, 2013

ADVANCING
TRINITARIAN THEOLOGY:
Explorations in Constructive
Dogmatics, 2014

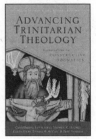

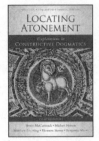

LOCATING ATONEMENT:
Explorations in Constructive
Dogmatics, 2015

THE VOICE OF GOD IN
THE TEXT OF SCRIPTURE:
Explorations in Constructive
Dogmatics, 2016

THE TASK OF DOGMATICS:
Explorations in Theological
Method, 2017

THE CHRISTIAN
DOCTRINE OF HUMANITY:
Explorations in Constructive
Dogmatics, 2018

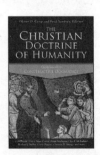

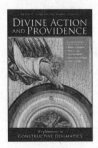

DIVINE ACTION
AND PROVIDENCE:
Explorations in Constructive
Dogmatics, 2019

THE THIRD PERSON
OF THE TRINITY:
Explorations in Constructive
Dogmatics, 2020

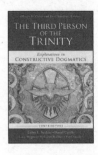

Oliver D. Crisp *and* Fred Sanders, Editors

CONFESSING
THE CHURCH

Explorations in
CONSTRUCTIVE DOGMATICS

— CONTRIBUTORS —

Natalie Carnes • Millard Erickson • Tom Greggs •
Jennifer Powell McNutt • Paul T. Nimmo

ZONDERVAN ACADEMIC

Confessing the Church
Copyright © 2024 by Oliver D. Crisp and Fred Sanders

Published in Grand Rapids, Michigan, by Zondervan. Zondervan is a registered trademark of The Zondervan Corporation, L.L.C., a wholly owned subsidiary of HarperCollins Christian Publishing, Inc.

Requests for information should be addressed to customercare@harpercollins.com.

Zondervan titles may be purchased in bulk for educational, business, fundraising, or sales promotional use. For information, please email SpecialMarkets@Zondervan.com.

ISBN 978-0-310-10696-8 (softcover)
ISBN 978-0-310-10698-2 (audio)
ISBN 978-0-310-10697-5 (ebook)

Cover design: Tammy Johnson
Cover photo: Everett Ferguson / CC by 4.0
Interior design: Kait Lamphere

Printed in the United States of America

24 25 26 27 28 LBC 5 4 3 2 1

To the many participants in the past nine years of LATC.

We couldn't have done it without your support.

CONTENTS

ACKNOWLEDGMENTS

THE EDITORS WOULD LIKE TO THANK Professor Clinton E. Arnold, dean of Talbot School of Theology, and the faculty and administration of Biola University for their support of the Ninth Los Angeles Theology Conference (LATC) in March 2023, out of which these published proceedings grew. We are also very grateful to Dr. Uche Anizor, associate professor of theology at Talbot School of Theology, Biola University, who was an enormous help behind the scenes. Dr. Anizor has graciously agreed to step up to become one of the organizers of the conference series going forward and will coedit future volumes in the LATC Zondervan Academic series with Professor Sanders. Meanwhile, Professor Crisp will step down as co-organizer and cofounder of the LATC series to take up new responsibilities in Scotland, including co-organizing the inaugural Scottish Dogmatics Conference in May 2024 with Professor Paul Nimmo at the University of Aberdeen and Katya Covrett, publisher for Zondervan Academic, who will be the conference sponsors and publish the proceedings.

LIST OF CONTRIBUTORS

Kimlyn J. Bender—is the Foy Valentine Professor of Christian Theology and Ethics at George W. Truett Theological Seminary, Baylor University. He holds a BA from Jamestown College, MDiv from Fuller Theological Seminary, and PhD from Princeton Theological Seminary.

Natalie Carnes—is professor of theology at Baylor University. She holds an AB in comparative religious studies from Harvard College, MA in religion from the University of Chicago, and PhD in Christian theological studies from Duke University.

Oliver D. Crisp—is Principal of St. Mary's College and Head of the School of Divinity, University of St. Andrews, where he is also Professor of Analytic Theology. He earned BD, MTh, and LLM degrees from the University of Aberdeen, a PhD from the University of London, and a DLitt from Aberdeen.

Stephen T. Davis—is Russell K. Pitzer Professor of Philosophy Emeritus at Claremont McKenna College in Claremont, California. He holds a BA from Whitworth University, MDiv from Princeton Theological Seminary, and PhD from Claremont Graduate University.

Steven J. Duby—is associate professor of theology at Phoenix Seminary, Phoenix, Arizona. He holds a BS from Moody Bible Institute, MDiv from Denver Seminary, and PhD in divinity from the University of St. Andrews.

Millard Erickson—is an unaffiliated scholar who has served as a pastor, theology professor, and seminary administrator. He earned a BA from the University of Minnesota, BD from Northern Baptist Theological Seminary, MA from the University of Chicago, and PhD from Northwestern University.

Tom Greggs—holds the 1616 Marischal Chair of Divinity at the University of Aberdeen. He earned an MA from the University of Oxford, PhD from the University of Cambridge, and DLitt from the University of Aberdeen. He is a fellow of the Royal Society of Edinburgh.

Daniel Lee Hill—is assistant professor of Christian theology at George W. Truett Theological Seminary, Baylor University. He holds a BA degree from Hampton University, ThM from Dallas Theological Seminary, and PhD from Wheaton College.

Matt Jenson—is professor of theology at the Torrey Honors College, Biola University. He holds a BA in literature and philosophy from Wheaton College and a PhD in divinity from the University of St. Andrews, and is ordained in the Evangelical Covenant Church.

Marguerite Kappelhoff—is executive dean at Sydney College of Divinity, Australia. She earned an MBA from Southern Cross University and a PhD in systematic theology from Charles Sturt University, Australia.

Kimberley Kroll—is assistant professor of biblical and systematic theology at Trinity Evangelical Divinity School, Trinity International University. She holds a BA in philosophy and English from Queens College, City University of New York, MDiv from Grace Theological Seminary, MA in philosophy from Biola University, and PhD in divinity from the University of St. Andrews.

Jennifer Powell McNutt—is Franklin S. Dyrness Chair of Biblical and Theological Studies and associate professor of theology and history of Christianity at Wheaton College. She earned a BA in religious studies at Westmont College, MDiv at Princeton Theological Seminary, and PhD in history at the Reformation Studies Institute at the University of St. Andrews. She is also an ordained Minister of Word and Sacrament in the Presbyterian Church (USA) and a fellow of the Royal Historical Society.

Steven Nemes—is instructor in Latin, Greek, and Humane Letters at North Phoenix Preparatory Academy, Phoenix, Arizona. He holds a BA in philosophy from Arizona State University and an MDiv and PhD from Fuller Theological Seminary.

Paul T. Nimmo—holds the King's Chair of Systematic Theology at the University of Aberdeen. He holds an MA from the University of Cambridge, an MTh from Princeton Theological Seminary, and a BD and a PhD from the University of Edinburgh.

Fred Sanders—is professor of theology in the Torrey Honors College, Biola University. He earned a BA in fine arts from Murray State University, MDiv from Asbury Theological Seminary, and PhD from the Graduate Theological Union, Berkeley.

Eric T. Yang—is associate professor of philosophy at Santa Clara University. He holds a PhD in philosophy from the University of California, Santa Barbara.

INTRODUCTION

We believe in one, holy, catholic, and apostolic Church.
—THE NICENE CREED

IN MANY AND VARIOUS WAYS, the church remains a subject of discussion and controversy in our contemporary world. Its place in Christian dogmatics is just as much the subject of debate, though that is often less widely reported in popular media. Dogmatic reflection on the nature and shape of the church has to do in part with the church's *confession*. That is, it has to do with what the church and those who self-identify as members of the church think the church is doing in, say, its liturgies and other practices such as almsgiving or mission, as well as in the theological content of its pronouncements in things like catechisms and creeds. This means that discussion of ecclesiology as a theological locus often also involves an act of religious self-awareness on the part of the theologian. What is the church? What is its nature as a community gathered around the teachings of Jesus of Nazareth and his immediate disciples? How is it related to other topics of Christian dogmatics, such as the Trinity or redemption? How should we think and speak about the church today?

An example will make the point more vividly. In one of his essays, the Anglican divine John Webster wrote that "ecclesiology is secondary. The life of the fellowship of the saints comes first, because it is in that fellowship that we keep company with God."[1] Yet what is this if it is not an expression of a *particular kind* of religious self-awareness about the dogmatic shape

---

1. John B. Webster, "The Visible Attests the Invisible," in *The Community of the Word: Toward an Evangelical Ecclesiology*, ed. Mark Husbands and Daniel Treier (Downers Grove, IL: IVP Academic, 2005), 113.

of discussion of the church? In Webster's case, the idea is that the formal structures that mark the church in theological discussion of ecclesiology should be secondary to the life and practices of the church as the community of the people of God. But of course, Webster's view is only one among many—and not just one among many views represented in different branches of the Christian church, though that is undoubtedly true. For even in his own tradition, Webster's position seems to be at odds with other ways of thinking about the dogmatic shape of the church. Consider, as a counterpoint, Article XIX "Of the Church" in the Thirty-Nine Articles of 1562, which are the confessional spine of Anglicanism. There we read,

> The visible Church of Christ is a congregation of faithful men [i.e. humans], in the which the pure Word of God is preached, and the Sacraments be duly ministered according to Christ's ordinance in all those things that of necessity are requisite to the same. As the Church of Jerusalem, Alexandria, and Antioch, have erred; so also the Church of Rome hath erred, not only in their living and manner of Ceremonies, but also in matters of faith.

According to the framers of the Articles of Religion the *sacramental* life of the church—that is, a particular theological understanding of its liturgical practices—is as important to a proper understanding of the dogmatic shape of the church as the preaching of the Word of God. This is seasoned with a little ecclesiastical humility in the recognition that other historic communions of the church have been mistaken in their views about matters of "living and the manner of Ceremonies" as well as matters of doctrine. No doubt such views would make Webster somewhat uncomfortable, even though they are indelibly etched into the foundations of the tradition in which he lived and served. Thus, confessing the church can be a theologically complex task, a dialectic between the views of the individual divine, the local ecclesial community, and the wider church.

As we have already indicated, this quick cameo of Webster and the Anglican Articles of Religion is supposed to illustrate the fact that there are many ways of thinking about the nature and shape of the church and her confession. Not all theological accounts of ecclesiology need to arise from *within* the church, however. These are matters that could be considered from outside the bounds of the church by those looking in upon it, so to speak. (What anthropologists call *etic* rather than *emic* accounts, which are articulated from "within" a particular tradition or perspective.) But this volume is concerned about the confession *of* the church or, more specifically, about how theologians representing various strands of the universal church understand various aspects and ramifications of its confession as being one, holy, catholic, and apostolic. And that is an emic practice if ever there was one.

So the essays contained within the covers of this volume express something of the diverse confession of the church. Yet there are also important signs of commonality and even convergence, as the reader will discover. Though we may sit in rather different places in our denominations and communions, we all confess the unity, holiness, universality, and apostolicity of each of our respective branches of the church—which is itself an ecumenical claim of some dogmatic importance. If no one view of the dogmatic shape of the church is privileged here, the emerging themes do perhaps represent some (informal) signs of ecumenical encouragement. For though our confession of the ideal creedal marks of the church may be a focus of unity, our understanding of the concrete form this takes in the life of the church is diverse, as a close reading of these essays will demonstrate.

Paul T. Nimmo's opening chapter takes up the theme of the church's holiness, considered especially with an eye to the issue of growth or progress in sanctification. Drawing on scriptural accounts of divine and ecclesial holiness, and on the work of John Calvin and Karl Barth, Nimmo proposes a chastened account of corporate sanctification. He argues that the sanctification of the church is entirely dependent on grace and that, as a result, growth and progress can only be thought of in relation to the development of obedient Christian practices that render the church as transparent as possible to that grace.

In chapter 2, "*Creatura Verbi*: Hearing the Living Word through the Spirit in the Church," Tom Greggs emphasizes the importance of the church receiving the good news of the gospel before proclaiming it. To consider this relation seriously is to bring doctrines of inspiration and the demands of hermeneutics into a larger ecclesiological meditation. On the practical side, Greggs considers how the church can actively cultivate a culture of receiving the Word before proclaiming it.

Kimlyn J. Bender's chapter 3, "Confessing Christ and Confessing the Church," examines the distinction and unity of Christ and the church. While acknowledging the dependence of ecclesiology on its Trinitarian and pneumatological groundings, Bender argues for the distinctive centrality of Christology for understanding the form and content of ecclesiology.

In chapter 4, Natalie Carnes "reconsiders the church-world divide," largely by comparing the distinction between world and church to the distinction between nature and culture. Carnes especially challenges the adversarial view of church versus world, proposing instead an approach in which the church is like leaven in the loaf, a witness to the world, and a participant in the world's flourishing.

Matt Jenson's chapter 5 takes up a number of these themes already introduced, setting them in fruitful dialogue. Jenson considers the distinction between church and world "necessary, but maverick," defending it while admitting its increasing implausibility. Beginning with a biblical-theological consideration of the relationship between Israel and the nations, Jenson directly engages Tom Greggs's recent proposal for a "non-binary" ecclesiology.

Kimberley Kroll's chapter 6 is, among other things, an example of the recent trend known as science-engaged theology. In "A New Creature: Holy Branches Grafted into a Single Vine," Kroll considers the detailed example of plant grafting as a metaphor for the relationship between Christ and his disciples/believers. A developed model like this can function not just illustratively but epistemologically, increasing the theologian's depth or range of understanding the possibilities of union.

In chapter 7, "The Church in a Postmodern Age," Millard Erickson considers how the church can navigate the challenges of postmodernity and remain relevant in today's world. Erickson approaches postmodernity as the cultural phenomenon associated with postmodernism, with its skepticism toward grand narratives and preference for personal experience. Erickson proposes a three-tiered model for understanding the church's role in a postmodern age: reflective/analytical (theology's intellectual environment), normative/doctrinal (the church's own beliefs), and functional/practical (how the church expresses itself effectively in culture).

In chapter 8, "The Community of the Apostles and the Spiritual Nature of Christian Unity," Steven Nemes proposes that the church be understood not so much as an institution with a certain intrinsic hierarchy and differentiation of roles, but as a spiritual community whose principle of unity is a shared experience of commitment to Jesus. He argues that the community of the original apostles gives insight into the nature of Christian unity. The apostles thought of themselves as independent messengers of the gospel of Jesus, each having the right to engage in his task freely without the consultation, intervention, and management of the others, all of which is not suggestive of a formal institution. Similarly, the community of the church as a whole arises out of a shared experience of faith and commitment to Jesus among many persons, which accounts for its unity in spite of its great diversity.

In chapter 9, "Exilic Ecclesiology: Suffering and Apostolicity in Early Modern Reformed Theology," Jennifer Powell McNutt explores how, "on the brink of the Reformation, the idea of 'apostle' had become so wedded to the notion of papal 'succession' that it was feared that apostolicity was in danger of losing its inceptive meaning and purpose in the confession of the church." Having retrieved the notion of suffering as a mark of apostolicity from the early French Reformed tradition (in which there was a tension between accepting and resisting suffering), McNutt tests it critically to assess its helpfulness for subsequent ecclesiology.

In chapter 10, Daniel Lee Hill takes up again the confession that the church is a holy people, set apart by God and called to a life of holiness. Acknowledging how difficult it is to reconcile this claim with the sins that mark the church's life, Hill argues that we can view the church as holy insofar as it is set apart as the means through which God bears witness to himself as reconciler and judge, prefiguring his eschatological reconciliation of the cosmos and judgment of the world. "The Christian confession of the church's holiness is first and foremost a claim that describes God's promise to present himself in and to this gathered community as reconciler and judge."

Chapter 11, coauthored by Stephen T. Davis and Eric T. Yang, considers the problem of ecclesial persistence: how much similarity and continuity of doctrine and organization is necessary for the church to be considered the same entity across time? Davis and Yang offer an approach that appeals crucially to the will of God and the narrative fittingness that follows from it, arguing that this "avoids a serious problem to mere similarity-and-continuity approaches." God's chosen story of Christ's church can account for "many different extant branches of Christianity today, thereby making each the same church as the one founded by Christ and the apostles."

In chapter 12, "The Triune God and the Marks of the Church," Marguerite Kappelhoff traces the traditional, creedal marks of the church to their origin within the nature and being of the triune God, and argues that this origin informs ecclesiology and its practices. Kappelhoff agrees with Barth that confessing the church's reality requires a faith that is "strong and certain and genuinely critical" in order to see the "unity of the church of Jesus Christ in its disunity."

In the final chapter, "Bond of Peace: Ecclesial Unity as Participation in the Son and Spirit," Steven J. Duby grounds ecclesial unity in Christians' participation in God the Son and God the Holy Spirit. Theologically grounded in this way, the unity of the church is a sign to the world of a deeper reality, namely, that the Father loves us just as he has loved his eternal Son and that the Spirit as the bond of love has enabled us to reflect his relationship to the Father and Son.

The essays collected together here represent some of the papers presented at the Ninth Los Angeles Theology Conference, held on the campus of Biola University in March 2023. May these essays extend discussion of the doctrine of the church today, *ad maiorem dei gloriam.*

Oliver D. Crisp and Fred Sanders
April 2023

CHAPTER 1

THE SANCTIFICATION OF THE CHURCH

Contemplating the Progress of the People of God

PAUL T. NIMMO

INTRODUCTION

This essay explores the somewhat occluded theme of the sanctification of the church. In works of theology, certainly of a Reformed stripe, the doctrine of sanctification often follows the doctrine of justification, these teachings together describing the *duplex gratia* of the applied work of Jesus Christ.[1] In such accounts, sanctification refers to the act or process by which an individual is and becomes holy, *sanctus*. However, it is less common to find the doctrine of sanctification thematised from a corporate perspective, with reference to the church and its becoming holy. Certainly, there is consistent affirmation of the holiness of the church, in line with the Nicene Creed, but in respect of Protestant circles at any rate, Herman Bavinck noted, "The Reformation . . . in practice all too often neglected [the holiness] of the church."[2]

This essay seeks to address this theme of the sanctification of the church directly, and in so doing, to offer one account of how one might contemplate

---

1. The classic expression is perhaps that of John Calvin, *Institutes of the Christian Religion*, vol. 2, ed. John T. McNeill, trans. Ford Lewis Battles, Library of Christian Classics (Philadelphia: Westminster, 1960), 3.3.1, 592–93, unfolded in the subsequent chapters of book 3 of the *Institutes*.
2. Herman Bavinck, *Reformed Dogmatics*, vol. 4, *Holy Spirit, Church, and New Creation*, trans. John Vriend, ed. John Bolt (Grand Rapids: Baker Academic, 2008), 321.

the progress of the people of God. After all, there are real questions here: Is the church—perhaps even a specific congregation—becoming holier? Is the church now any holier than it was two thousand years ago? And if not, what is going on theologically? The result of these reflections will be a fairly chastened and relatively modest account of church holiness, but one that seeks explicitly to do justice both to the broad witness of Scripture and that may also reflect something of the very ambiguous story that is church history.

The essay falls into two major sections. The initial exegetical section explores the scriptural depictions, first, of the holiness of the triune God, and, second, of the holiness of the church. In this way, not only their distinction, but also their deep interconnection is illuminated. The subsequent section moves to theological reflection on two problems arising from the exegesis. The first problem is how the holiness of the church can be affirmed given the systematic failure of the people of God to be holy in the course of history. The second problem is whether and how it is possible to speak of the progress of the church in history. Here the works of John Calvin and Karl Barth are explored in particular. The essay concludes with a fairly modest proposal regarding how one might contemplate and affirm the progress of the people of God.

1. Scriptural Reflections on Holiness

To begin, it is helpful to turn to the witness of Scripture, seeking to discern the contours of its portrayal of the holiness of God and the holiness of the church.

The Holiness of God

To speak of holiness in the Christian tradition is to speak first, and last, of God, the one whose very nature it is to be holy. Scripture is replete with testimonies to the divine holiness. The seraphim in the heavenly temple seen by Isaiah declared, "Holy, holy, holy is the LORD of hosts; the whole earth is full of his glory" (Isa. 6:3). And in the Revelation of John, the four living creatures sing without ceasing, "Holy, holy, holy, the Lord God the Almighty, who was and is and is to come" (4:8).

Indeed, God is the one whose very name is holy: a holy name in which one is to glory, for which one is to build a house, to which one is to give thanks—a name which is to be blessed.[3] Such scriptural testimony to the

---

3. See respectively 1 Chronicles 16:10; 29:16; 16:35; and Psalm 103:1.

irreducibility of the divine holiness could easily be multiplied. And a repeated claim of such references is that this holiness is *sui generis*—unique in kind. In Exodus the song of Moses and the Israelites declares, "Who is like you, O LORD, among the gods? Who is like you, majestic in holiness, awesome in splendor, doing wonders?" (15:11).[4] And in the book of Revelation again, the heavenly conquerors of the Beast sing, "Lord, who will not fear and glorify your name? For you alone are holy" (15:4).

The essential uniqueness of the holiness of God is worth highlighting, even at this stage. Emil Brunner captured the insight well: "To be holy . . . is that which sets the Being of God apart from all other forms of being."[5] God is holy on God's own account, not from outwith, and is holy without reserve and without measure. There is a separation between God and all that is not God, a separation that is zealously guarded by God, who is a "jealous God" (Ex. 20:5), and that—as will be noted—finds its distant echo in the idea of holiness on earth being linked with being in some way set apart.

There is a further specification to register at this point, and that is the Trinitarian aspect of divine holiness as it is attested in the New Testament. Holiness is predicated here not only of the divine being—that is, of the divine nature—but of each of the three persons of the Trinity, and in emphatic terms. Jesus himself prayed to his "Holy Father" (John 17:11),[6] while the unclean spirit in the first chapter of Mark cried out, "What have you to do with us, Jesus of Nazareth? Have you come to destroy us? I know who you are, the Holy One of God" (Mark 1:24).[7]

As for the Holy Spirit, well, the clue is in the name—holy is the one who descends upon Jesus at his baptism and leads him to the wilderness, who teaches the followers of Jesus, fills them, inspires them, and assists them—this one is explicitly called the Holy Spirit.[8] To this Spirit above all is ascribed the work of sanctification.[9]

To this point, however, no material definition of holiness has yet been provided. As a starting point, one might adapt the definition of Petrus van

---

4. See also the evocative 1 Samuel 2:2: "There is no Holy One like the LORD, no one besides you; there is no Rock like our God."

5. Emil Brunner, *Dogmatics*, vol. 1, *The Christian Doctrine of God*, trans. Olive Wyon (London: Lutterworth, 1949), 158.

6. Compare also Luke 1:49, and Mary's testimony that "the Mighty One has done great things for me, and holy is his name."

7. Further references to the holiness of Jesus Christ can be found at Luke 1:35; John 6:69; Acts 3:14; 4:27; and Hebrews 7:26.

8. See respectively Luke 3:22; 4:1; John 14:26; Acts 11:24; 1 Thessalonians 1:15; and 2 Timothy 1:14.

9. See among other references Romans 15:16; 1 Peter 1:2; and 2 Thessalonians 2:13.

Mastricht and recognise holiness as "an absolute goodness, by which God is inclined to all moral purity and recoils from all impurity of sin."[10] The Leiden Synopsis similarly opines that "holiness . . . is the virtue whereby [God], being most pure, approves everything that is pure, and whereby [God] is repulsed by its opposite."[11] There is a twofold disposition that is thus in effect in the intrinsic holiness of God—towards purity and against sin.

The holiness of the triune God with its double disposition is no abstract holiness—there is here no holy mystery, no abstract *noumenon*. The holiness of God is made known as God reveals Godself to creation as holy, as majestic and sovereign Lord. The God of Scripture is thus holy both in nature and in act. Ezekiel reported God saying, "I will display my greatness and my holiness and make myself known in the eyes of many nations. Then they shall know that I am the LORD" (38:23).

This making known of the holiness of God takes place in God's works in creation. Indeed, van Mastricht offers a catalogue of the works of God in which God reveals the divine holiness: from the decrees, through creation, providence, redemption, calling, and sanctification, to glorification.[12] As the comprehensive nature of the list indicates, God displays the divine holiness *throughout* these acts—at each point opposing and overcoming sin, and advancing and promoting purity. And in the process of these divine acts, the holy God is revealed to be the God who covenants with God's people. It is little wonder that John Webster wrote of holiness as "a mode of God's activity," such that to speak of it "identifies the manner of [God's] relation to us."[13]

This holiness of God is therefore not an annihilating purity that destroys the creature when it draws near. Rather, it is an uplifting purity that cancels out that which threatens creation and raises up the people of God. God proclaimed through Hosea, "I am God and no mortal, the Holy One in your midst, and I will not come in wrath" (11:9). Indeed, precisely in the revelation of God's unique holiness, there is an evocation and empowerment of an echo, a correspondence to holiness from within creation itself.

It would be possible to linger longer on the divine holiness itself: to

---

10. Petrus van Mastricht, *Theoretical-Practical Theology*, vol. 2, *Faith in the Triune God*, trans. Todd M. Rester, ed. Joel R. Beeke (Grand Rapids: Reformation Heritage Books, 2019), 407.

11. *Synopsis Purioris Theologiae*, vol. 1, *Disputations 1–23*, trans. Riemer A. Faber, ed. Dolf te Velde (Leiden: Brill, 2015), 6.40, 179.

12. Van Mastricht, *Theoretical-Practical Theology*, 2:411. He noted that the divine holiness is also revealed in Scripture, worship, God's people, God's ministers, angels, and particular places and times (2:411–12).

13. John Webster, *Holiness* (London: SCM, 2003), 41.

insist upon the way in which the simplicity of God ensures that the divine holiness is not separate from the divine love and the divine mercy, to think through the appropriate construal of the divine wrath in relation to the divine holiness, and to reflect on the relation between the divine holiness of the nature of God and the divine holiness of God's works.

Yet, as noted, the holy God is not content simply to reveal this holiness to creation: the holy God evokes also a response. And here arises the doctrine of the church.

THE HOLINESS OF THE CHURCH

The holiness of God is purposeful, with a clear telos. As mentioned already, at the heart of the purpose and works of the holy God in creation is the establishment of a holy community in covenant relationship with God. It is for this reason that Paul wrote, "[God] chose us in Christ before the foundation of the world to be holy and blameless before him in love" (Eph. 1:4). The reference to "choosing" indicates that the sphere of the divine election, that gracious and merciful decree of God, is relevant here. The reference to "us" is to "the saints . . . in Ephesus" (Eph. 1:1) and—by extension—to the church everywhere. Their sanctification was simply, for Paul, "the will of God" (1 Thess. 4:3).[14]

This holy community is grafted into the people of Israel, similarly chosen for holiness by the electing grace of God. The Lord said to Moses and Aaron, and thus to all Israel, "I am the LORD your God; sanctify yourselves, therefore, and be holy, for I am holy" (Lev. 11:44).

This Israel is called to be "a priestly kingdom and a holy nation" (Ex. 19:6),[15] just as the writer of Hebrews described his sisters and brothers as "holy . . . partners in a heavenly calling" (3:1).[16] Yet the calling is also a command. There is not just an invitation to but a demand for holiness, an expectation of lived obedience. And the new covenant repeats identically this call and its ethical implication: "As he who called you is holy, be holy yourselves in all your conduct, for it is written, 'You shall be holy, for I am holy'" (1 Peter 1:15–16).

The covenant between God and the people of God therefore has clear expectations; one might even venture the language of a conditional

---

14. One might compare 1 Thessalonians 4:7: God did "not call us to impurity but in holiness" or 2 Timothy 1:9–10: God "saved us and called us with a holy calling, not according to our works but according to his own purpose and grace, and this grace was given to us in Christ Jesus before the ages began, but it has now been revealed through . . . Jesus Christ."

15. See among many possible examples of this logic Deuteronomy 28:9.

16. See for the divine calling especially Romans 1:7 and 1 Thessalonians 4:7.

covenant. The people of God are to be holy, just as the Lord their God is holy. In a distant yet important analogy to the nature and acts of God, they, too, are to seek purity and to reject impurity. They, too, are to set themselves apart in creation without being separate from it.

At the same time, remarkably, Scripture relates that the sanctification of the people of God has happened *already*, has already been effected in Jesus Christ. Paul wrote, "To the church of God that is in Corinth, to those who are sanctified in Christ Jesus, called to be saints, together with all those who in every place call on the name of our Lord Jesus Christ, both their Lord and ours" (1 Cor. 1:2). Or again, Peter wrote in his first epistle to those "who have been chosen and destined by God the Father and sanctified by the Spirit to be obedient to Jesus Christ and to be sprinkled with his blood" (1:2).

There is therefore a sense in which the recipients of these letters—and thus all Christians—are *already* sanctified, *already* saints.[17] Hence, the church is identified as the *communio sanctorum*, the communion of saints. Those chosen and called are already somehow set apart, not from the world, but in the world—and, it should be added, for the world, in a distant creaturely echo of the revealed holiness of God. Here, too, there is a faint proto-Trinitarian grammar attested in Scripture: this creaturely sanctification is from God,[18] in Jesus Christ,[19] and by the Holy Spirit.[20]

This objective, completed aspect of sanctification does not diminish the ethical imperative, but it does frame it. Thus the writer of Colossians exhorted the church, "As God's chosen ones, holy and beloved, clothe yourselves with compassion, kindness, humility, meekness, and patience" (Col. 3:12). In other words, it is precisely those chosen, already holy, already loved, who are called to obedience. Elsewhere Paul exhorted Christians to present themselves as "a living sacrifice, holy and acceptable to God" (Rom. 12:1), and even to "making holiness perfect" (2 Cor. 7:1). Correspondingly, there is ethical counsel and instruction throughout the New Testament.[21] Van Mastricht wrote of holiness as God's "moral goodness, by which God

---

17. One might compare 1 Corinthians 1:30: "God is why you are in Christ Jesus, who became for us wisdom from God, and righteousness and sanctification and redemption," and 1 Corinthians 6:11: "You were washed, you were sanctified, you were justified in the name of the Lord Jesus Christ and in the Spirit of our God."

18. See 1 Thessalonians 5:23, corresponding to the petition of Jesus at John 17:17.

19. Sanctification takes place specifically through the offering of the body of Jesus Christ in death (see Heb. 10:10; Col. 1:22). Jesus is said to be the "one who sanctifies" at Hebrews 2:11.

20. For references, see n. 9 above.

21. For a classic exploration, see Richard B. Hays, *The Moral Vision of the New Testament: A Contemporary Introduction to New Testament Ethics* (London: T&T Clark Continuum, 1996).

is most especially imitable."[22] There is thus a simultaneity of indicative—"you are saints"—and imperative—"be saintly." The demands of the latter, however, are never framed as moral requirements in the absence of faith. And so Paul told Agrippa of his conversion and reported being sent by the Lord "to open their [gentile] eyes so that they may turn from darkness to light and from the power of Satan to God, so that they may receive forgiveness of sins and a place among those who are sanctified by faith in me" (Acts 26:18).

Paul similarly wrote later of sanctification as being "by the Spirit and through belief in the truth" (2 Thess. 2:13). Sanctification, then, is never a human work, even as ethical striving becomes intrinsic to the life of the church under grace.

This corporate sanctification of the chosen community has two purposes, one soteriological, one doxological. Regarding the former, the Lord declared in Isaiah that he gave his Servant "as a light to the nations, that my salvation may reach to the end of the earth" (49:6).

And Peter wrote that the reason the holy, chosen people of God are what they are is "in order that you may proclaim the excellence of him who called you out of darkness into his marvelous light" (1 Peter 2:9).

The holiness of the church is thus to bring others to the Lord. And regarding the latter, there is an ultimate end for the people of God. In the book of Daniel, one reads, "The holy ones of the Most High shall receive the kingdom and possess the kingdom forever—forever and ever" (7:18). And the Apocalypse of John similarly points to the future glories to come: "Blessed and holy are those who share in the first resurrection. Over these the second death has no power, but they will be priests of God and of Christ, and they will reign with him a thousand years" (Rev. 20:6). Hence, the telos of the holiness of the church ultimately relates to a "beyond," a destiny in heaven beyond this life and this world.

2. THEOLOGICAL ISSUES WITH HOLINESS

The exegetical account sketched above has outlined key contours of thinking about the primary, essential holiness of God and the secondary, derivative holiness of the church. Yet both aspects of this account come under significant pressure from the existence of sin: the very fact of sin seems to compromise both the holiness of God and the holiness of the church. The interest of this essay is specifically in the latter concern.

---

22. Van Mastricht, *Theoretical-Practical Theology*, 2:407.

There can be little doubt that sin diminishes the body of Christ. The church may well be holy with reference to its calling and its cleansing, but it is rather more difficult to speak of its holiness in practice. To say the very least, the church has not always fulfilled the high ethical imperatives that confront it in Scripture. Francis Turretin defined a church as "true" when it is "said to be holy," and this is the case where "it contains nothing false as to doctrine of faith, nothing unjust as to doctrine of morals, [and] can be known from no other source than a comparison with the Scriptures."[23] Yet it is not clear that, in this time between the times, such a church has ever existed. Turretin himself acknowledged that "every particular visible church can fall into deadly error, in faith as well as in practice . . . such errors are the proximate causes corrupting and destroying the church"—in other words, the church militant is vulnerable; it "creeps in the mire."[24] Of course, it is a consistent refrain across theology that the church as a whole will not fail: God will not be left entirely without witness in the world.[25] But it can be a very fragile witness: the church prior to the consummation is not entirely holy. Rather than turning to purity and away from sin, the church has done the reverse. Far from being a light to the nations, the church has been at points an agent of darkness. And even where the church appears to be holy, there is a caution that "external holiness is deceitful and doubtful."[26] Turning from textbooks and treatises to the real world, there is little space among actual churches for the anticipated "lovely portraits" and "ideal paradigms."[27] There can arise here a disjunction between what Nicholas Healy describes as "blueprint ecclesiologies" and the mixed ecclesiastical situation that is empirically confronted.[28] In a contemporary context, as Joseph Small writes, "Church sin is evidenced in systemic ignoring of ecclesial racism, indifference to doctrine, sexual misconduct and abuse, . . . and a host of other grand and

---

23. Francis Turretin, *Institutes of Elenctic Theology*, vol. 3, *Eighteenth through Twentieth Topics*, ed. James T. Dennison Jr., trans. George Musgrave Giger (Phillipsburg, NJ: Presbyterian and Reformed, 1992), 18.13.8, 113.

24. Turretin, vol. 3, 18.9.5, 53; 18.11.26, 81.

25. For a typical statement of this belief, see the Second Helvetic Confession, ch. 17: "Meanwhile God has in this world and in this darkness his true worshippers, and those not a few, but even seven thousand and more (I Kings 19:18; Rev. 7:3ff.). For the apostle exclaims, 'God's firm foundation stands, bearing this seal, "The Lord knows those who are his,"' etc. (II Tim. 2:19)," in *Reformed Confessions of the Sixteenth Century*, ed. Arthur C. Cochrane (Philadelphia: Westminster, 1966), 266–267.

26. Turretin, *Institutes of Elenctic Theology*, vol. 3, 18.13.10, 113.

27. The phrases are from Joseph Small, *Flawed Church, Faithful God: A Reformed Ecclesiology for the Real World* (Grand Rapids: Eerdmans, 2018), 3.

28. Nicholas Healy, *Church, World, and the Christian Life: Practical-Prophetic Ecclesiology* (Cambridge: Cambridge University Press, 2000), 25–51.

petty transgressions."[29] It is easy to understand Job asking, "How then can a mortal be righteous before God?" (Job 25:4), and concluding, "God puts no trust even in his holy ones" (Job 15:15). Perhaps even Martin Luther's claim that "there is no greater sinner than the Christian Church" comes into perspective and becomes understandable.[30]

The church itself thus appears to be in a *simul-simul* position: it is at one and the same time both holy and sinful, *simul sanctus et peccator*.[31] This is no partial situation such that one group or congregation or denomination is holy and another is sinful. Rather, one might here think of a *totus-totus* dynamic, such that the church is both entirely holy by way of its union with the holiness of Jesus Christ and entirely sinful on the basis of its failure to live in obedience to his commands.

With this reflection in view, the pressing questions arise. The first is the question of how to conceive the actual, objective holiness of the church that is affirmed in Scripture. The second is the question of how to view the movement towards holiness of the church in history, how to contemplate the progress of the people of God. In what follows, each of these pressing questions will be addressed in turn.

OBJECTIVE HOLINESS AND THE CHURCH

The first question relates to a theological conundrum. If Christians desire to claim that the church is holy at the same time as the empirical church gives the impression of being rather less so, then in what way is it meaningful to describe the church as holy?

One recourse to answer this question is to turn to the important and necessary doctrine of the invisible church, to indicate that it is the *invisible* church of the true saints that is the locus of holiness. But this is not a fully satisfactory answer, in so far as it still locates holiness in a community of individuals, all of whom—at least to the extent that they are still alive in this world—are both righteous *and sinful*. In other words, assuming that the holiness of the church pertains to the church of this world at all, recourse at this point to the invisibility of the church simply shifts the problem.

---

29. Small, *Flawed Church*, 117. Small writes, "Thinking of the church as a company of criminals is not a cynical denigration of the church, but a counter to the church's proclivity to justify itself, to promote itself as a virtuous, holy enclave in a sinful world." *Flawed Church*, xiv.

30. Martin Luther, cited in Webster, *Holiness*, 73.

31. It is clear that to speak of the church itself as sinful has proven to be problematic or impossible in certain traditions, notably that of Roman Catholicism, which recognises clearly the sins of its clergy and laity yet does not ascribe sinfulness to the church itself. Yet one may wonder whether this rather defensive position adequately captures the bathos of the history of the church.

However, the implicit parallel to the doctrine of justification in the language of simultaneous holiness and sinfulness may indicate a more felicitous way of speaking of the holiness of the church. In this trajectory, holiness *does* truly belong to the church but only *improperly*, that is—more precisely—by attribution or imputation. It is a quality alien to it, passively received and recognised only in faith. And it is conceivable and recognisable only when the church is regarded in light of its union with Jesus Christ. Bavinck alluded to this idea of the *alien* holiness of the church when he wrote that Christians are "objectively counted as saints in Christ by virtue of God's imputation to them of the righteousness of Christ."[32] And Webster similarly opined, "To be a saint is to have one's holiness in Christ Jesus,"[33] and thus alluded to "the passivity which is at the heart of the Church as a creature of divine grace."[34] The holiness of the church is only to be grasped along such extrinsic, ec-centric lines: it is truly and really "holy" by virtue of its union with Jesus Christ in the Spirit, even in its problematic present: its holiness is located originally and properly in Jesus Christ in the uniting power of the Spirit and only derivatively and improperly in itself.

This conception of the holiness of the church as imputed brings three theological gains. First, considering the present holiness of the church as an ecclesial virtue that is imputed rather than original renders it clear that holiness is entirely a matter of grace. The holiness of the church must always be petitioned for and received from the hand of God with gratitude and humility. Second, considering the present holiness as an ecclesial virtue that is dependent on union with Christ by the power of the Spirit emphasises that the holiness of the church is profoundly relational and covenantal. Christ is head of the body, the church, not only in the past, but also in the present, while the Spirit not only gathered, upbuilt, and sent the church of the past but also gathers, upbuilds, and sends the church today. Indeed, ongoing provision of this holiness of the church is part of the heavenly priesthood of Christ, through his continuing heavenly intercession and, by the agency of the Spirit, his continuing earthly ministry. And third, considering the essential holiness of the church as an ecclesial virtue that is properly located in the union of the church with Christ indicates that the life of the church is ec-centric, that it lives from a centre beyond its own boundaries.

The holiness of the church is therefore not under its own control or

---

32. Bavinck, *Reformed Dogmatics*, 4:321.
33. Webster, *Holiness*, 83.
34. Webster, *Holiness*, 55.

visible by its own powers but is "hidden with Christ in God" (Col. 3:3), and the true life of the church is lived in Christ, from and in and to a perfect centre beyond the reach of the church in its broken humanity.[35] Such an orientation of the holiness of the church to its Head and its living from and in this source by the gracious power of the Spirit is at the heart of the being of the church. Karl Barth highlighted this radical dependence of the church, observing that Christians live spiritually only as they live ec-centrically: "They can only look beyond themselves, clinging to God . . . and to God only in Jesus Christ, and this only as they are freed to do so, and continually freed to do so, by the Holy Spirit."[36]

In the same way, the church can only live—and can only be holy—as it lives ec-centrically, looking beyond itself, clinging to God, and to God only in Jesus Christ, and this only as it is freed to do so, and continually freed to do so, by the Spirit.

SUBJECTIVE HOLINESS AND THE CHURCH

The second question that arises from the situation of the church is how to reflect upon its actual progress in history, what might be called its active or subjective sanctification. Stated differently, the question is one of whether and, if so, to what extent the church truly becomes holy over time. To reflect upon how the progress of the church in holiness might be conceived, two classic approaches to the issue are to be explored—the first from John Calvin, the second from Karl Barth.

JOHN CALVIN

Calvin readily recognised the problem of the holiness of the church, and his focus in his ecclesiology was very much on the visible church in the world. The presenting issue that governs much of his attention in this regard is the question of schism and its legitimacy—a question with particular traction in relation to his dealings both with Swiss Anabaptists and with Roman Catholics. Calvin wrote that his opponents "claim that the church of Christ is holy," and he certainly agreed on this point; however, he continued that "the church is at the same time mingled of good men

---

35. It is noteworthy that Webster in *Holiness* hesitated to draw on the trope of participation, preferring instead the language of reconciliation, fellowship, and relation with reference to Ephesians 2 (62).

36. Karl Barth, *The Christian Life: Church Dogmatics*, IV/4, Lecture Fragments (Edinburgh: T&T Clark, 1981), 94. For further detail on Barth's vision of the ec-centricity of the Christian life, see Paul T. Nimmo, *Being in Action: The Theological Shape of Barth's Ethical Vision* (London: Continuum, 2007), 97–99.

and bad,"[37] and he cautioned that in the present age, prior to the Day of Judgement, his opponents "are vainly seeking a church besmirched with no blemish."[38] The truth is that the church is inevitably a mixed society, and because of this, Calvin argued that schism on the basis of morality is both undesirable and unjustifiable. On his account, such a rigorous concern for ecclesial perfectionism is misguided, a zealous behaviour that arises out of "pride and arrogance and false opinion of holiness [rather] than of true holiness and true zeal for it."[39]

Yet this begs the question, he noted, of "in what holiness [the church] excels."[40] Here Calvin turned back to the work of Christ, who "gave himself up for the church that he might sanctify her [Eph. 5:25–26]" and who remains "daily at work in smoothing out wrinkles and cleansing spots."[41] In light of this activity of Christ, Calvin acknowledged, "The church's holiness is not yet complete. The church is holy, then, in the sense that it is daily advancing and is not yet perfect: it makes progress from day to day but has not yet reached its goal of holiness."[42]

Three observations might be ventured regarding this acknowledgement. First, and most simply, Calvin clearly affirmed that there is progress in the church—a "daily advancing." Second, Calvin acknowledged that this progress is ongoing and has not reached its end. In the immediate context of writing, Calvin's conclusion—supported by the behaviour of prophets and apostles as well as by Christ himself—is that schism is never justified by moral failure, as long as "the Word of God is preached and the sacraments are administered."[43] This, of course, is the qualification to which Calvin did ultimately resort in order to justify the Protestant schism from the Roman Catholic Church.[44] But the wider theological point is that while Calvin did not deny the ongoing need to encourage Christians to perfection, he recognised that one can never be *sure* of attaining such perfection; it is for this reason that "in the Creed forgiveness of sins appropriately follows mention of the church."[45] Christians are not only received and adopted into the

---

37. Calvin, *Institutes*, 4.1.13, 1027.
38. Calvin, *Institutes*, 4.1.13, 1028.
39. Calvin, *Institutes*, 4.1.16, 1030.
40. Calvin, *Institutes*, 4.1.17, 1031.
41. Calvin, *Institutes*, 4.1.17, 1031.
42. Calvin, *Institutes*, 4.1.17, 1031.
43. Calvin, *Institutes*, 4.1.19, 1033; cf. 4.2.1, 1041: "As soon as falsehood breaks into the citadel of religion and the sum of necessary doctrine is overturned and the use of the sacraments is destroyed, surely the death of the church follows"; at this point, separation is necessary, *Institutes*, 4.2.10, 1051.
44. Calvin did acknowledge, however, that vestiges of the true church might remain even at points within the Roman Catholic Church, *Institutes*, 4.2.11–12, 1051–53.
45. Calvin, *Institutes*, 4.1.20, 1034.

church through forgiveness, but are preserved and protected there by the same: "Unless we are sustained by the Lord's constant grace in forgiving our sins, we shall scarcely abide one moment in the church."[46] The reason is that "however great the holiness in which God's children excel, they still—so long as they dwell in mortal bodies—remain unable to stand before God without forgiveness of sins."[47] And third, the true goal of the church is identified as holiness, but there is no sense that this will be achieved before the eschaton, at which point there will be a Day of Judgement.[48] In the interim, it is God alone who foresees "who are unfeignedly holy and will persevere to the very end."[49]

The limited attention Calvin devoted to the holiness of the church was governed by his treatment of the issue of schism. Further insight can be gained from a brief review of his exploration of individual sanctification, an exploration which is itself framed with a corporate intention in so far as the language used is regularly plural. Here Calvin wrote of sanctification as falling under the work of Christ, and as constituting "a singular gift from God."[50] In a statement that sums up its purpose well, he observed, "Sanctified by [God's] Spirit we may cultivate blamelessness and purity of life."[51] Calvin explained, "Through his Holy Spirit [Christ] dwells in us and by his power the lusts of our flesh are each day more and more mortified; we are indeed sanctified, that is, consecrated to the Lord in true purity of life, with our hearts formed to obedience to the law. The end is that our especial will may be to serve his will and by every means to advance his glory alone."[52]

It is small wonder that Joel R. Beeke suggests that, for Calvin, "faith, repentance, sanctification, and assurance are all progressive."[53] Yet immediately, any optimism or lassitude regarding this growth is exposed and

---

46. Calvin, *Institutes*, 4.1.21, 1035.

47. Calvin, *Institutes*, 4.1.22, 1036. It is against this backdrop that the prophecy that the unclean shall not enter the holy temple (Isa. 35:8) is to be understood. Calvin explained, "Let us not understand this prophecy as if all the members of the church were without blemish; but because they zealously aspire to holiness and perfect purity, the cleanness that they have not yet fully attained is granted them by God's kindness." *Institutes*, 4.1.17, 1032. There is here a mirror image of the divine acceptance by grace of the good works of the individual Christian, however imperfect: "for believers uprightness, albeit partial and imperfect, is a step toward immortality." *Institutes*, 3.17.15, 820.

48. Calvin, *Institutes*, 4.1.13, 1028.

49. Calvin, *Institutes*, 4.1.8, 1022.

50. Calvin, *Institutes*, 3.3.21, 615.

51. Calvin, *Institutes*, 3.11.1, 725.

52. Calvin, *Institutes*, 3.14.9, 776.

53. Joel R. Beeke, "Appropriating Salvation: The Spirit, Faith and Assurance, and Repentance," in *A Theological Guide to Calvin's Institutes*, ed. David W. Hall and Peter A. Lillback (Phillipsburg, NJ: P&R, 2008), 282.

countered. Calvin continued, "But even while by the leading of the Holy Spirit we walk in the ways of the Lord . . . traces of our imperfection remain to give us occasion for humility"; indeed, even the best human work is corrupted and "savours of the rottenness of the flesh"; and finally, "this mortal life is never pure or devoid of sin" and "no perfection can come to us so long as we are clothed in this flesh."[54] Calvin starkly recognised the pervasive presence and unresting effect of sin in the life even of the regenerate. The result is an incomplete transition—a position affirming growth, insisting upon growth, yet brutally realistic about its progress and its reverses—and a constant rhetorical swing from one position to the other and back.

It might be wondered, then, whether this position is stable, whether in light of this strong insistence upon the unavoidable fallenness of regenerate action, talk of progress is misplaced. Yet it should be noted that there is an overarching forward dynamic to it. As Richard B. Gaffin Jr. notes, sanctification for Calvin brings a disposition to holiness, a concern for godliness, no matter "how weak and sin-plagued that disposition and how imperfectly manifested subsequently."[55] The final impression is one in which progress is affirmed.[56] This led Calvin to a pastoral approach to progress in the Christian life:

> Let us not despair at the slightness of our success; for even though attainment may not correspond to desire, when today outstrips yesterday the effort is not lost. Only let us look toward our mark with sincere simplicity and aspire to our goal; not fondly flattering ourselves, nor excusing our own evil deeds, but with continuous effort striving toward this end: that we may surpass ourselves in goodness until we attain to goodness itself.[57]

Calvin thus did affirm progress in the church but was aware of its fragility.

KARL BARTH

In turning to Barth's account of the holiness of the church, one enters his ecclesiology. For Barth the church is certainly a visible, empirical institution

---

54. Calvin, *Institutes*, 3.14.9, 10, 776, 777.
55. Richard B. Gaffin Jr, "Justification and Union with Christ," in *A Theological Guide to Calvin's Institutes*, ed. David W. Hall and Peter A. Lillback (Phillipsburg, NJ: P&R, 2008), 255–56.
56. Calvin, *Institutes*, 3.7.3, 692.
57. Calvin, *Institutes*, 3.6.5, 689.

in the world, susceptible of all manner of attention and analysis. Yet in so far as the church is *more* than this, in so far as it is a spiritual reality, this is a gracious and interruptive work of the Spirit.

In his treatment of the notes of the church in *Church Dogmatics*, Barth opens his section on the church as "holy" by observing that the term "indicates the contradistinction of the Christian community to the surrounding world."[58] For all that it remains a human society, it has a very different basis and goal than all other societies—namely, the Spirit. But Barth immediately registered a crucial distinction: "The holiness of the church is not that of the Holy Spirit . . . but the holiness caused [*geschaffen*] by [the Spirit] and ascribed to [the church]."[59] In other words, the church is only holy as it receives its holiness from outwith itself, and even as it becomes holy, it "is still a part of the creaturely world."[60] Its holiness can therefore only be a "reflection [*reflex*] of the holiness of *Jesus Christ* . . . which falls upon it as he enters into and remains in communion with it by the Holy Spirit."[61] As a creaturely institution, absent this "third dimension" of its being, "[the church] in and of itself is not holy; it is nothing special"; indeed, it is "as unholy as Adamic humanity; with [that humanity] it sins and makes itself guilty; with [that humanity] it is in absolute need of justification and a share in his holiness."[62] Barth thus echoed Calvin here with regard to the sinful nature of the church as human.

In what follows, we'll see that Barth made two critical observations that are of particular import.

First, Barth posited that the distinction (*Aussonderung*) of the church from the world—that which precisely constitutes its holiness as set apart—is not under its own control. It is, Barth averred, quoting Luther, a "*passiva sanctitas* [passive holiness]."[63] Thus, although the church is *active*, the church does not have control over the *holiness* of its activity: Barth noted that "it does not lie in its power or at its disposal to bestow the predicate 'Christian' upon its own activities."[64] The church acts, but it cannot make

---

58. Karl Barth, *Church Dogmatics*, ed. G. W. Bromiley and T. F. Torrance, trans. various, 4 vols. in 13 pts. (Edinburgh: T&T Clark, 1956–75), here at IV/1, 685. For occasional references to the original text, see Karl Barth, *Die Kirchliche Dogmatik*, 4 vols. in 13 pts. (Munich: Chr. Kaiser, 1932; and Zürich: EVZ-Verlag, 1938–65), with page numbers in square brackets. All references to this work hereafter: *CD*.
59. Barth, *CD*, IV/1, [767] 686.
60. Barth, *CD*, IV/1, 686.
61. Barth, *CD*, IV/1, [767] 686.
62. Barth, *CD*, IV/1, [767] 687.
63. Barth, *CD*, IV/1, 693.
64. Barth, *CD*, IV/1, [774] 693.

its acts holy. Of course, Barth noted, some actions of the church actually "*are* holy, i.e., have the character of real witness to [Jesus Christ]."[65] But precisely this character and this holiness are "in every single case dependent on the counter-witness of [Jesus Christ], the matter of his particular blessing, of his free grace."[66] And while Jesus Christ has promised to direct this grace to his community, he does not give it "into their hands."[67] The church depends always on his active presence: the church must always pray for its holiness.[68]

Second, Barth observed that to affirm the *passive holiness* of the church does not mean that this holiness has "only . . . theoretical, but no concrete practical significance."[69] For Jesus Christ is one who asks "continually, whether and to what extent [the church] might correspond to the fact that it is his body . . . in its visible existence."[70] In other words, Jesus Christ continually poses the question of the holiness of the church. Barth observed, "The holiness [of Jesus Christ] is not given to it as a kind of umbrella, under which it could either rest or walk here and there according to its preference, but as the pillar of cloud and fire was given to the Israelites in the desert to determine their way, as the mystery by which it has to orient itself in its human-churchly work."[71]

The church is thus called to travel a particular way, to move in a particular direction in which it seeks to act obediently in the world to witness to Jesus Christ. But the success of that venture, the degree to which it becomes a *true* witness and thus holy—the "third dimension" of its reality, as Barth called it—remains entirely outwith its control. The holiness of the church remains utterly extrinsic: for this holiness to be realised requires the dynamic intervention of grace that renders its activity a true witness of Jesus Christ.[72]

In this account, Barth portrayed the church as possessing a holiness that is alien to it, extrinsic to it, that must be received by grace in the event of revelation. Small wonder that Gerald McKenny ventures that "our freedom for God is not dependent on whatever growth, however great or little, occurs in the tendency of our capacities to such action. It is therefore a

---

65. Barth, *CD*, IV/1, 693.
66. Barth, *CD*, IV/1, [775] 693–94.
67. Barth, *CD*, IV/1, [775] 694.
68. Barth, *CD*, IV/1, 693.
69. Barth, *CD*, IV/1, [782] 700.
70. Barth, *CD*, IV/1, [782] 700.
71. Barth, *CD*, IV/1, [783] 701.
72. Karl Barth, *God Here and Now*, trans. Paul M. van Buren (London: Routledge & Kegan Paul, 1964), 62.

mistake on [Barth's] view to look to any such process."[73] The church thus never disposes over the divine grace of the Spirit by which it witnesses.

ANALYSIS

Both Barth and Calvin characterised sanctification as falling within the work of Christ and the Spirit. There is a shared resounding affirmation of the objective holiness of the church; but there is a shared clear recognition that the church—the communion of saints—is on a journey of sanctification. The reason is again common to both: the ongoing and virulent limitations on the regenerate life brought about by the ongoing power of sin. Perfection remains command and aspiration but not a goal achievable in this world.

At the same time, there are significant differences of interest. First, Barth was insistent that in the case of sanctification, the holiness of Christians remains external to them, in Jesus Christ. Not only justification, but also sanctification, is alien to the believer, and is theirs only through this participation in Jesus Christ. Now, certainly Calvin also wished to ascribe sanctification to this same participation, but nonetheless had no reservations about predicating this sanctification directly of the believer. The decentring of the sanctified identity of the Christian thus seems more thoroughgoing in Barth. And this leads to the second distinction. For Barth was consequently far more hesitant to affirm any growth in holiness on the part of Christians. The church only ever begins at the beginning with empty hands, depending always on the arrival of grace from beyond. The church is holy only in so far as it becomes so in the event of witnessing to the alien holiness of Jesus Christ. Hence, on this account, it is difficult to conceive of the church—to use Calvin's words—advancing daily. Instead, every day the believer begins again at the beginning, and by the end of the day has not advanced in personal holiness at all. In one sense, there is little movement forward at all—no increasing approach to perfection, no gradual increase of righteousness over sin, only the movement from one event of faithful obedience to another, from one disruptive entry of grace to the next.

CONCLUSION

This essay has sought to offer an exploration of the holiness of the church. It began with exegetical reflections on the holiness of God and of the

---

73. Gerald McKenny, *Karl Barth's Moral Thought* (Oxford: Oxford University Press, 2021), 166.

church before turning to consider two theological problems arising—how to conceive of the holiness of the church given its sinfulness and—with the aid of Calvin and Barth—how to construe the progress of the church. It is time to draw some preliminary conclusions.

If the holiness of the church is to be construed in a way that comports both with the ethical exhortations of Scripture and with the empirical reality of sin, then it seems that an account along the lines of Barth may offer clear insight. Certainly, Christians are holy, as Scripture says, in Jesus Christ: he is their sanctification, complete once for all. But in terms of describing the Christian life as sanctified—whether on a personal or an ecclesial level—it seems that holiness always remains alien as a quality. To speak of Christians as holy—or rather becoming holy—is to speak of them only as witnessing truly to the holiness of Jesus Christ. Yet the truth of their witness is itself utterly dependent on an event of grace. Hence, sanctification can take place only as a blessing of the Spirit upon their activity, lifting creaturely and fallen works to testify to Jesus Christ. Christians are, of course, called to undertake these works; there is no dismissal of the third use of the law, no trace of antinomianism. But with reference to the effects of these works, while great things should be the object of hope, modesty should accompany all expectations.

On this account, sanctification is an event that takes place, as the Spirit comes to Christians and blesses their activities, but sanctification correspondingly never remains with them or their deeds as a perduring quality. Sanctification retains here a *jenseitig* (that-sided) character, always representing the activity of Jesus Christ toward the Christian or the church in the Spirit, sanctifying in the event in which faithful response is called forth. This needs to be re-enacted afresh each time by a new movement of the Spirit, and those movements—moments—leave a legacy in history but cannot be captured. Christians can and do pray for this sanctifying blessing of the Spirit, but the arrival of the person of the Spirit is not something over which they dispose. They always arrive with empty hands. And the result is that it is very difficult here to speak of "making headway," "making progress," and "advancing" in sanctification in the way that Calvin did. It seems rather that Christians are always beginning again from the beginning, that they daily start with nothing, that they have to start with "that daily drowning of the old Adam which is always so doubtful a matter because he can unfortunately swim."[74]

---

74. The memorable quip is from Barth, *CD*, III/2, 631, cf. *CD*, IV/3, 253.

On this account, then, the answers to the questions of whether the church grows in holiness or whether the church is holier today than at the outset are negative. Is there, then, any way in which one can speak of the progress of the people of God?

One helpful way to speak of the church making progress might be in the sense of the church being on a journey. One might reach here for the language of pilgrimage, but—as explored elsewhere—it may be that the language of *peregrinatio* is more suitable instead.[75] This idea describes a journey that is undertaken in love and at cost but that is unsure of its earthly destination because it seeks the place of its resurrection that is not to be found here. On this journey, the church is called to obedience, to engage in practices that seek to be open to the kingdom of God. This will involve a continual dying to vested interests and selfish desires, a mortification of the old self. But it will also involve—God willing—a graceful and dynamic regeneration, and thus moments of vivification in the power of the Spirit. And as the church is always called to move from and to grace, it will develop practices of worship and mission—of knowledge and confession; of penitence, gratitude, and joy; of relatedness within to each other and outwith to the world and to the creation; finally, of prayer and proclamation.

All these practices have a dimension that lies entirely within human control—they are human activities. Growth in this connection might then refer to an increasing interest in, attention to, and frequency for these Christian disciplines. This would involve the development of a creaturely pattern of behaviour, a creaturely disposition or *habitus*. In connection with this, then, there could be genuine improvement and increase in the extent to which these activities shape the life of the Christian and of the church. The power of such a *creaturely* habitus would lie in the ability not to bring forth the Spirit in and of itself, not to increase in possessed holiness, but in the ability to instill in a life of discipleship obedient patterns of action as open as possible to the grace of God. Stated differently, through such patterns of action the church can seek on its journey under heaven—even in and with all its creaturely and sinful limitations—to render itself as *transparent* to divine grace as possible. Again, this seeking would not, in itself, effect grace: grace remains at the divine disposal, and can only be the object of prayer. But at a creaturely level, such a disposition and its accordant activities could grow in depth and increase in sincerity, frequency, and intensity.

---

75. See Paul T. Nimmo, "Ecumenism: Gospel Imperative, Harsh Reality, and Pilgrim Journey," *Theology in Scotland* (forthcoming, 2023).

Amidst the creatureliness and sinfulness of the life of the church, this might be one vision of its progress in the Christian life.

Such will never reach perfection. But perhaps perfection is best saved for another time.[76]

76. The sincere thanks of the author are due to attendees at the Systematic Theology Research Seminars of the University of Cambridge and the University of St. Andrews, who engaged with an earlier version of this material; to Daniel Pedersen, who helpfully commented upon an earlier version of this essay; and to the attendees of the 2023 Los Angeles Theology Conference for their insightful conversations.

CHAPTER 2

CREATURA VERBI
Hearing the Living Word through the Spirit in the Church

TOM GREGGS

IF AS PROTESTANTS WE CONSIDER the church a *creatura verbi*, the focus on the church should be on its *creation* (passively) not its *creating* (actively). All too often, Protestant accounts of the church focus on the activity of preaching the word in this: what that word is to be preached or how it is to be proclaimed in word and sacrament. But to be a creature of the word requires a prior and primary passivity in the activity—a receiving before a proclaiming. For the church, corporately, to be a creature of the world, it is necessary for us to ask, How do we *hear* or *know* the good news of the gospel? This is a question that has been surprisingly neglected in our current theological age. Of course, we might point to the fact that in recent years both the doctrine of inspiration and the practice of hermeneutics have come to the fore. In response to a century of liberal dominance of theology, the objective significance of Scripture as *theopneustos* (inspired, or God-breathed) has been of considerable significance for evangelical theologies,[1]

---

1. An important dividing line in approaches to the Spirit's role in biblical interpretation is between those who see the role as restricted to the past or to the general constitution of faith communities in which the Bible is read and those who find a role for the Spirit in episodically illuminating the mind of the hearer/reader directly in the present. Hans Frei, "Theology and the Interpretation of Narrative: Some Hermeneutical Considerations," in *Theology and Narrative: Selected Essays*, ed. George Hunsinger and William C. Placher (New York: Oxford University Press, 1993), 94–116; David Tracy, *The Analogical Imagination: Christian Theology and the Culture of Pluralism* (New York: Crossroad, 1998); and to a large extent Francis Watson, *Text, Church, and World: Biblical Interpretation in Theological Perspective* (Edinburgh: T&T Clark, 1994), take the former approach, whereas the more ambitious latter approach can be found in Kevin Vanhoozer, *Is There*

as well as what are now called "biblical theologies."[2] The rediscovery of
the "strange new world within the Bible," as Karl Barth's essay is titled,
has led to a revived sense of the significance of the biblical message.[3] The
practice of writing "theological" commentary is an effect of this, as the two
horizons of hermeneutics are employed for those who have a newfound
respect for the particularities and significance of the inspired Word of God.[4]
But such approaches tend rarely to give any significance to the task of the
sinful, finite, human reader being able to hear, read, and receive the Word
of God in a fallen world unaided. Where questions of the reader and the
reader's response do arise, they are far more likely to arise in relation to
modern or postmodern theories of epistemology than they are to account
for the divine operation of God.[5] It is surely true to note that, in the words
of Webster, most approaches to hermeneutics "betray a pervasive naturalism
which separates divine communicative activity from human acts, authorial
or hermeneutical, one of whose chief effects is to make language about God
redundant in talking of the biblical texts and their reception."[6] We answer
the question of how we know and understand the text with little or no
discussion of the activity and economy of God in this knowing.

Until the seventeenth century (the century in which the fact, like the
telescope, was invented),[7] however, the doctrine of illumination was at least
a means by which theologians were able to address how the inspired Word of
God came to be implanted and received in the fallen, limited creaturely *ratio*.[8]

a Meaning in This Text? The Bible, the Reader, and the Morality of Literary Knowledge (Grand Rapids:
Zondervan, 2009); and Darren Sarisky, Scriptural Interpretation: A Theological Exploration (London:
Wiley-Blackwell, 2012).

2. The classic reference is to Geerhardus Vos, Biblical Theology: Old and New Testaments (Grand
Rapids: Eerdmans, 1948), but see also Graeme Goldsworthy, According to Plan: The Unfolding Rev-
elation of God in the Bible (Downers Grove, IL: InterVarsity, 2003), and Peter Gentry and Stephen
Wellum, Kingdom through Covenant: A Biblical-Theological Understanding of the Covenants (Wheaton,
IL: Crossway, 2018), among others.

3. Karl Barth, "The Strange New World within the Bible," in The Word of God and Theology,
trans. Amy Marga (London: T&T Clark, 2011), 15–29.

4. See, e.g., Willie James Jennings, Acts, Belief: A Theological Commentary on the Bible
(Louisville: Westminster John Knox, 2017); Joseph L. Mangina, Revelation, Brazos Theological
Commentary on the Bible (Grand Rapids: Baker, 2017); Michael Wilcock, Jeremiah and Lamenta-
tions: The Death of a Dream and What Came After, Focus on the Bible (Fearn, UK: Christian Focus,
2013), as well as other offerings from all three series.

5. This is true, for instance, of the approach taken by Anthony Thiselton, The Two Horizons:
New Testament Hermeneutics and Philosophical Description (Grand Rapids: Eerdmans, 1980), the essays
in Paul Ricoeur, Figuring the Sacred: Religion, Narrative, and the Imagination (Philadelphia: Fortress,
1959), and Kevin Vanhoozer, First Theology: God, Scripture and Hermeneutics (London: Apollos, 2003).

6. John Webster, "Illumination," Journal of Reformed Theology 5, no. 3 (2011): 327.

7. Alasdair McIntyre, Whose Justice? Which Rationality? (South Bend, IN: Notre Dame University Press, 1988), 357.

8. It is worth noting that the notion of ratio up to this point did not simply include intellectual faculties but was a means by which the creature responded to the God who is the source of

Rather than naturalistic accounts of knowing or of experience discussed in relation to philosophic epistemology, phenomenology, or hermeneutics, the doctrine of illumination aimed at giving a properly *theological* account of the activity of God in not only graciously speaking divine truth, but graciously enabling the creature to hear and receive divine truth. While there were different forms of the account of illumination (whether it be Augustine or Aquinas, Bonaventure or Luther, Calvin or Owen), accounts were offered of the economic operation of the Holy Spirit in bringing the Word to the creature's hearing. While strands of theology that had experiential cores and traditions (such as certain Franciscan theologies and Wesleyan theologies)[9] continued to try to account for the aspect of the economy that brought about genuine experience of the Word and its assurance, the triumph of empirical and rational knowledge incurred itself upon theological accounts to such an extent that theological accounts of the means of creaturely knowing diminished. Very few recent theological accounts subsequently have attended to the doctrine of illumination, replacing this theological locus with often non-theological methodological

---

all knowledge. Therefore, music, for example, could be considered rational and a response to it (in whatever form) a rational response. In the Platonist tradition, where *ratio* (or διάνοια) is the movement of the soul by which it arrives at both theoretical and practical knowledge (ἐπιστήμη), the same point about music falling under the wide scope of "rational" or "rational response to the divine" could be made for statecraft, ethics, hermeneutics, architecture, artisanal crafts, poetry, gymnastics, theatre, dance, and the general art of rhetoric, which in one form or another enters into almost every domain of public and private life. It would also apply to what we think of as characteristically religious activities of prophecy and ritual worship, which Plato, perhaps ironically, cites as forms of "divine madness" or enthusiasm, along with the various arts that are inspired by the Muses and, perhaps most importantly, the activity of love (*Phaedrus* 245b7–c1). This is because in the Platonic philosophy all such activities are alike in being preconditioned by our ability to grasp and be inclined toward the ultimate cosmic and divine realities (*Republic* 5.477bff.) Any activity that purports to disclose such fundamental knowledge is apt to move the soul by persuasion. The often-alleged "suspicion" of the arts and rhetoric in Plato is better understood as Plato's appreciation that such practices are both capable of being revelatory and also capable of confusing the soul through images and distracting that person from the task of recollecting what God has done for them (*Phaedrus* 249c2). One can see the same ambivalence in Augustine's description of the Western church's attitude to the liturgical use of music (hymnody): an initially stern caution, owing to the motive power of its beauty, spontaneously yielding to its legitimacy as God-sanctioned, inspiring, and revelatory (*Confessions* 9.7.14–15, 10.33.49, *De Musica* 6.57–58). See Férdia J. Stone-Davis, *Musical Beauty: Negotiating the Boundary between Subject and Object* (Eugene, OR: Cascade Books, 2011). This is the expression of ratio that is to be understood by this essay: not intellectual capacity but response to the omniscient source of all knowing through whatever means, including those that are available to those with even the most extreme physical disability.

9. Bonaventure's understanding of illumination and its relation to Augustine's theory is contested, but see Lydia Schumacher, *Divine Illumination: The History and Future of Augustine's Theory of Knowledge* (London: Wiley-Blackwell, 2011), who claims that he followed a Victorine and Avicennist understanding that is "extrinsicist" about illumination and so less faithful to Augustine's orthodox Trinitarianism than Aquinas's understanding of illumination. According to Schumacher, what is at stake is, among other things, the recognition of a contributing role for autonomous natural cognition that depends on experience for its production of abstract universals. By this standard, Bonaventure's account wanders while Aquinas's succeeds.

discussions of hermeneutics. Within the field of theological hermeneutics, indeed, the only significant figure to devote time to the doctrine is Kevin Vanhoozer, relating the doctrinal content to speech-act theory; and even then this account is not fully developed.[10] Vanhoozer distinguishes between the written word of Scripture, as God's locution, from the illocutionary force (or meaning) thereby revealed.[11] The former remains historical but the latter is intended to be encountered by the audience in the living present. Moreover, because of the limits of human understanding, *the Holy Spirit* must illumine the mind of the hearing subject, in the moment of hearing, in order for the meaning of God's speech act to be received as the revelatory speech act that it is intended to be:

> The Bible *is* the word of God insofar as its inspired witness—which is to say the inspired locutions and perlocutions—really do present Jesus Christ. Yet the Bible also *becomes* the word of God when its illuminated readers receive and grasp the subject matter by grace through faith, which is to say, when the Spirit enables what we might call illocutionary uptake and perlocutionary efficacy [the effects of the speech act on the audience].[12]

---

10. Cf. Vanhoozer, *Is There a Meaning in This Text?*, 413–14.

11. Albeit Vanhoozer discusses this in a way that unhelpfully negates and fails to appreciate the complexity of Barth's account of Scripture.

12. Kevin Vanhoozer, "A Person of the Book? Barth on Biblical Authority and Interpretation," in *Karl Barth and Evangelical Theology: Convergences and Divergences*, ed. Sung Wook Chung (Grand Rapids: Baker Academic, 2006), 57; cf. 54–58. Vanhoozer is echoing a concern similar to the one put forward by Nicholas Wolterstorff, *Divine Discourse: Philosophical Reflections on the Claim That God Speaks* (Cambridge: Cambridge University Press, 1995). Wolterstorff claims Barth is at tension with himself in holding on the one hand that revelation is God's speech and on the other that God's word only becomes revelation to us after God's speech has ended: "God speaks in Jesus Christ, and only there; then on multiple occasions, God activates, ratifies, and fulfils in us what God says in Jesus Christ" (*Divine Discourse*, 73). The concern is that what makes God's speech revelatory, then, is not itself speech, but some other "speechless" activity of the Spirit, which would also seem to exacerbate evangelical concern for the all-sufficiency of the written word of Scripture. Space does not allow a detailed response to the points about Barth, but suffice it to say that there is a failure to note the constancy of God such that while God is of course sovereign over God's Word (who could think otherwise?), God is constant in God's speaking and our reception: it is the same God who does both. Moreover, as Edward Epsen recently pointed out to me, even if one were to agree wholesale with Vanhoozer, the same problem remains. A divine speech act's meaning would be featured in the intended illocutionary force of the act, which recursively includes certain effects by means of recognition of that intention. Vanhoozer confuses this and takes the meaning of a divine speech act to be the perlocutionary effects themselves. But if the meaning of divine speech were just its effects, then Wolterstorff's concern would still remain operative: spiritual illumination of the hearer would be disconnected from what was historically spoken; in such a case, we would have to say, unacceptably, that God did not mean anything, or at least did not accomplish his self-revelation in Christ, until the hearing of the audience. We should say instead that the meaning of God's speech is already accomplished, but that illumination of the audience by the Spirit in the present is necessary and included in the act's intention.

It should be noted that Darren Sarisky has also offered something heading toward a doctrine of illumination in his *Scriptural Interpretation*. He uses Basil of Caesarea (in particular, *On the Holy*

What remains clear, however, is that there has been little attempt to consider what it means for the fallen, limited creature to read Scripture aided by the God who desires the gospel to have a terminus in the creature.

None of this is to decry the need to exercise the human intellect in the reading of Scripture and to deploy the critical faculties which God has given us (as will be seen below), but it is to note that the creature does not read or hear the Word of God unaided. We need, therefore, to consider the *reading, hearing, and receiving* of Scripture *theologically* and not naturalistically. This will require a discussion of the church and the Word in their relation to other doctrinal loci, principally the work of the Spirit in illumining grace, the relationship between the Word and the Spirit, and the human subject.

Indeed, the very texts that hermeneutics interpret includes within them the following from St. Paul:

> [These things] God has revealed to us through the Spirit, for the Spirit searches everything, even the depths of God. For what human knows what is truly human except the human spirit that is within? So also no one comprehends what is truly God's except the Spirit of God. Now we have received not the spirit of the world but the Spirit that is from God, so that we may understand the gifts bestowed on us by God. And we speak of these things in words not taught by human wisdom but taught by the Spirit, interpreting spiritual things to those who are spiritual. (1 Cor. 2:10–13)

It is, therefore, to the question of what it means for the human to comprehend the things of God by God's Spirit to which it is necessary to turn.

1. WORK OF THE SPIRIT

The human knower only knows the things of God by virtue of the act of God. In illumination, the Holy Spirit enables the creature to receive, hear, and understand the objective act of God's divine illumination. As St. Paul wrote, "Those who are unspiritual do not receive the gifts of God's Spirit, for they are foolishness to them, and they are unable to understand them

---

Spirit) to offer a theological description of reading as a threefold process of purgation, participation, and spiritual contemplation (*pneumatike theoria*). For Sarisky, as for Vanhoozer, illumination corresponds to this third stage: "a reading of scripture in which one turns to the Spirit and partakes of his glory" (220). As with patristic accounts, this can sound lofty but Sarisky also says that illumination is whatever allows the reader to make a connection (a recognition of divine intention?) between the text and the reader's present life circumstances.

because they are spiritually discerned" (1 Cor. 2:14). To discern spiritually is to be open to the movement of the Spirit's grace and to move within those movements. The Spirit who searches the very depths of God (1 Cor 2:10) is the same Spirit who opens the ears of the creature, so that seeing she may see, and hearing she may understand (cf. Isa. 6:9; Mark 4:12).

The activity of the creature's (limited) understanding is one that stems from *the Spirit's* economy as the one who spoke through the prophets and the apostles. Following the ascension of Christ, it is the Spirit who continues to reveal the deep things of God *to the creature*. While Christ as the Word of God is objectively the revelation of God the revealer, the Spirit is the person of the divine life who brings this revelation to its terminus in creaturely hearing and understanding.[13] As creatures who have fallen, we are unable even to see, hear, and receive the revelation of God unaided: we cannot "bear" unaided by the Spirit what God desired to instruct us with. St. John recorded Jesus teaching the disciples,

> I still have many things to say to you, but you cannot bear them now. When the Spirit of truth comes, he will guide you into all the truth; for he will not speak on his own, but will speak whatever he hears, and he will declare to you the things that are to come. He will glorify me because he will take what is mine and declare it to you. All that the Father has is mine. For this reason I said that he will take what is mine and declare it to you. (16:12–15)

Here there is no division between the message of the Son and the message of the Spirit. But in the time after the ascension, it is the divine gift of the Spirit that guides the believer in truth to the glory of God. This is not the same as natural reason, but is an operation of grace aimed at glorifying the divine life, rather than singularly a creaturely aptitude. As Johann Quenstedt asserted, "Theology is a God-given practical aptitude of the intellect given to man by the Holy Spirit through the written Word, regarding true religion, by which man after the Fall is to be brought to life eternal through faith in Christ."[14] Crucially, for Quenstedt, the theologian is not a class of Christian, or even a preacher, but any Christian who learns of salvation through the Spirit's gracious relating of the Word to the

---

13. Cf. Barth, *CD*, I/1.6, 12.

14. Johann Andreas Quenstedt, *The Nature and Character of Theology: Introduction to the Thought of J. A. Quenstedt from Theologia Didactico-Polemica Sive Systema Theologicum*, abr., ed., and trans. Luther Poellot (St. Louis, MO: Concordia, 1986), 73.

believer by the Spirit. As with Clement, countering so-called Gnosticism in the early centuries of the Christian era, there is no specialist "gnostic" knowledge associated with being a Christian here. Instead, this receiving and hearing of divine things is an aspect of creaturely salvation: "It is not, then, that some are enlightened Gnostics and others are only less perfect Spirituals in the same Word, but all, putting aside their carnal desires, are equal and spiritual before the Lord."[15] It is not that, therefore, there is a genus of "theologian" as if this were some advanced, illuminated gnostic.[16] It is, rather, that the Spirit makes the revelation of God available to creaturely minds. This is offered universally to the Christian, though the effect of it may be different. Owen made this point well when he wrote, "There is an illumination which is an especial effect of the Holy Ghost by the word on the minds of men. . . . This light variously affects the mind, and makes a great addition unto what is *purely natural*, or attainable by the mere exercise of our natural abilities."[17] That the activity of illumination is not "attainable by mere exercise of our natural abilities" is an indication that illumination is not a doctrine that somehow addresses the intellectual Christian. To *know* God and the things of God is not to speculate philosophically about principles of metaphysical fancy, but it is to have been reached by the Spirit's grace in our natural, fallen lives with their natural, limited, fallen intellects: "By the Holy Spirit who searches even the depths of God (1 Cor. 2:10), God reveals what has not been seen or heard or conceived by the human heart (1 Cor. 1:9f.)."[18] Those with cognitive disability, for example, are not less likely to have been reached by the Spirit's grace than those with vastly high IQs. The cause of illumination is not the intellect that reaches up to the Spirit but the Spirit who condescends to the creature.

Illumination is, thus, not simply an act of the Spirit, but more specifically an act of the Spirit's *grace* and *mercy*. In the current lapsarian context of humanity, it is not only the grace of the Spirit that is responsible for the Spirit's work *ad extra* in illumination, but also the mercy of the Spirit in illuminating the fallen creature. Not only are we those who cannot hear, see, and receive all the Lord has done for us; we are also those who in our

---

15. Clement of Alexandria, *Christ the Educator*, trans. Simon P. Wood (Baltimore: Catholic University of America Press, 1954), 31.

16. Webster, "Illumination," 336: "By the Holy Spirit who searches even the depths of God (1 Cor. 2.10), God reveals what has not been seen or heard or conceived by the human heart (1 Cor. 1.9f.)."

17. John Owen, *The Works of John Owen*, vol. 4, *The Work of the Spirit* (Carlisle, UK: Banner of Truth Trust, 1991), 232.

18. Webster, "Illumination," 336.

sin do not wish to hear, see, and receive all the Lord has done for us. After the fall, the capacity to be illumined does not lie within us, but we "are made" able to be taught by God—something which is "acquired through the assisting grace of the Holy Spirit."[19] While objectively, revelation in the life of Christ and in Scripture as it testifies to Christ may be considered to exist for the theologian, those without the Spirit find themselves like those outside Jesus' circle in the Gospels: "they may indeed look but not perceive, and may indeed hear but not understand" (Mark 4:12). Just as during his own life, people did not recognise or receive Jesus for who he is, so today in their sin people fail to see revelation—reading dead words of religion in the Bible as a book, rather than the living word of God, "active and sharper than any two-edged sword, piercing until it divides soul from spirit" (Heb. 4:12). In their sin, outside of faith, the message people hear is not received to their benefit (cf. Heb. 4:2). It is not only, therefore, that we are reached in grace with the merciful story of God's revealing grace. But the mercy of God also extends through the Spirit's act of grace to the capacity to overcome the fallen propensity to reject the revelation of God's salvation in Christ. There is no *Anknüpfungspunkt* in the creature—even in the creature's capacity to hear and receive divine revelation.[20] The ultimate and proximate cause of the creature's capacity to hear the good news and to behold and receive salvation rests in the mercy of the Holy Spirit's grace to creatures who have rejected God. As Joseph Bellamy said, "When the gospel, which is hid from all natural men, comes to be revealed, internally revealed to us by the Holy Spirit, in all its divine glories, agreeable to Matt. xi.23; 2 Cor. iii. 18, iv. 6, it is known to be from God, from the divinity of its nature."[21] It is by God that God is known. This knowing of God is by virtue of not only God's revealing but also God's mercy to sinners in enabling them to know and hear the Word of God. Indeed, the proclamation of the Word of God by humans stems from the prior hearing and receiving of the Word by the illuminating grace of the Spirit.

Through the Spirit's merciful grace, the Word of God actually *reaches* the human. This means, therefore, that there is a human response to this hearing. While we cannot hear unaided, once we hear, the Spirit frees us

---

19. Quenstedt, *Nature and Character of Theology*, 73.

20. Cf. the debate between Barth and Brünner in Emil Brünner and Karl Barth, *Natural Theology: Comprising Nature and Grace by Emil Brünner and the Reply No! by Dr Karl Barth* (Eugene, OR: Wipf & Stock, 2002).

21. Joseph Bellamy, "An Essay on the Nature and Glory of the Gospel of Jesus Christ," in *The Works of Joseph Bellamy*, vol. 2 (Boston: Doctrinal Tract and Book Society, 1853), 423.

to make an appropriate response. This response is one of moving within the movements of the Spirit. Moved, the creature moves in the Spirit's movements. Hearing, the creature seeks to understand the deep things of God. Through the Spirit's light, the creature beholds and receives salvation. This is a human response aided by grace. It is the response of desiring (through the Spirit's redeeming work) to hear, understand, and see more of the unfathomable depths of the love of God. This human response is that having received the prevenience of the Spirit's grace, the creature is called to engage in a cycle of epicletic calling for the Spirit's aid to search ever-deeper the things of God. Having been enabled to hear the Word, the creature is called in a virtuous cycle to call ever more for the Spirit's gracious mercy to accompany her as she seeks to love God's Word and know God's revelation. In *Contra Celsum*, Origen stated this well:

> If the law of Moses had contained nothing which was to be understood as having a secret meaning, the prophet would not have said in his prayer to God, "Open Thou mine eyes, and I will behold wondrous things out of Thy law;" whereas he knew that there was a veil of ignorance lying upon the heart of those who read but do not understand the figurative meaning, which veil is taken away by the gift of God, when He hears him who has done all that he can, and who by reason of habit has his senses exercised to distinguish between good and evil, and who continually utters the prayer, "Open Thou mine eyes, and I will behold wondrous things out of Thy law."[22]

Leaving aside the question of figurative interpretation, this continual utterance of "Open Thou mine eyes" is the prayer of the one who, illumined by the Spirit's merciful grace, seeks the illumination of the continual Spirit so as not to hear or read revelation with "a veil of ignorance lying upon" them.

Although the divine activity of moving towards and into the creature with revelation is incalculably greater, the human response still involves action and effort: there is an *asymmetrical* creaturely action to correspond to the divine event. This action might even precede conversion, in a response to the convicting grace that leads a person to search or enquire into God's revelation to creation.[23] Indeed, Owen still spoke of the first "degree" of

---

22. Origen, *Contra Celsum* 4, 50, trans. Henry Chadwick (Cambridge: Cambridge University Press, 2008), 520.

23. See, e.g., John Wesley, *Doctrinal and Controversial Treatises II*, ed. Paul Wesley Chilcote and

illumination (preceding conversion) as "an industrious application of the *rational faculties* of our souls to know, perceive, and understand the doctrines of truth as revealed to us."[24] This account of Owen is no natural theology: it is the attempt to know truth *revealed*, but it is still a human action—one of response. Illumination is then "a light superadded" to this action of the human beyond the agential response of the human creature.[25] The creature can respond to the divine event: she can open her eyes, and as she does (so aided by the Spirit's prevenient grace) she is enabled to see to the glorious wonders of God's salvation through the illuminating light of God. Clearly, even in this opening of her eyes, the person's mind is aided by God,[26] and, of course, the power of that light reaches and touches everywhere and everything,[27] and its intensive extensity makes the small act of the creature's faltering, blinking eye pale in insignificance. As through a mirror dimly (1 Cor. 13:12), by the Spirit's proleptic event in illuminating the believer, we see what one day we shall see face-to-face. As Augustine put it (using different metaphors),

There the one and only and all-embracing virtue is to love what you may see, the ultimate bliss to possess what you love. There, after all, the blessed life is to be drunk from its own fountain, from which something splashes over to this human life of ours, so that in the trials and temptations of this age we may live temperately, bravely, justly and prudently. In order to attain that state of undisturbed rest and that vision of inexpressible truth, we undertake here the labor of restraining ourselves from pleasure and enduring adversity and assisting the needy and resisting the fraudulent. There the glory of the Lord is to be seen, not through some significant vision, whether of the bodily kind such as was seen on Mount Sinai, or the spiritual such as Isaiah saw or John in the Apocalypse, not in code but clearly, to the extent that the human mind can grasp it, depending on God's grace as he takes it up, so that God may speak mouth to mouth with any whom he has made worthy of such conversation.[28]

Kenneth J. Collins, The Bicentennial Edition of the Works of John Wesley, vol. 13 (Nashville: Abingdon, 2013), 179.

24. John Owen, *The Works of John Owen*, vol. 3, *The Holy Spirit*, ed. William H. Goold (Carlisle, UK: Banner of Truth Trust, 1966), 331, italics original.

25. Owen, *Works of John Owen*, 3:331–32.

26. Augustine, *On Genesis*, The Works of St. Augustine, a Translation for the 21st Century, trans. John E. Rotelle (New York: New City Press, 2003), bk. 12, 494.

27. See Daniel Hardy, *Wording a Radiance: Parting Conversations about God and the Church* (London: SCM Press, 2010), esp. ch. 6 but also passim.

28. Augustine, *On Genesis*, bk. 12, 495.

For all the overwhelming imagery of divine activity and glory, for all of the asymmetry, nevertheless, the creature acts here. Indeed, Augustine helpfully moved the discussion away from purely intellectual endeavours, seeing the activity of the creature to involve other labours: "Restraining ourselves from pleasure and enduring adversity and assisting the needy and resisting the fraudulent." It is not only an intellectual response that comes from illumination, but also an affective, moral, and doxological response.

But there is, nevertheless, also an intellectual response. Having opened the eyes of her mind to the radiant illumination of God, the creature is called to an activity of discipline to keep being able to see. It is here, and only now, that there is a need to consider what Owen called the "disciplinarian" means of interpreting Scripture, by which he meant "due use and improvement of *common arts and sciences*, applied unto and made use of in the study of the Scriptures."[29] We might call this the activity of reading and study. But there needs to be proportion in the manner in which we account for these things, lest the university professor consider herself or himself a gnostic teacher of our enlightenment age's naturalistic hermeneutical special advanced knowledge. It is hard to acknowledge that the world's oldest English-speaking university has as its motto *"Dominus illuminatio mea"* ("The Lord is my light") in an age in which the efforts of the human intellect are considered primary and the role of God in knowing has disappeared even in theology. Webster managed here to strike the right balance (though perhaps in his general argument with too much of a continuous and not interruptive sense of grace, and with too little acknowledgement of sin). When considering the event of divine illumination and the divine activity of aiding the creature, he wrote, "None of these properties eliminates the work of reception or makes the activity of reading superfluous."[30] There is a clear role for the human intellectual endeavour, but there is a clear order and proportion required here: "Hermeneutical reason is, of course, subservient; it is pupil, not *magister*; its readiness for instruction does not precede the Spirit's coming."[31] Hermeneutics is neither the proximate nor ultimate *res* of the creature's receiving of revelation. It is rather the response of the disciple who desires to learn from the master she has encountered; it is the eyes that squint open to behold the glorious light; it is the movement of the creature with (and not against) the movements of the Spirit.

---

29. Owen, *Works of John Owen*, 4:209.
30. Webster, "Illumination," 336.
31. Webster, "Illumination," 338.

Of course, even here there is need for care. We cannot presume that the manner in which we interpret a theological position, or read a text, from the exercise of human intellect is a Spirit-given truth. Indeed, the most likely illuminated readings of texts will be those that engender humility and repentance, and those that point back to Christ since the Spirit testifies to the message of Christ (John 16:13). But we can presume that what we know of truth comes from the illumination of God, that what we *receive* of revelation is because God's Spirit has aided us. We will only know the extent of this truth once we know as we are known (1 Cor. 13:12): it is only eschatologically that we will see the extent to which our minds were illuminated by the Spirit's truth. But any truth we have is truth that has not only been revealed but has reached our minds by the Spirit's illuminating action. As Augustine argued, it is not the teacher in this world who teaches truth but "by the realities themselves made manifest to him by the enlightening action of God from within."[32] The degree of illumination and spiritual truth in the efforts of our human response will come only in light of the eternity we will spend journeying ever deeper into God's own life as we behold the glories of the light whose rays we see through blinking eye now: "To the degree that the rational soul is united to Him by charity, by so much does it contemplate these intelligible principles (*rationes*), through whose vision it is made supremely happy being bathed, so to speak, and illumined by Him with spiritual light."[33]

2. Word and Spirit

There are, however, clear objective bounds to the extent to which any believer can claim illumination from the Spirit, and these result from the teaching of Jesus that the Spirit will "not speak on his own, but will speak whatever he hears" and take what is Christ's and declare it to us (John 16:13).

---

32. Augustine, *The Teacher*, trans. Robert P. Russell (Washington, DC: Catholic University of America Press, 1968), 54. Augustine was happy to credit Plato's doctrine of *anamnesis* or recollection as imparting something important about the nature of cognition: in unitizing, sortally classifying, predicating, and otherwise forming objects of thought, we must act in accord with innate cognitive structuring principles, habits, or what we would call concepts. These cannot be taught or even learned experientially because they are presupposed in all learning activity, just as a word's lexical definition cannot give you a concept but presupposes you already have it and merely offers you a new sign for it. By making use of native concepts, there is a meaningful sense in which knowledge is "recollective" in that it grows from within as it is occasioned by external signs. But while Augustine agreed with Plato that concepts are innate, as part of our God-given endowment, he rejected any association of recollection with the transmigration of pre-existent souls.

33. Augustine, *Eighty-Three Diverse Questions*, trans. David L. Mosher (Washington DC: Catholic University of America Press, 1977), q. 46.

The principal discipline, therefore, to which the believer must attend in seeking illumination is the discipline of reading, studying, and meditating on Scripture. Illumination may well have its immediate dogmatic *res* within economic pneumatology, but it also has its proximate dogmatic *res* in relation to the doctrine of the revelation of the Word of God in Jesus Christ and in Scripture: it is *the Word* which the Spirit illumines. Here, the magisterial Protestant dogmatic principle of the unity of Word and Spirit must never be forgotten. The Spirit illumines the Word of God *to the creature*, making this Word alive and aiding the creature in her reception of it. But in this activity, the Spirit never teaches anything contrary to the Word. The Spirit is the person of God who enables the creature to receive the revealedness of revelation in her contingent spatio-temporal existence.[34] The Spirit takes what happens there and then in Israel-Palestine and brings that revelation to its telos and terminus in the creature. There is no independence in the Spirit's activity just as there is no independence in the Son's activity: the Word who is incarnate of the Holy Spirit is in its written form inspired by the Spirit; the Word which is spoken by the Son to which Scripture pays testimony is heard and received by the creature through the Holy Spirit. There is a twofold, symbiotic relationship of Word and Spirit. If the doctrine of inspiration deals with the writing of Scripture, it is the latter sense of the hearing and receiving of that Scripture that the doctrine of illumination concerns. In its most primal sense, illumination is an expression of the church's recognition of a canon—of the church's hearing of the gospel as it is read, and the church's ascent to the authority of the canon over it. More specifically, we might say, "Illumination refers to the Spirit's work of so enlightening the church's reading and contemplation of the words of the prophets, evangelists, and apostles that regenerate intelligence comes to know the mind of God."[35] Crucially, this is not a limitation pertaining to creaturely intellectual cognisance: "The workings of the Spirit in illumination, as in all things, are mysterious, exceeding creaturely capacity."[36] But this mystery is a revealed mystery in the Word of God: it is a mystery which brings the revelation of the mystery of God in the face of Jesus Christ (2 Cor. 4:6) to creaturely cognition as mystery.

---

34. Cf. my Tom Greggs, *Barth, Origen and Universal Salvation: Restoring Particularity* (Oxford: Oxford University Press, 2009), pt. 2.

35. Webster, "Illumination," 325. Here intelligence needs to be referred to in the broader sense. It is knowing the mind of God, which is the sign of regenerate intelligence, not intelligence as the condition for knowing God. There can be problems perhaps in Webster's account where intellect is construed in an overly narrow way.

36. Webster, "Illumination," 325.

In this way, it is not a mysticism or expression of an inward light unfettered by canonical rule: illumination is the illumination *of Scripture, of the Word.* As Quenstedt said, any aptitude to know is "called God-given not because it is such through some fantastic ecstacy or enthusiasm, as the new prophets, Schwenkfelders, Weigelians, and Shakers or Quakers in England boast of their aptitude, but because it is such through a divine gift, not direct but indirect and drawn from the Word of God."[37]

Illumination is not the freedom to claim authority for ourselves, but the freedom to live under the instruction of Scripture in a way that does not valorise the modern banality of either fundamentalism or intellectual naturalism. When we enquire into illumination, we are concerned with Scripture as it speaks—without certainty we know exactly what it says, what it means, or that we are able to hear it without being inhibited by sin, and yet through illumination hearing Scripture as "the communication of *divine revelations* unto the minds of men."[38] Illumination concerns Scripture as the means by which the Spirit effects the Spirit's "infinite wisdom and care of the church" through the speaking of Scripture to the here and now.[39] Illumination in Protestant theology is also not an expression of natural theology, as if the book of creation could be read except through the book of Scripture.[40] Illumination does not free believers from the Word but binds them to it: through illumination the Word reaches its terminus in the creature; the Word becomes alive and living; the Word is heard, and—from this hearing—is proclaimed by the church. Vanhoozer articulates this point well (though with particular emphasis on speech-act theory):

> The Spirit illumines the letter by impressing its illocutionary force on the reader. Thanks to the illumination of the Spirit, we see and hear speech acts for what they are—warnings, promises, commands, assertions— together with their implicit claim in our minds and hearts. In so doing, the Spirit does not alter but ministers the meaning: "The spiritual sense is the literal sense correctly understood." The distinction between "letter"

---

37. Quenstedt, *Nature and Character of Theology*, 74–75.

38. Owen, *Works of John Owen*, 4:187, italics original.

39. Owen, *Works of John Owen,* 4:187.

40. It should be noted, however, that such an understanding of natural theology has only become mainstream recently. In early modern Protestant theology, natural theology was valued as a search for divine revelation that was posterior to the encounter with Scripture and the regenerate acquisition of faith. See John Henry, "Religion and the Scientific Revolution," in *The Cambridge Companion to Science and Religion*, ed. Peter Harrison (Cambridge: Cambridge University Press, 2010), 39–58.

and "spirit" is precisely that between reading the words and grasping what one reads. Likewise, the difference between a "natural" and an "illuminated" understanding is that between holding an opinion and having a deep sense of its profundity.[41]

Illumination is not an inward, free-ranging direct inspiration, therefore, but an event of the Spirit's grace always in relation to the already objectively revealed Word of God in the person of Jesus Christ. Illumination does not offer another source of authority separate from the Word of God, but is a means of hearing, beholding, receiving, and experiencing the Word of God in the contingent contemporaneities in which the church and its believers live.

One should not, therefore, set up a false competition between the doctrines of inspiration and illumination, or between the sufficiency of the Word of God and the ongoing work of the Spirit enabling the believer to receive it, as if there were a zero-sum game between these options.[42] Rather, these two events of merciful grace are symbiotic events of the one act of God in divine grace. They are the objective and subjective works of revelation;[43] or else the speaking and hearing works of the Word; or else the outward and inward works of the gospel. Although his emphasis was always on the Word of God and the accounts of the Holy Spirit he offered were often underdeveloped, Martin Luther made this point powerfully:

> Now when God sends forth his gospel he deals with us in a twofold manner, first outwardly, then inwardly. Outwardly he deals with us through the oral word of the gospel and through material signs, that is, baptism and the sacrament of the altar. Inwardly he deals with us through the Holy Spirit, faith, and other gifts. But whatever their measure or order the outward factors should and must precede. The inward experience follows and is effected by the outward. God has determined to give the inward to no one except through the outward. For he wants to give no one the Spirit or faith outside of the outward Word and sign instituted by him. . . . Observe carefully, my brother, this order, for everything depends on it.[44]

---

41. Vanhoozer, *Is There a Meaning in This Text?*, 413.

42. Douglas Kennard creates such a zero sum in his "Evangelical Views on Illumination of Scripture and Critique," *Journal of the Evangelical Theological Society* 49, no.4 (2006): 797–806.

43. See Barth, *CD*, I/1.

44. Martin Luther, *Church and Ministry II*, Luther's Works, vol. 40 (Minneapolis: Augsburg Fortress, 1959), 146.

This order and asymmetry are of crucial importance. There is no moment in which we hear something that has not been spoken by God; no moment in which we can experience something that has not been done by God in Christ; no moment in which we subjectively appropriate something that has not been objectively enacted. But without the hearing, without the experience, without the subjective, how can we ever know that which is spoken, completed, and objective? This twofold manner of the gospel cannot be divided: inspiration is meaningless without illumination, just as illumination is meaningless without inspiration. Illumination not only rests on the presumption of the sufficiency of Scripture but is also an expression of what sufficiency means: "Scripture is not an 'unsupplemented text'; its sufficiency is not self-sufficiency. There is inspired Scripture, and there is a set of Spirit-moved persons and activities (to avoid hermeneutical inflation, call them 'readers' and 'reading') which constitute creaturely intelligence and learning."[45]

Inspiration and illumination belong inextricably together as doctrinal expressions of the one act of God in the events of the Spirit's inspiration of and illumination of God's Word to humanity.

Illumination, therefore, does not undermine a doctrine of perspicuity but is a means of expressing it. Unnuanced understandings of perspicacity actually allow the reader to claim more authority for herself without a sense of the mediated forms. If the text is perfectly perspicuous alone without the reader needing to be aided by the Spirit, then this enhances the claims of any individual, since her own natural capacity is claimed as the authority for the interpretation of Scripture as if no mediating activity of God between the text and reader were required and as if no humility in relation to a life (and, in that, a life of sin) beneath the objective reality of the text were needed. That the Spirit's illuminating mercy is required to interpret a text opens the possibility of any individual's interpretation being ultimately authoritative and expresses the sovereignty of Scripture (and not any individual's interpretation) over the believer.[46] Quenstedt helpfully set up a hierarchy of

---

45. Webster, "Illumination," 336.

46. Kennard, "Evangelical Views on Illumination," is wrong, therefore, in his sense of perspicuity when he claims meaning is "clearly indicated in the divinely accommodated biblical text itself without need of an intuitive work of the Spirit to render this clear" (799). This enhances the interpretation of any individual, suggesting no other interpretation is possible, and it also enhances the singular interpretation of one Christian or group in relation to the text. It is not Scripture that is clear in such an approach, but it is rather the particular interpretation that is claimed as clear. In Zwingli's 1522 sermon "On the Perspicuity and Certainty, of Infallibility, of the Word of God," in *Huldrych Zwingli Writings: The Defense of the Reformed Faith*, trans. Edward Julius Furcha, vol. 1 (Allison Park: Pickwick, 1984), 328–84, Zwingli argued that any authoritative interpretation has

causation in terms of theological reflection (his term for receiving the Word of God). Clearly, for him, the principal efficient cause of our knowledge and hearing the Word of God is the triune God Godself.[47] But he then listed as the "moving cause" the economy of God. This economy is described in a twofold manner. First, there is "the boundless goodness and inexhaustible mercy of God, by which God, as it were the good especially communicative of itself, deigned to impart His wisdom to men and, coming forth from the hidden seat of His majesty, to reveal Himself to mankind." Second, following the fall, there is the mercy of God by which God saves us from perishing, and in this God brings us to know God by God's divine Word.[48] Following this moving cause, there is the "mediating cause," which is the written word of the Bible: "We know nothing of the divine mysteries but by divine revelation comprehended in the Sacred Scriptures."[49] There is, then, what Quenstedt described as the "ministerial causes": the writers who were directly inspired, and the great company of the orthodox.[50] Only following this can we begin to reflect on the reception of this (in Quenstedt's terms) theology in the "form of theology":

> The form of theology is gathered from its genus, and the specific differ-
> ence is drawn from the other causes. Now there is (1) a remote genus,
> namely intellectual aptitude, or that which perfects our intellect, (2) a
> near [genus], namely the practical aptitude, and (3) the nearest [genus],
> namely the practical aptitude given by God, or conferred on man by the
> Holy Spirit through the Word.[51]

The most proximate event or moment for the creature in this hierarchy is the God-given aptitude to know, hear, and receive revelation "by the Holy Spirit through the Word." Moving from the Bible as an objective reality to its interpretation through an overemphasis on inspiration in an account of perspicacity is tantamount to the very naturalistic interpretations offered

---

its source in no less and no more than the self-disclosure of the Spirit. This is as much true for the average believer as it is for the pope or church father. It is not that the average believer should have any special confidence in the prospects of an unassisted reading; Zwingli's point is rather that the individual cannot expect any "outsourced" temporal authority to substitute for the illuminative work of the Spirit. After all, to discern truth in any instruction received or sermon preached, individuals would need to test the message against their own Spirit-led interpretation.

47. Quenstedt, *Nature and Character of Theology*, thesis 31, 54.
48. Quenstedt, thesis 32, 55–56.
49. Quenstedt, thesis 33, 56.
50. Quenstedt, thesis 34, 56–57.
51. Quenstedt, thesis 35, 57.

in academic hermeneutics and historical criticism. Perspicacity is, instead, an account of all these events of the one act of God in God's movement toward and within the creature through the Spirit and the Word—not simply an account of rational and natural exercise of human intelligence in relation to an objective text that is considered objectively clear in relation to a particular person's or church's interpretation. John Owen put this well:

> It is supposed, when we assert the *clearness and perspicuity* of the Scripture, that there is unto the understanding of it use made of that *aid* and *assistance* of the Spirit concerning which we do discourse. Without this the *clearest revelations* of divine supernatural things will appear as wrapped up in darkness and obscurity: not for want of *light in them* but for want of *light in us*. Wherefore, by asserting the necessity of supernatural illumination for the right understanding of divine revelation, we no way impeach the *perspicuity* of the Scripture.[52]

And what remains unclear or obscure is so "for the *exercise of our faith, diligence, humility, and dependence on God*, in our inquiries into them."[53] It is to make us humble in our interpretation and diligent in faith that there continue to be aspects of Scripture that are unclear to the human reader. Scripture might well be objectively perspicuous, but we cannot see the clarity of its light unaided—not because there is not perfect light in Scripture but because there is no light in us and our eyes are closed by sin. We cannot confuse our sinful or naturalistic readings with the perspicuity of the inspired Word of God: without illumination, we can never see this.

3. Human Reader

It is incumbent, therefore, on any account of illumination to address not only loci of pneumatology and of the revelation of the Word, but also the locus of theological anthropology. Illumination is a response to the question of who the person is who is interpreting, and as such illumination must attend to an account of the human reader. Interpretation does not happen without a human interpreter, and that human interpreter must not fail to be considered as a theological object. What it is to be human is a question for theology in a theological account of the interpretation of Scripture. This

---

52. Owen, *Works of John Owen*, 4:194, italics original.
53. Owen, *Works of John Owen*, 4:197, italics original.

subject can be treated no more atheistically or naturalistically than the question of the text itself, or of revelation or of interpretation. Who it is who is interpreting is central to the question of what the task of interpretation is.

The human creature reading the text of Scripture and receiving revelation is both limited and sinful. The limits of the creature make her unable to receive the revelation of God unaided. The magnificent plenitude of the divine life is such that the revelation of it comes only in a veiled form even as it is unveiled.[54] There are two forms of this limitation. First, even in the form of the Scripture itself, the Bible is indirect as a revelation. It is, primarily, a *witness* to revelation, but it is not in itself the encounter of revelation with the human. It is in its own form (unaided by the Spirit's grace) a set of limited, human words spoken and written by limited, human authors. The Spirit is needed to overcome by illumination the limitations of the creaturely human words of Scripture from its authors, and by an event of grace, make it become the revelation of the Word of God to which its words witness. Second, the Spirit is needed to overcome the barriers and limitations of the contemporary human reader. The limitations of her own creatureliness require the Spirit's aid in order that she might receive even in its veiled form the unveiling of God's revelation. John Owen put the matter strongly: "This defect ariseth not from any blamable *depravation of our nature* as corrupted, but from the very *essence and being* of it as created; for being finite and limited, it cannot perfectly comprehend things infinite."[55] And it is worth quoting Barth here at length in terms of the interrelation of these two barriers:

> It is not only that we cannot attribute to ourselves any capacity or instrument for recognising the Word of God either in the Bible or elsewhere. It is also that if we are serious about the true humanity of the Bible, we obviously cannot attribute to the Bible as such the capacity—and in this it is distinguished, as we have seen, from the exalted and glorified humanity of Jesus Christ—in such a way to reveal God to us that by its very presence, by the fact that we can read it, it gives us a hearty faith in the Word of God spoken in it. It is there and always there as a sign, as a human and temporal word—and therefore also as a word which is conditioned and limited. It witnesses to God's revelation, but that does not mean that God's revelation is now before us in any kind of divine

---

54. See Barth on the veiled-unveiled dialectic in the word of God's one-sided encounter with us, *CD*, I/1.6, 207.

55. Owen, *Works of John Owen*, 4:196, italics original.

revealedness. The Bible is not a book of oracles; it is not an instrument of direct impartation. It is genuine witness. And how can it be witness of divine revelation, if the actual purpose, act and decision of God in His only-begotten Son, as seen and heard by the prophets and apostles in that Son, is dissolved in the Bible into a sum total of truths abstracted from that decision—and those truths are then propounded to us as truths of faith, salvation and revelation? If it tries to be more than witness, to be direct impartation, will it not keep from us the best, the one real thing, which God intends to tell and give us and which we ourselves need? But if it does not try to do this, if it is really witness, we must understand clearly what it means and involves that in itself it is only witness. It means the existence of those barriers which can be broken down only by miracle. The men whom we hear as witnesses speak as fallible, erring men like ourselves. What they say, and what we read as their word, can of itself lay claim to be the Word of God, but never sustain that claim.[56]

Simply as creatures, we need the supernatural grace of God to receive the revelation of the divine life, since such reception "transcends our ability to understand."[57]

What makes these limitations even greater is that the human creature is fallen and sinful:[58] not only does she live in a condition of creaturely limitation but in that creaturely limitation, she moves further away from the grace of divine life and lives in revolt and resistance to it. As John Webster put it, "Before theology can proceed, such resistance may need to be healed. To understand illumination, theological reason needs illumination."[59] The first step of this illumination is an awareness and conviction of sin. Indeed, this awareness (and the humility that stems from it) is an indication of the illuminating grace of the Spirit. If the reader is convicted and humbled, there is evidence of the Spirit's illumination of the text. Wesley made this point when he wrote, "How is this testimony to be distinguished from the presumption of a natural mind? It is certain, one who was never convinced

56. Barth, *CD*, I/2, 506–7.
57. Quenstedt, *Nature and Character of Theology*, thesis 15, 39.
58. It is worth noting that, for example, for Owen conviction of sin is a discussion that follows on directly from the discussion of illumination; see Owen, *Works of John Owen*, 3:233–34. And Quenstedt, too, was very aware of sinfulness (34–35).
59. Webster, "Illumination," 327, saw this resistance in terms of hermeneutical naturalism. There needs, however, to be a stronger account of sin. Webster saw the *opus gratiae* to accord with the work of the Spirit in *opus naturae*. But there is not enough emphasis on the interruption of grace in relation to a world of sin. Webster did note, however, that "the depravity of our nature is such that we resist acquiring the knowledge of God's mind."

of sin is always ready to flatter himself, and to think of himself, especially in spiritual things, more highly than he ought to think."[60]

We might say the light shines into the darkness and makes us aware of the darkness in which we did not know we were. Only as we are illuminated do we become aware of sin and the need for our illumination. The sin of which we are convicted is an indication of the Spirit's gracious aid in helping us to hear revelation: through the Spirit we encounter the speaking Jesus saying, "Repent and believe."

Illumination is not, therefore, a continuity with the creature's capacity, as if unaided the creature could ascend toward the Lord's revelation. Instead, the Spirit works in salvation, bringing the God-breathed, redeeming, sanctifying grace of salvation. While being sanctified, we are able proleptically to move within the divine movements of grace: our movements within and in correspondence to God's own movement of grace are always brought by the Spirit's "assisting grace."[61] Clement of Alexandria in his *Paidagogos* viewed enlightenment as a means of expressing salvation: "This is what happens with us, whose model the Lord made Himself. When we are baptized, we are enlightened; being enlightened, we become adopted sons; becoming adopted sons, we are made perfect; and becoming perfect, we are made divine."[62] Our illumination or "enlightenment" does not precede but succeeds the saving grace of God, and is part of the ongoing salvific work of God in us as creatures as we are illumined.[63] An account of illumination requires, therefore, an account of the renewing grace of the Spirit in the human.[64] In the words of John Webster:

> The renewal of creaturely nature includes renewal in the knowledge of God, for the Spirit is "the spirit of wisdom and of revelation" (Eph. 1:17). This work of the Spirit is the environment for a theology of revelation, and therefore of Holy Scripture as its prophetic and apostolic form, and therefore of the illumination of the regenerate mind for the reading of Scripture. The Spirit is given that, having the eyes of their hearts enlightened, the saints may *know*.[65]

---

60. John Wesley, *The Works of John Wesley*, vol. 1, *Sermons I* (Nashville: Abingdon, 1984), 277.

61. Quenstedt, *Nature and Character of Theology*, 74.

62. Clement, *Christ the Educator*, 26.

63. Bonaventure, *The Works of Bonaventure: Itinerarium Mentis in Deum* (Franciscan Institute Publications, 2002), ch. 4, made a similar point: the pilgrimage of perfection is one of illumination.

64. Sanctification is at once complete and objective in Christ; ongoing by the Spirit who forms us into the form of Christ; and awaiting us in completion in the eschaton, throughout which all creatures will journey into the divine life.

65. Webster, "Illumination," 329, italics original.

The knower who encounters revelation does so as she is being redeemed and sanctified.

The limited sinful and sanctified creature also comes by illumination to be open to different forms of knowledge and knowing. Learning through the illumination of grace is different from simply reading to gain other modes of knowledge.[66] Since illumination is a mode of knowing for the believer who is being sanctified by grace, both the mechanism of knowing and the knowledge that is gained is distinctive from other modes of knowing and other forms of knowledge. John Wesley accounts for this in his extracts from Norris as follows:

> Men famed for learning are often infamous for living; and many that study hard to furnish their heads, are yet very negligent in purifying their hearts; not considering, that there is a moral as well as a natural communication between them; and that they are concerned to be pure in heart and life, not only upon the common account in order to happiness hereafter, but even in order to their own particular end here.[67]

In the here and now, therefore, through the illumination of the Spirit, we are enlightened not in gnostic information, but in the purification of our hearts and our moral lives. The human knows but the knowledge the human has is a knowledge that comes not from willful exercise of our intellects but from the light that comes from God, exposing and banishing the darkness within the creature.[68] By illumination, the human becomes capable of knowing that of which she was previously incapable in terms of knowledge of God and God's ways with the world and with us as individuals.

The mode of knowing and receiving revelation for the human is a mode that is not only done, furthermore, with the mind, but also through prayer. The immediate means of knowing the revelation of God comes from "fervent and earnest prayer for the assistance of the Spirit of God revealing the mind of God."[69] Indeed, Wesley's edition of Norris's *Reflections on the Conduct of Human Life*, affirms Norris in saying that prayer is the "way of consulting God": "This we know was the method whereby the wisest of men obtained his unparalleled wisdom. For as wisdom was his choice, so

---

66. John Wesley, *Reflections upon the Conduct of Human Life; with Reference to Learning and Knowledge. Extracted from Mr. Norris*, 5th ed. (London: Methodist Preaching Houses, 1798), 13.

67. Wesley, *Reflections*, 14.

68. Webster, "Illumination," 333, put this in an inverted way that is equally helpful: "It is *in God's light* that creatures see light; but in God's light creatures really do *see* (Ps. 33:9)."

69. Owen, *Works of John Owen*, 4:201.

the method of his seeking and obtaining it was by prayer."[70] Those who read Scripture and seek to know the deep things of God must attend to their studies but must do so also on bended knee and in a posture of prayer. The words of Norris apply even more now in an age that prioritises methodological naturalism and atheism more than in his own times:

> The generality of students do not apply themselves to this at all. Pray indeed (it is to be hoped) they do for other things which they think lie more out of their reach; but as for learning, they think they can compass this well enough by their own industry, and the help of good books, without being beholden to the assistance of heaven. But did they attentively consider, that God is truth, it is not to be imagined they would be so indifferent in using prayer, or any of the preceding methods of consulting God for his own light.[71]

In the context of prayer, we read the Word of God that we may hear and receive its words. Prayer becomes the context in which the Spirit's work of sanctifying the creature enables her to receive the Word in what John Henry Newman called the "illative" sense[72]—a context in which the Spirit takes the Word of God in prayer and particularises this Word in the concrete contexts of contingent contemporaneity in a manner that brings about wise, moral, holy behaviour.[73] This illuminating work of the Spirit through prayer in and for a particular context, and in forming the believer, enables the Word of God to be heard and then spoken in any place or time: "Where God the Spirit discloses the truth of God's story in Israel and in Jesus to us and so creates faith, the particular story of Jesus becomes the key to our particular life-story. God the Spirit discloses the universal truth of the story of God with Israel and with Jesus by particularising it for particular people at particular times."[74]

The human subject not only hears the Word of God through the Spirit's merciful and gracious work of illumination, but hears the Word spoken to (and heard in) a given context in its spatio-temporal contingency and particularity.

---

70. Wesley, *Reflections*, 15.

71. Wesley, *Reflections*, 15.

72. John Henry Newman, *An Essay in Aid of a Grammar of Assent* (London: Longmans, Green, 1903).

73. Cf. Quenstedt, *Nature and Character of Theology*, 29–30: inspiration of God is "acquired by experience and intuitive by excellence."

74. Christoph Schwöbel, "Introduction," in *Theology through Preaching: Sermons for Brentwood*, ed. Colin E. Gunton (Edinburgh: T&T Clark, 2005), 8.

CONCLUSION

What is it for the church to be a creature of the Word? To be a creature of the Word is to focus first and foremost on how the living Word of God creatures us. It is the active passivity of *hearing* and *knowing* and *receiving*. We know and hear through the Spirit's illuminating merciful grace in enabling the creature to hear the Word of God as a fallen, limited human being sanctified in the here and now as she prays to know the Lord's ways and Word. It is only by the grace of God that we can hear the words of the grace of God. We are not illuminated through Enlightenment means of knowing, but Scripture itself teaches that we are strengthened to this purpose through the work of the Spirit. This is, in the end, a mode of knowing that has a telos that roots and grounds us in love. The knowledge we receive from God and the words we hear surpass our natural knowledge or capacities. We are strengthened by the Spirit, and Christ dwells deeply in our hearts through faith. The Word of God and the Spirit of God can never be prized apart: the Word is inspired by the Spirit just as the Spirit illuminates the Word. Should we ever rest singularly on our own capacities (however much we believe these to be fitting) to understand God's Word, we deceive ourselves in our pride and sin that we can know the love of Christ that "surpasses knowledge." For the church to be a *creatura verbi* is not an expression of what Daniel Hardy called "a purism of the word" or primarily an account of the preaching office.[75] It is rather an expression of the hearing of the whole church of the sovereign word of God spoken to it by the Spirit, and a receiving of the gospel by the church.

---

75. Daniel Hardy, *Finding the Church* (London: SCM, 2001), 33.

CHAPTER 3

CONFESSING CHRIST AND CONFESSING THE CHURCH

KIMLYN J. BENDER

CENTURIES AGO, IN 1431, a young warrior was tried and put to death on religious grounds, though her reputation would in time be restored and the Roman Catholic Church would grant her sainthood in 1920. Before her accusers at trial, asked about Christ and the church, Joan of Arc gave a remarkable confession: "About Jesus Christ and the Church, I simply know they're just one thing, and we shouldn't complicate the matter."[1] Her response, evincing both firm conviction and simple piety, highlights one answer to a question that is fundamental for Christian faith, specifically, what is the relation of Christ to the church? Such a question may indeed complicate the matter, but such complication seems inescapable upon reflection. This reflection might begin with the direct question of the relation of Christ and the church, though it may begin with a consideration of ecclesiology itself as a theological topic and how such a question might find its place within it.

To consider ecclesiology is to consider a doctrine that must be recognized as a derived one, though the immediate question that follows is, derived from what, exactly? Broadly speaking, ecclesiology is an implicate of the work of God in the economy of salvation, the end result of God's

---

1. Quoted in the *Catechism of the Catholic Church*, 2nd ed. (New York: Doubleday, 1995), §795, 229.

salvific will and action, of Christ's earthly and ascended threefold ministry, of the Spirit's power that calls the church into existence, adds to its number, and equips it for its witness in the world. In this sense, ecclesiology follows upon the work of the triune God, and insofar as this God determines to be for the world as its creator, reconciler, and redeemer, yet is not of the world or dependent upon it, the church is grounded in the election of God. The church is enclosed within the intentions of God even as it is instantiated within the world and, like all creatures, stands over against God as well. In this regard, God's freedom and perfection are as fundamental in relation to the church as they are to creation, for the church is a created reality. For this reason, ecclesiology is a doctrine ultimately situated under the doctrine of the Trinity.[2]

If this divine election in freedom is the ultimate grounding of the church's existence, the proximate cause of the church's appearance in history is the enlivening work of the Holy Spirit, which is nowhere in Scripture so evident as in the founding of the church at Pentecost. Regardless of understandable attempts to speak of the church in the Old Testament or with regard to the apostolic band around Jesus during his earthly ministry, the church proper—as the confessing community that now, as at its inception, proclaims the crucified Christ as the risen Lord and attends to the teaching of the apostles, to fellowship, to the breaking of bread, and to prayer (Acts 2:42)—this church came to be through the miraculous and promised arrival of the Spirit in power at Pentecost. For this reason, ecclesiology stands as a subdiscipline within pneumatology, and in point of fact the church finds itself placed under the third article of the creed.[3]

Yet while the church is grounded in the triune God of eternity and called into being in time by the Spirit of power, the result of the divine freedom and faithfulness, the church stands in a special relation to Christ such that ecclesiology is also a derived doctrine of Christology. Indeed, it may be argued that it is from this particular vantage point that ecclesiology is best framed and understood. This is the case not only because the concrete form of God's election of the church is itself enclosed within the larger election of God to be for us in Christ Jesus, in whom the church was chosen "before the foundation of the world" (Eph. 1:4; see vv. 3–14),

2. See John Webster, "'In the Society of God': Some Principles of Ecclesiology" in Webster, *God without Measure: Working Papers in Christian Theology*, vol. 1, *God and the Works of God* (London: T&T Clark, 2016), 177–94.

3. See Tom Greggs, "Proportion and Topography in Ecclesiology: A Working Paper on the Dogmatic Location of the Doctrine of the Church," in *Theological Theology: Essays in Honour of John Webster*, ed. R. David Nelson, Darren Sarisky, and Justin Stratis (London: T&T Clark, 2015), 89–106.

but because the church's coming into existence at Pentecost by the Spirit also finds its meaning within the larger range of events, including the prior call of Christ to his disciples and his revelation of the Father to them, his death and resurrection for their salvation and that of the world, his promise to send the Spirit upon them for their empowerment and to lead them into truth (John 16:7–15), his commission to them to "go . . . and make disciples" (Matt. 28:19), and his ascension and promised return for which the church hopes and waits. In short, the church lives between the first and second advent of Christ and takes its place in the salvific economy precisely as a community in view of and attesting to Christ's earthly ministry and ascended lordship. Moreover, that ecclesiology is properly an implicate and derived doctrine of Christology becomes clear when it is appreciated that ecclesiology sets forth not only the ultimate *grounds* upon which the church rests and the proximate *means* by which it is established, empowered, and equipped, but also the particular *content* of its proclamation and confession and the particular *form* such witness takes in its life. The content of the church's proclamation is the gospel, and the form of its witness is a suffering love for the sake of the world. The church proclaims, as Paul insists in his first canonical letter to the Corinthians, a word of the cross even as it lives a cruciform life, both resting upon resurrection hope in the crucified and risen Christ.[4]

To put this in the language of Martin Luther, the church lives not for itself but in Christ and in the world—it lives "in Christ through faith," and it lives in its "neighbor through love."[5] That the church's faith is a faith in Christ crucified and risen and its love a cruciform love entails that Christology and ecclesiology are intricately intertwined. The fact that this order of Christ's perfect sacrifice received in faith precedes and gives intelligibility to Christ's paradigmatic example of love, and that these cannot be reversed in order, ensures that Christology and ecclesiology are themselves irreversibly ordered and distinct. Luther's irreversible order

---

4. Indeed, all of Paul's advice to the Corinthians in very practical matters is given in view of the cross, since "there is no church or church practice for Paul without the cross, nor any that is not in the end cruciform in character." See Kimlyn J. Bender, *1 Corinthians*, Brazos Theological Commentary of the Bible (Grand Rapids: Brazos, 2022), 199. As Joseph Fitzmyer observed, "The one norm by which Paul judges almost every problem in the Corinthian church is its relationship to Christ Jesus, who is for him not only the content of the gospel that he preaches or the motivation of his exhortations, but also the norm of conduct for all individual Christians and of the activity of the community as a whole." Joseph A. Fitzmyer, *First Corinthians*, Anchor Bible Commentary (New Haven, CT: Yale University Press, 2008), 75.

5. Luther, *The Freedom of a Christian*, in Martin Luther, *Luther's Works*, ed. Jaroslav Pelikan and Helmut T. Lehmann, 55 vols. (St. Louis: Concordia; Philadelphia: Fortress, 1958–86), 31:371. All references to this work hereafter: *LW* followed by the volume and page number(s) (e.g., *LW*, 31:371).

of faith in Christ and works of love for others is uninfringeable not only soteriologically but ecclesiologically. Christ's perfection in person and work cannot be confused with the church's own identity and activity such that soteriology gives way to moralism.[6] Nevertheless, the proclamation and life of the church are both christologically determined.

The proclamation of Christ crucified and risen is therefore at the heart of the church's identity, evident from the very first day of the church's existence at Pentecost, for the purposes of God, grounded in the mystery of his eternal will, are revealed by means of the power of the Spirit now poured down upon the disciples—and what is revealed is the very salvation that has come to the world in Jesus Christ. The church, first through the mouth of Peter and through countless persons thereafter, proclaims and confesses Christ—crucified, risen, ascendant, and glorious. It announces the gospel—that Jesus, crucified at the hands of sinners, yet all according to the plan and foreknowledge of God and with larger salvific intent, is now risen and ascended and is both Lord and Christ, his name the only one given for our salvation (Acts 2:22–24, 36; 4:12).

This gospel, the constitutive mark of the church's apostolicity that grounds its unity, gives rise to its catholicity, and declares and specifies the basis of its holiness, is the confessing of Jesus as both Christ crucified and risen Lord, raised by the Father through the power of the Holy Spirit. Jesus is the one who has revealed the Father's heart, who promised to send the Spirit, who is now seated at the right hand of God, interceding for, addressing, and ruling, his church. Ecclesiology is consequently an implicate of Christology—for as Christ was sent by the Father, so Christ sent the apostles, and by extension, sends the church into the world (John 20:21; Matt. 28:18–20). The works he did, he promised they themselves would do (John 14:12); the love he has for them, he commanded they should have for one another (John 15:12–13). There is thus an analogue between these two commissions and movements, and therefore between the unique, incomparable, and perfect work of Christ in his passion and the correspondent suffering of the church in its earthly witness to that work, a fact that is never lost on the apostle Paul (e.g., Rom. 8:17; cf. Col. 1:24).

---

6. "For the Christian life is profoundly disoriented if it asks only *what the Christian ought to do*, without first asking *what God has done for him or her*." Eberhard Jüngel, "The Sacrifice of Jesus Christ as Sacrament and Example" in *Theological Essays II*, trans. Arnold Neufeldt-Fast and J. B. Webster (Edinburgh: T&T Clark, 1995), 166–67. The same holds as true for the church as for the Christian in this respect.

When this particular relation of Christ and the church is appreciated, it is then unsurprising that the most dominant images for the church in the New Testament and those that have played the most significant role in the history of the church's self-reflection are christological ones. Moreover, the fact that the election of Christ encloses the election of the church, so that the sending of Christ by the Father finds a corresponding echo in the sending of the church by Christ through the Spirit, entails that the relation of Christ and the church and the clarification of their respective ministries become matters of particular dogmatic and practical importance.

In view of this intimacy of Christ with his church, one might then return to our initial inquiry and reasonably ask—how should the unity of Christ and his church be understood; and remembering Joan of Arc's response, is confessing Christ and confessing the church one thing or two? The remainder of this paper will attempt to provide a provisional answer to these questions. In brief I will argue that rightly framing such questions depends on taking account of three determining factors: *who* is making the proclamation of identification and unity, *how* such unity is understood, and *when* and in what context this claim is being made.

Before we can address such themes, however, it is important to appreciate the trajectory and broad convictions of the biblical witness and the resultant trajectory in the West on the question of the relation of Christ and the church. Due to limitations of space, we are here only able to paint with the broadest brush and present brief examples rather than detailed examinations of biblical passages. Yet the conclusion that is reached, when examining the entire New Testament, is that Christ is portrayed both as the unique divine Lord who alone effects the world's salvation through his sacrificial death, as well as the true human exemplar who serves as the pattern for the church's life and behavior. For instance, it is the very supremacy and singularity of Christ's humiliation and exaltation for our salvation to which Paul appealed when arguing that others should live in a way that they might "Let this mind be in you, which was also in Christ Jesus" (Phil. 2:1–11 [v. 5] KJV). Such a view of Christ as both incomparable Savior and exemplary pattern is also witnessed in the fact that Christ is both the unique Lord who has the divine authority to give an absolute command and the paradigm for human obedience to such a command (see John 13:13–15). This is a consistent portrait across the witness of the New Testament. What must also be added, however, is that the careful distinction of Christ and the church in the New Testament was softened in Augustine's conception of the *totus Christus*, wherein Christ and the church were portrayed as a single "person."[7] It was later sacrificed in florid christological ecclesiologies of the nineteenth and twentieth centuries, such as those of Johann Adam Möhler, Matthias Joseph Scheeben, Karl Adam, and Émile Mersch, in which the church was understood as an extension of Christ, ecclesiology itself effectively subsumed into Christology.[8]

Now, the temptation in view of past excesses in christological ecclesiology is of course to abandon Christology as of distinctive importance for understanding the church. Such is an understandable reaction, but it is not a helpful one. It is understandable because straightforward comparisons of Christ's being and work and the church's own—such as conceptions of the church as an extension of the incarnation and the prolongation of Christ's ministry in the world, as seen so often in metaphysical ecclesiologies of the modern period—fail to preserve Christ's perfection and the singular character of his unique existence and accomplishment. The reaction is likewise understandable when it is recognized that Augustine's conception of the relation of Christ and the church as a single person, however pastorally helpful in its context and unsystematic in its construal, was nevertheless the beginning of a deeply misguided trajectory. As T. A. Lacey observed decades ago, "To say that the Church is the body of Christ is not the same as to say that the Church is Christ."[9]

Therefore, in view of the testimony of the scriptural witness, the "basic dogmatic rules" of Christ's perfection and preeminence,[10] and past historical excesses (and rightly in that order), the answer to our earlier question must be that confessing Christ and confessing the church are two irreducible acts of confession, for Christ and the church can never be incorporated under

---

7. While Augustine did not invent the notion of the *totus Christus*, he is the most important person for its articulation and development in the ancient church. See Tarsicius van Bavel, "The 'Christus Totus' Idea: A Forgotten Aspect of Augustine's Spirituality," in *Studies in Patristic Christology*, ed. Thomas Finan and Vincent Twomey (Dublin: Four Courts, 1998), 84–94; Kimberly Baker, "Augustine's Doctrine of the *Totus Christus*: Reflecting on the Church as Sacrament of Unity," *Horizons* 37 (2010): 7–24; James K. Lee, *Augustine and the Mystery of the Church* (Minneapolis: Fortress, 2017); and Kimlyn J. Bender, "Christology and Ecclesiology," in *The T&T Clark Handbook of Ecclesiology*, ed. Kimlyn J. Bender and L. Stephen Long (London/New York: T&T Clark/ Bloomsbury, 2020), 327–30 (323–43). Also insightful are the articles by David Moser and Kevin Vanhoozer (and Moser's response to Vanhoozer) on Augustine's conception of the *totus Christus* in *Pro Ecclesia* 29 (2020): 3–30; 31–42; and 53–67, respectively.

8. For a brief survey of this Augustinian trajectory in these figures, see Bender, "Christology and Ecclesiology," 330–35.

9. T. A. Lacey, quoted in J. Robert Nelson, *The Realm of Redemption: Studies in the Doctrine of the Nature of the Church in Contemporary Protestant Theology*, 6th ed. (London: Epworth, 1963), 91. Nelson himself provides a more sober path ahead: "As Head of the Body, then, Christ is considered both distinct from the Body and inseparable from it. He unites the Body in Himself, and is yet not to be identified with it. His Spirit gives the Church life and direction, but He is not just the soul of the Church" (93).

10. See Webster, "'In the Society of God,'" 187 (186–87).

the conception of a single and identical subject, nor can their work be brought under a single appellation of salvific "causes," even if distinguished by the notions of primary and secondary ones. Karl Barth once said that only someone who could say "Jesus Christ" in one word could take pride in not being a dialectical theologian.[11] And in analogy to this, one cannot speak of Christ and the church as enclosed within a single subjectivity or agency. While there may be suspicions of stark dualism with relation to theological anthropology and the understanding of the human person as body and soul, there can be no such suspicion here, but only firm conviction in an irreducible and irrevocable duality. To confess Christ and to confess the church are to confess two different realities. In this respect, to speak of Christ and the church in their irreversible distinction requires not only a dialectical imagination but dialectical conviction and confession.[12]

Yet however much the extravagant Augustinian ecclesiologies of the nineteenth century have shown themselves deficient in preserving this distinction, it is nevertheless a mistake to cast aside the real union of Christ with his church for a model of ecclesial voluntarism. It will no more do to place the unique relation of Christ and his church under a general category of sociality than it does to place it under a general category of sacramentality or unified subjectivity. Christ's words to Paul that his persecution of the church was a persecution of Christ himself (Acts 9:4; cf. Matt. 25:40, 45), and Paul's own descriptions of the church as the body of Christ (e.g., Rom. 12:4–5; 1 Cor. 12:12–27; cf. also Eph. 4:12; 5:23; Col. 1:24), should not be dismissed, even if they cannot be brought under the general category of either (organic) metaphysics or mere (voluntaristic) metaphor. It is not only the inviolable distinction of Christ and the church but the nature of their irrevocable union that merits serious reflection and its own form of confession, for it is a real relation of a unique fellowship (*koinonia*) and intimacy (see 1 Cor. 1:9). What can be said of it, and how should it be understood? While confessing Christ and confessing the church display an irreducible duality, we can rightly speak of the inseparable and proper

---

11. "Only one who could say Jesus Christ, that is, could say God become flesh, God and man, in *one* word, and that word a true word, could pride himself on *not* being a 'dialectical theologian.'" Karl Barth, "Church and Theology," in *Theology and Church: Shorter Writings 1920–1928*, trans. L. P. Smith (New York: Harper & Row, 1962), 301.

12. A christological ecclesiology thus must be able, in the words of John Webster, "to determine the point at which Jesus stops and the church begins." John Webster, "On Evangelical Ecclesiology," in Webster, *Confessing God: Essays in Christian Dogmatics* (London: T&T Clark, 2005), 163; see also Webster, "'In the Society of God,'" 184–87. In short, we might say that any discussion of *totus Christus*, if retained at all, must be disciplined by an even more fundamental, and preceding, *solus Christus*.

union of Christ and the church when three things are remembered, namely, the three initial elements earlier mentioned: it must be remembered *who* is making the proclamation of union and how such union is established, *how* in turn such union is claimed, and *when* it is most properly professed. The following discussion of these three elements can be understood as an explication of the logic and implications of Christ's pronouncement to Paul on the road to Damascus recorded in Acts 9:4, the very verse that meant so much to Augustine.

First, the unity of Christ and the church can be established and properly proclaimed only by Christ himself, and precisely because the union is predicated on his prerogative and will. The glorious personal appearance of the risen Christ to Paul displayed, in its very occurrence, the unmistakable distinction of this Lord from his church. Yet in Jesus' pronouncement he claimed the church and its members as his own, closer to himself than they are to one another. "Paul, why do you persecute me?" Christ declared, and in view of that proclamation, Paul's conception of the church as Christ's earthly body took on a realistic and relational rather than purely metaphorical meaning. Here was no triumphal assertion by the church of its glory, authority, salvific power, or worldly status, but rather the declaration by Christ of undeserved and unexpected association and fellowship. Christ declared his identification with his church, and even if such identification is best understood in terms of gracious intimate association rather than organic personal identity, it is nevertheless mistaken to think that such a brief verse can be cast aside as of no exegetical or dogmatic import, for it points to Paul's own understanding of the church as found "in Christ" and "with Christ," echoed in the later Pauline assertion that the church is essentially defined by the reality of "Christ in you, the hope of glory" (Col. 1:27).

Yet the unity of Christ with his church is not a declaration the church can make for itself. The church cannot secure a claim upon Christ or identify itself with him. From the side of earth, there can be but an acknowledgment of Christ's otherness and supremacy in heavenly splendor. He has no equal, no rival, and no earthly vicar. But in sovereign lordship and grace, he has joined himself through the Spirit to the church nonetheless—the church truly is his earthly body insofar as the singular assumption of flesh by the Word is reflected—though in no way repeated or extended—in the annexation of the church.[13] This relation of Christ and his church

---

13. Barth could go so far as to say that the church is Christ's "earthly-historical form of existence" and, with Christ, is the *totus Christus*, though with great qualification. See Karl Barth, *Church Dogmatics*, ed. G. W. Bromiley and T. F. Torrance, trans. G. W. Bromiley, G. T. Thomson,

is a reflection—but in no way a repetition or prolongation—of the one perfect and unique union of God and humanity in the person of Jesus Christ.[14] As Barth put this, the relation between Christ and the Christian, and by implication between Christ and the church, stands "in analogy to the mystery and miracle of Christmas."[15] In turn, this unique relation of Christ to the church bears an intimacy that has, for Paul, itself but one analogical reflection, the unity of husband and wife in marital union.[16] And like marital union, where the integrity of each partner is preserved and not lost even as they become "one flesh," Christ is not subsumed into the church, nor the church subsumed into Christ.[17] Rather, Christ announces himself to the church, and in his announcement he reveals his assumption of the church as his earthly body, the taking of the church as his bride. The church's own task is to proclaim the perfection of Christ as its Savior and Lord even as it does so in correspondence to the exemplary service of Christ as its pattern. In this, the supremacy and preeminence of Christ over his church, and the precedence of Christology to ecclesiology, is always of paramount and fundamental importance.

And it is precisely in this way, as stated by Ernst Käsemann, that "Christology is the permanent measure of all ecclesiology."[18] They exist in an irreversible relation, as do Christ and the church.[19] Through the same

---

et al., 4 vols. in 13 pts. (Edinburgh: T&T Clark, 1936–77), IV/2, 59–60. All references to this work hereafter: CD followed by the volume/part and page number(s) (e.g., CD, IV/2, 59–60).

14. "The church is the analogate which points to Jesus Christ as the analogue. As analogate, the church reveals that Jesus Christ himself is the one who brings men and women into correspondence with himself as the church." See Eberhard Jüngel, "The Church as Sacrament?," *Theological Essays*, trans. J. B. Webster (Edinburgh: T&T Clark, 1989), 206.

15. Barth, *CD*, IV/3.2, 542; cf. 554.

16. See 2 Cor. 11:2; Eph. 5:21–33; cf. Rev. 19:7; 21:2, 9; 22:17.

17. The church confesses both Christ's freedom over and over-against it as well as his faithfulness to it. The voice of Christ is therefore not subsumed into the church's teaching office and dogma, his priestly work not extended in the church's sacramental practices, nor his kingly lordship entrusted and thus transferred to the church's governance. As Barth put this point, "Christ's bestowal of his power on his Church cannot be reasonably understood to mean that he had partially relinquished his own power, that in relation to the Church he had ceased to be wholly God." Barth, *Theology and Church*, 293.

18. Ernst Käsemann, *New Testament Questions for Today*, trans. W. J. Montague (Philadelphia: Fortress, 1969), 258; see 257–59. There is a relation of Christology and ecclesiology, but these must be rightly ordered. "The question as to what is prior to faith in the sense that it supplies the criteria of faith can in the last resort only be answered christologically; and answered in a such a way as to keep Christology distinct from ecclesiology and anthropology and in no circumstances to substitute either for it. Christ alone is the ground, the Lord and the Judge of faith, of the individual Christian as of the whole community. The kerygma which is worthy of the name does not, then, simply make Christ present; it creates at the same time a proper distance between him and the hearer. . . . He [Christ] may awake eschatological self-understanding and the common life of the believers, but in so doing he is not absorbed into either, but challenges them to discipleship and service" (see Käsemann, 60).

19. Käsemann, 258. Käsemann acknowledged that the church is a scandal in the world, but (contrary to the position of his teacher Rudolf Bultmann) it is not the same scandal as the cross itself:

gospel, the word of the cross, Christ simultaneously calls the church into existence through the Spirit and gives it the pattern for its corresponding life.[20] Ecclesiology finds its proper convictions and emphases in the discernment between the exclusive office of Christ and the vocation of the church's cruciform witness and service, a discernment resting upon a rightful discrimination between Christ's substitutionary and exemplary work, as well as between the church's proper passivity and activity. As Luther stated, "Therefore he who wants to imitate Christ insofar as He is an example must first believe with a firm faith that Christ suffered and died for him insofar as this was a sacrament."[21] Yet here, too, the proper relation is one of order rather than choice, for the unique sacrifice of Christ does not undermine but establishes the pattern of ecclesial emulation. Thus, Paul pronounced the perfection of Christ's work, but he also urged the church to imitate him precisely as he imitated Christ in a life lived in service to God and others (1 Cor. 11:1; cf. 4:16; 2 Thess. 3:7, 9).

This leads to the second element of a proper understanding of Christ and the church, namely, how such a claim of union with Christ is made. The unity of Christ and the church can only be claimed by the church as a promise predicated on the freedom of God and of Christ. This freedom is evident in the judgment that came to Paul in Christ's words of identification with his church, for in Christ's question, "Paul, why do you persecute me?" is not only a word confirming Christ's union to the church, but also a word of judgment against the self-deception of one who acted with the intention of serving God yet whose actions were indicted as displaying a "zeal without knowledge" (Gal. 1:13–16a; Phil. 3:4–11; cf. Rom. 10:2). Christ's promise to be near the church therefore does not preclude the possibility of his opposition to its specific actions. Paul as an apostle was

---

"For the Cross creates the Church, and the Church represents, and does not replace, the Cross" (58). Nor can the Church put itself on the same plane as the Cross" (58). Put similarly, "A community which is not created by the Word is for us no longer the community of Jesus," for the Word precedes the church (261). One perhaps could not find a more pointed contrary position to that of Henri de Lubac, who famously stated, "Thus, if one thing is certain in this world, it is that, for us, the Church precedes the Gospel." Henri de Lubac, *The Motherhood of the Church*, trans. Sergia Englund (San Francisco: Ignatius Press, 1982), 8. These statements articulate two very different understandings of the relationship of Christ and the church. See also Webster, "On Evangelical Ecclesiology," 154.

20. The church is therefore the daughter, not the mother, of the Word, a creature of the gospel, as are all Christians. See Jüngel, "Church as Sacrament?," 208–9.

21. Luther, "Lectures on Hebrews," *LW*, 29:124. Elsewhere Luther wrote, "The chief article and foundation of the gospel is that before you take Christ as an example, you accept and recognize him as a gift, as a present that God has given you and that is your own." And then, "Now when you have Christ as the foundation and chief blessing of your salvation, then the other part follows: that you take him as your example, giving yourself in service to your neighbor just as you see that Christ has given himself for you." Luther, "A Brief Instruction on What to Look for and Expect in the Gospels," *LW*, 35:117, 120.

prescient and wise enough to know, in no small part in view of his former life, that a church was not insulated from its own forms of self-deception (cf. Rom. 10:2), whether in the danger of embracing another gospel (e.g., 2 Cor. 11:4; Gal. 1:6–9) or, as evident in the first canonical letter of Paul to Corinth, of simply failing to live into the gospel's entailments of renouncing the idolatry, immorality, and greed of the present age. In view of this oppositional element of Christ to the church, ecclesiology must not simply be a static presentation of the church's placement in the divine economy or of its intrinsic formal relations to God, Christ, and the Spirit. It must also set forth the necessary means to test the church's confession with regard to both its content and form in view of Christ's own lordship over it.[22]

It is therefore not only Christ's mercy, but Christ's judgment, that begins with the household of God, and can begin precisely because the church is distinct from Christ himself. The unity of Christ with his church is a promise that can be trusted but not asserted by the church in pretentious self-affirmation or as a talisman to ward off divine rebuke. In this life, the church must hear not only the overarching pronouncement of grace, namely, Christ's promise to be with the church to the end of the age (Matt. 28:20), but also Christ's opposition to the church's sin and failure. As the Old Testament accounts reminded the Israelites that the gifts of the ark of the covenant as well as the tabernacle and later temple were not to be taken as simplistic guarantees of God's presence and blessing, so the new covenant is no naive assertion of God's domestication or warrant to equate Christ's promised presence to the church with a blanket approval of its actions. Rather, as with Christ's own appearance to Paul on the Damascus road, Christ's identification with his church takes place in the very act of its *confrontation*. Such confrontation is not opposed to, but a form of, Christ's mercy to the church. It ensures, in Barth's words, that the church is not abandoned to the fate of having a conversation solely with itself.[23] Christ's confrontation now takes concrete form precisely in the objectivity of the canonical witness that not only is read within the church but also stands over against it.

Moreover, such confrontation reminds the church that, like God's marriage to Israel in the Old Testament, Christ takes to himself not an intrinsically virtuous bride but makes her so in a declaration that entails

---

22. It is precisely for this reason that the doctrine of Scripture must be dogmatically placed in relation to Christology and pneumatology and cannot be subsumed into the doctrine of ecclesiology itself.

23. Barth, *CD* I/2, 583–85.

a future fulfillment. The present assurance and future hope of the church is grounded in the perfect and glorious exchange between Christ and his bride, one and the same as that between Christ and the Christian.[24] This is not a mutual exchange of being, agency, or authority as it was for many of Augustine's later disciples. It is, instead, an exchange of the righteousness of the one for the sin of the other. The union of Christ with the church is not the union of two partners in mutual sanctification or salvific action, but of a holy Lord who embraces the church even as he absolves her guilt and extinguishes the power of her sin. In the most profound words of Paul, for our sake God "made the one who knew no sin [Christ] to be sin, so that in him we might become the righteousness of God" (2 Cor. 5:21). The intimacy of Christ and the church is realized not in spite of but precisely through the fact that Christ has come to save not the righteous but sinners.[25] This union of Christ with his bride is an eschatological hope as much as it is grounded in a present promise and reality (2 Cor. 11:2; Rev. 21:2). As Barth captured this point, "The Church is the Church of forgiven thieves, who wait for their redemption."[26]

The unity of Christ with the church must therefore be understood in eschatological rather than in timeless terms. In effect, the declaration of a word of judgment by Christ to the church in time expresses a necessarily temporal element to the relation that should not be ignored in ecclesiology. Such judgment cannot be set aside with appeals to a timeless metaphysical union or even to an irrevocable divine election of the church in eternity past. Akin to Bonhoeffer's recognition with regard to the doctrine of justification, so the claim of Christ's unity with his church must be confessed by the church humbly in response to a divine promise, and not as a pretext for the self-justification of its actions. To borrow and extend Bonhoeffer's pastoral advice, ecclesiology confesses that Christ may confront a church that is "hiding behind cheap grace" or succumbing to historical indifference.[27]

This observation leads to the third and final element that must mark the union of Christ and his church. If the first is that only Christ can effect and declare this union, if the second, correspondingly, is that the church

---

24. "Who can understand the riches of the glory of this grace? Here this rich and divine bridegroom Christ marries this poor wicked harlot, redeems her from all her evil, and adorns her with all his goodness." Luther, "The Freedom of a Christian," *LW*, 31:352.

25. See Jüngel, "Church as Sacrament?," 211. Here Luther's distinctive use of the bridal imagery of Christ with the church to speak of the exchange of Christ's righteousness and the believer's sin is apposite. See "The Freedom of a Christian," *LW*, 31:351.

26. Barth, *Theology and Church*, 294.

27. Dietrich Bonhoeffer, *Discipleship*, ed. Geffrey B. Kelly and John D. Godsey, trans. Barbara Green and Reinhard Krauss (Minneapolis: Fortress, 2001), 68.

must claim this unity only in present promise and eschatological hope, the third element is that Christ's present unity with his church is nowhere so properly claimed by the church as in the midst of its suffering.

The unity of Christ with his church is preeminently made in an identification with its suffering witness, a witness that reflects the suffering of Christ's own work. Christ's words to Paul on the road to Damascus came precisely during the church's suffering at the hands of Paul's work of persecution against it: "Paul, why do you persecute me?" The profound unity of Christ with the church implied in this statement cannot be separated from the suffering the church undergoes for the sake of Christ himself—and specifically as set within this narrative, upon the martyrdom of Stephen and Paul's participation in that act which directly preceded this confrontation of Paul by Christ (Acts 7:58–8:2). In this regard, it is noteworthy that here not only the agent who makes a statement and the manner in which it is made, but also the context in which it is uttered, have bearing upon our rightful understanding of it. Christ's unity with his church is most powerfully indicated when it is confessed in the church's suffering witness. It is confessed by the church not as a pretext for the assertion of its authority and splendor but as a promise it clings to in the midst of the tribulations and tragedy of its existence.

This is not to say that suffering is itself the basis for a claim of righteousness or union with Christ. As Paul insisted, the knowledge of Christ comes precisely in the reception of a righteousness that is not one's own but that comes by faith (Phil. 3:9). Yet it is also true that for Paul this faith and righteousness led to a desire to know Christ in his suffering and to be united with him in his death (Phil. 3:7–11; cf. Rom. 6:5). Such is no masochistic aspiration, but a mysterious admission that Christ is known not in spite of but in such affliction. And for Paul this was not only an apostolic vocation but the church's own existential reality (Rom. 5:3–5; 8:18; cf. 12:12). In other words, not only the apostle but the church itself can never be so confident in the promise of Christ's presence to it, of Christ's very identification with it, as when it is in the midst of suffering for the sake of gospel witness.

This claim in no way mitigates the truth that the salvific passion of Christ is solely his own.[28] Nor does it make suffering either a prerequisite

---

28. To put this in the terms of the perfection of Christ's priestly work, the finality of Christ's sacrifice entails that the language of the Christian life as a sacrifice offered to God is now that of metaphor, for the spiritual sacrifices of the lives of Christians who are built into a holy priesthood do not replicate, extend, or augment Christ's own, but in their own sphere embody the spiritual life

for Christ's promise and presence or an empirical mark and guarantee of faithful witness to the gospel. Yet there is a reason that the transfiguration accounts in the Gospels are enclosed on both sides with Christ's instruction to the disciples that he would have his singular cross but they would have their own.[29] Nor is it a matter of coincidence that the vision of Christ in his ascended glory is given to Stephen precisely in the moment of his death, as Stephen, as Christ before him, prayed so that God might have mercy even upon his executioners (Acts 7:60 [54–60]; cf. Luke 23:34). The church that might dare to assert its unity with Christ can only be the church that is joined in the ministry of his sufferings. Attempting to articulate the church's fundamental identifying characteristics, Luther identified the seventh and last of its marks succinctly: "The holy Christian people are externally recognized by the holy possession of the sacred cross."[30] One of the tragedies of the Reformation was that this recognition of Luther, so deeply held as well by the Anabaptists, could not lead to a deeper understanding between them. Bonhoeffer, mediating these magisterial and radical Reformation commitments in the twentieth century, expressed this shared conviction anew: "The cross is neither misfortune nor harsh fate. Instead, it is that suffering which comes from our allegiance to Jesus Christ alone."[31] In view of this, *solus Christus* is not only the proclamation of the exclusivity of Christ's salvific work, but also the church's confession of an exclusive allegiance to a singular Lord, and implicitly, the price of such allegiance.

Here things must be brought to a close. A healthy ecclesiology will embrace all three of these elements: Christ's self-proclaimed identification with his church, its reception as gospel promise, and the church's corresponding suffering witness. All point to the specificity of the relation of Christ and the church and its proper elucidation. Christ's relation to the church is a mystery confessed in faith precisely because, in analogy to the incarnation itself, it is a unique relation between God and the world and a very specific one. In service to expressing this unique relation is the biblical

---

of conformity of the church and the Christian to the pattern of Christ's own self-giving in service to others (e.g., Rom. 12:1; 1 Peter 2:5, 9 [4–12]). As Jüngel described this, "The story of Jesus Christ, understood as a sacrament, might be an *exemplum* for our own conduct, that is, the extent to which our lives can and should follow after his example and *conform to his story*." Jüngel, "Church as Sacrament?," 183 (181–83). But the church's activity and suffering themselves "have no sacramental function whatsoever" (188). Jüngel continued, "The Christian community may not ascribe any soteriological function or significance to itself or allow such to be ascribed to itself" (188). Such is the inviolable difference between Christ's atoning death and those of Christians who witness and attest to it.

29. See Matt. 16:21–26; 17:1–8; 17:9–13; 22–23; cf. Luke 9:18–25; 9:28–36; 9:43b–45.
30. Luther, "On the Councils and the Church," *LW*, 41:164.
31. Bonhoeffer, *Discipleship*, 86.

imagery of the church as the body of Christ and of the church as his bride. Such images must themselves be disciplined and contextualized by the larger biblical patterns of divine and christological prevenience, perfection, and freedom, and they have their own limitations, which are in turn revealed and offset by the multiplicity of other biblical images and conceptions for the relation of Christ and the church, God and his people, the Spirit and his community and temple.

Nevertheless, while it would be tempting to abandon a specifically christological ecclesiology in view of historic distortions of such images of body and bride, ecclesiology cannot limit itself to explicating the eternal grounds of the church in the divine triune perfection or to elucidating the Spirit's work of the church's equipping and empowerment, as important as these indeed are. It cannot rest content with these because the pattern for the church is not found in a speculative form of triune perichoretic life, in social forms of Trinitarian relations, or in general or even charismatic forms of human sociality or giftedness. Moreover, it is not possible for ecclesiology to retreat either to descriptions of triune perfection or to ethnography or social science, for the church as a mystery is grounded in eternity but lives very much in time, and it is called and created to do so. Ecclesiology must for this very reason give great consideration to the substance and character of the gospel, and it is precisely in expositing the gospel of Christ that the church finds both the content of its proclamation and the form such proclamation should take in its witness of both word and deed as empowered by the Spirit of God.

And what it finds, if it clings to the biblical witness, is that it is called, in Barth's words, to give a reflection of the love with which God loved the world, which in its concrete display is the unique sacrifice of Christ, now proclaimed by and indeed reflected in the suffering of his earthly body.[32] Ecclesiology cannot ignore this particular correspondence to Christ. While ecclesiology must be grounded in an explication of the work of the triune God, resting in God's eternal perfection and election, and while ecclesiology must be understood in view of the Spirit's work of calling, equipping, and empowering the church for its earthly witness and ministry, it remains the case that the church's confession and life are given their specific content and concrete form in view of Christ's own incarnate life, sacrifice, and service. In other words, the gospel of the cross is both the subject matter of the

---

32. "What the community owes to the world, and each individual within it, is basically that in its life, and in the lives of all its members, there should be attempted an imitation and representation of the love with which God loved the world." Barth, *CD*, III/4, 502.

church's proclamation and the pattern of its life.[33] And in the gospel, the church finds both the grounds of the firm distinction between itself and the Lord it proclaims and follows, but also the announcement of his union with it, for his name of Emmanuel stands at the very heart of the gospel. It is the name of the one who inquired of Paul, "Why do you persecute me?"

We turn now at the end to leave Joan of Arc to consider an earlier witness that Barth found of particular resonance. John the Baptist said that Christ must increase and he must decrease (John 3:30). The same holds true in our age—Christ must become more, and the church must become less, proclaiming Christ and not itself (2 Cor. 4:5). In this assertion, the demarcation of Christ and the church is announced and confessed. In an age when the church is seemingly receding in the West, this may nevertheless and without irony be the confession that is in fact needed. What we require today is not an ecclesiology obsessed with self-preservation, self-assertion, or incessant moral browbeating whether of the left or the right. What we need, rather, is a deflated, rather than expansive, ecclesiology. Such a disciplined and circumscribed ecclesiology might be placed in service to the larger and more fundamental doctrines of Christology and pneumatology and Trinity from which it is derived. In turn, the church might again find its rightful center in gospel proclamation and celebration amid innumerable peripheral tasks and concerns. Such may sound irresponsible or evasive in this age of ecclesial moralism, but it would not be the first time the church found itself, the clarity of its proper task, and the hidden source of a renewed vitality not only for the center of its witness but also for its circumferential engagements, by losing itself in Christ and the gospel.

---

33. And, again, it is so precisely in this order, for the primary task of the church is found not first in its obedience but in its recognition of what God in Christ has already accomplished. The church thus narrates and testifies the passion account of Christ, not its own passion story (see Jüngel, "Church as Sacrament?," 188). That the church is defined by Christ's finished work of atonement and not defined by its own activity and practices is made clear "by the first and fundamental act of the Christian life, that is, by its first and fundamental answer to the question: what should we *do*? The answer is: we should *celebrate*. The first and fundamental act of the Christian life is the celebration of Christian worship. The fact that Christians become *active* in the act of *celebrating*, that is, in an event which sovereignly excludes any idea that life is characterized by *performance*, makes it abundantly clear that the service demanded of Christians is itself a matter of *thankfulness* for the sacrifice or gift of Jesus Christ. Christian life, Christian action, is forged by the primal human act of thankfulness." Jüngel, "Church as Sacrament?," 183, italics original.

CHAPTER 4

NATURE, CULTURE, CHURCH

Reconsidering the Church-World Divide

Natalie Carnes

I RECENTLY CAME ACROSS an article titled "World versus Church: Who Is Winning?"[1] I laughed when I read it. I pictured a grim scorekeeping angel drawing neat little rows of lines, meticulously tracking the points gained and lost by the two sides. *Soul worships the Lord in spirit and in truth?* Point church. *Baptized soul gives up on Christianity?* Point world. *Widow gives two mites?* The grim angel draws a satisfied line for the church, trying not to appear smug. *Inequality grows to staggering levels as the marginalized continue to be exploited?* The grim angel—well, I don't know how the grim angel would quantify this one. But as I searched for articles on the church and world, I discovered more titles framing their relation adversarially. One called "The Church versus the World" warns churches against catering to fads. Another called "Church vs World . . . Win, Lose, or Draw?"[2] surprised me by critiquing a win-lose trade-off between the church and the world. Then the author suggested a win-win approach, quoting Stephen Covey's *7 Habits of Highly Effective People* like the book of Proverbs.

All of these articles, even the win-win article, are funded by an antagonistic and territorial view of church versus world, which, even when

---

1. "World versus Church: Who Is Winning?" Christian Today, https://christiantoday.com.au /news/world-versus-church-who-is-winning.html, last accessed 16 December 2021.
2. John MacArthur, "The Church versus the World," Grace to You, October 7, 2009; https:// www.gty.org/library/articles/A267/the-church-versus-the-world; "Church vs. World . . . Win, Lose, or Draw?" Discipleship Ministries, the United Methodist Church, June 17, 2010, https:// www.umcdiscipleship.org/resources/part-three-continue-to-change-the-world-series.

articulated in subtler and more sophisticated forms than these headlines, paints what I will argue is a problematic picture of ecclesiology. For a different approach, I want to turn to recent conversations in the humanities around nature and culture that provide an analogy for elaborating a better model. Because this comparison is happening at a high level of abstraction, I want to fill in the difference this alternative model makes by contrasting two ecclesiologies exemplary of the different positions: Rod Dreher's very popular antagonistic ecclesiology and what I am calling a protagonistic ecclesiology, representative of the nature-culture relation I sketch, and which is found in one of Rowan Williams's latest books. The contrast between them is interesting because of how much the two models share and yet how different they are. I conclude the talk by taking one step further into the concrete, describing some lives and movements in the history of the church where we can glimpse the protagonistic ecclesiology at work in the world. What it looks like, I want to suggest, is a deep solidarity that can help tend some of the colonialist wounds the church has inflicted over the centuries.

DREHER: CHURCH VERSUS WORLD

I want to illustrate the antagonistic church-world relation I have in mind by turning to the work of Rod Dreher, specifically his book *The Benedict Option*. I'm guessing most of you have at least heard of this book. I know at Baylor it was the subject of book groups and informal discussions; it inspired lifestyle reevaluations and gave Christians additional vocabulary for articulating their lives in the world. The basic argument is that as St. Benedict of Nursia's monastic program gave light and strength to the Christian church in the "Dark Ages," so can it, in modified form, do the same for our own "Dark Ages." More specifically: in response to what he sees as a worrying trend of secularization coupled with a weakening of the church, Dreher recommends that Christians form communities that withdraw from certain aspects of society to intensify their Christian practices and strengthen their faith commitments. The choice, as he puts it, is stark: "Make a decisive leap into a truly countercultural way of living Christianity, or . . . doom our children and our children's children to assimilation."[3] His book is a blueprint for avoiding such doom and leaping into a countercultural world of Christianity.

After noting the gathering "storm clouds" of "the breakdown of the

---

3. Rod Dreher, *The Benedict Option: A Strategy for Christians in a Post-Christian Nation* (New York: Sentinel, 2017), 2.

natural family, the loss of traditional moral values, and the fragmenting of communities," Dreher dramatically declares early on in his book that the culture war is over. "Today we can see that we've lost on every front. . . . [The] sexual Revolution triumphed decisively, and the culture war . . . came to an end. . . . The public square has been lost."[4] We are not yet out of the first chapter, and victory has slipped away, the war ended.

The loss was not, to Dreher, one event but occurred in stages. Antagonistic ecclesiologies often spawn declension narratives. An antagonistic frame is structured, definitionally, by what one is against and, relatedly, by a sense of the limits of one's power, which always feels more limited than it should. And so it tempts the antagonist into a declension narrative to explain *why* these powers are more limited than they should be. To be clear, there is nothing wrong with a declension narrative as such. As the church, we're committed to a pretty powerful declension narrative. It's called the fall, and the narrative tells us that we have never known an unfallen world. The problem with these "versus"-spawned declension narratives is that they historicize the fall, locating it at some temporal moment like the institutionalization of the early church, the reign of Constantine, the Reformation, the advent of modernity, or Vatican II. And in historicizing the fall, the narratives also tempt us to historicize "paradise"—finding it in the community of the disciples, in pre-Nicene Christianity, in the medieval church, in the early Protestant communities. But as Christians, we know, or should know, that no time escapes the curse of the fall. There is sinfulness, violence, and exploitation all the way down through the history of the church and humankind. The "versus" narratives avert our attention from the ubiquity of fallenness and can, in their critical mode, also fuel false visions of utopia and engender a warlike mentality to preserve attempts at recapturing that utopia.

Dreher's declension narrative occupies his second chapter. It is a centuries-spanning narrative of decline. There is a downward movement in every century since the 1300s, according to Dreher, from nominalism's defeat of realism, to the triumph of an anthropocentric over theocentric social imagination, onward through the Reformation, scientific revolution, Enlightenment, and Industrial Revolution, until we arrive at the woes of the twentieth century: the sexual revolution, technocracy, and world wars.[5]

---

4. Dreher, 9.

5. For Dreher, it is specifically the Reformation's crisis of religious authority in the sixteenth century, the wars of religion and scientific revolution's alienation of humanity from the cosmos in the seventeenth century, to the Enlightenment's enthronement of reason in the eighteenth century. Dreher, 22, 45–46.

I won't spend time disputing this declension narrative, but I do want to note that one of the questions elided is who exactly this narrative is for. There is a telling moment near the beginning of the chapter as Dreher is framing this narrative of decline when he writes, "In the 1940s . . . the out-of-wedlock birth rate among whites was 2 percent. It is now nearly 30 percent."[6] And he follows that statistic up with the report of a woman sighing, "It's like the whole world is coming apart."[7] Whose world? Why are we framing a narrative of decline with what is happening to *white* babies? What are the motivating concerns and hopes of this narrative?

I leave these questions hanging to pursue another issue haunting Dreher's book. Despite declaring the war over, Dreher cannot let go of martial language. His descriptions of the situation of church in the world are saturated with the metaphor of war: a "world growing ever more hostile to [our faith and our values]" versus a church "largely ineffective in combating the forces of cultural decline."[8] The words *war* and *wars* show up over thirty times in the short book; same with versions of the word *fight*. At one point, he writes, "Don't be deceived by the ordinariness of this charge [of the Benedict Option]. This is politics at its most profound level. It is politics during wartime, and we are fighting nothing less than a culture war over what C. S. Lewis called 'the abolition of man.'"[9] The war is over, and then it's not over, because Dreher cannot imagine himself into another structuring metaphor of the relationship of church and world. It is, for him, fundamentally antagonistic.

But, of course, it's more complex than that because it is not that Dreher *never* entertains another kind of relationship. There is a lovely moment at the end of the first chapter when he reaches for an image of protagonism, writing, "If we are going to be for the world as Christ meant for us to be, we are going to have to spend more time away from the world."[10] Let's bracket the suggestion that Christ's way of being for the world is withdrawal from it (a claim I disagree with) because what I want to highlight here, positively, is the insistence that Christians should be *for* the world. There are throughout the book other avowals of for-ness, voiced by monks Dreher quotes, such as Father Cassian, who says of his posture toward the world, "There's not just a *no*; there's a *yes* too. . . . It's both that we reject what is

---

6. Dreher, 22.
7. Dreher, 22.
8. Dreher, 2, 1.
9. Dreher, 97.
10. Dreher, 19.

not life-giving, and that we build something new. And we spend a lot of time in the rebuilding, and people see that too, which is why people flock to the monastery. . . . We are rebuilding. That's the *yes* that people have to hear about."[11] Later he quotes Father Benedict saying, "I think too many Christians have decided that the world is bad and should be avoided as much as possible. Well, it's hard to convert people if that's your stance. . . . It's a lot easier to help people to see their own goodness and then bring them in than to point out how bad they are and bring them in." The monks he quotes were more consistent about articulating this protagonistic relationship than Dreher, whose one avowal of for-ness slips quickly back into the language of militaristic antagonism.

To be fair, the monks also, in some places, used militaristic language. Brother Ignatius, for example, wrote, "Let's attack by expanding God's kingdom—first in our hearts, then in our own families, and then in the world."[12] But what is interesting about this version of the martial metaphors of attack and expansion is that the church and world are not territorialized. The work begins not with an external threat but with what exists *within a person*. And this theme recurs in the words of the monks, who spoke of the rule working "to channel your spiritual energy," and "to train your heart and spirit," and to work with one's passion to train the person with "spiritual and moral self-discipline."[13] Dreher is worried about the heart too; he wants to protect it from external threats. But to the monks, the threat is not first and foremost external to my community; it is not even external to my own soul. The danger is already there in the heart that resists God's coming kingdom. The world is not imagined as a territory spatially distinct from the church but as naming some reality that goes all the way through my own desires, my own self. And that reframes the struggle of church and world, not as a contest for power but as a part of my own continual call to rebirth into the likeness of the Word.

There are moments when Dreher rises to the level of this monastic insight, but by the end of the book, church and world have hardened back into a spatialized antagonism. The world is the external threat that the church overcomes by strategies like, for example, buying from Christian rather than non-Christian people, building hiring networks to hire Christians rather than non-Christians, and sending kids to classical schools or homeschooling

---

11. Dreher, 50.
12. Dreher, 73.
13. Dreher, 52, 57, 64.

them rather than exposing them to the secularisms of public school.[14] Most of all, it seems to be about holding at bay what Dreher consistently refers to as the LGBT agenda. That is the problem with public schools, where your daughter may come home, tell you her friends are bisexual, and defends that claim with "a lot of babble about gender being fluid and nonbinary."[15] It is the problem with the workplace, where workers are asked to "burn incense to Caesar" by attending diversity and inclusion trainings that affirm the sexuality and gender identity of LGBTQ individuals. For Dreher, the "LGBT agenda" essentially functions as an avatar for the world, and so the legalization and normalization of same-sex relationships and transgender identities speaks to territory the church has lost. It dramatizes the way the world for Dreher is imagined as a threat external to the church, constantly encroaching on the territory of the church, and therefore something to be battled. LGBTQ communities are for him grace-free zones, and his vision of church is a fortress against them. The martial metaphor emerges from and feeds this imagination.[16]

To be clear, I do not believe it is *necessarily* problematic to conceptualize any church-versus-world dynamic, and I understand that such rhetoric can be a way of capturing the distinctiveness and integrity of the church and its commitments. There is, moreover, a way that "world," like "flesh," has in Scripture a secondary meaning of "that which is actively opposed to God's purposes"—particularly in the epistles of James, Peter, and John. It is important that these secondary meanings not become confused with the primary ones, lest we degrade God's creation.[17] And it is also important to keep in view the myriad other images of church-versus-world like the leaven in the loaf. Nevertheless, church-versus-world rhetoric is present

14. Dreher, 188, 157.

15. Dreher, 157.

16. The liturgy and monastic practice also become a type of strategy, which Elizabeth Bruenig commented on in her article "City of Rod": "In [Dreher's] last chapter, however, he reflects on a conversation with a pastor who said: 'The moment the Benedict Option becomes about anything other than communion with Christ and dwelling with our neighbors in love, it ceases to be Benedictine. . . . It can't be a strategy for self-improvement or for saving the church or the world.' One is then left unsure what this Benedict Option is, if not a strategy for saving the church, given that Dreher has already stated rather plainly that it is a strategy for saving the church." Elizabeth Stoker Bruenig, "City of Rod," *Democracy: A Journal of Ideas*, March 1, 2017, https://democracyjournal.org/magazine/city-of-rod/.

17. The world is figured in these epistles as that from which we must keep ourselves "unstained" (James 1:27). Friendship with the world is "enmity with God" (James 4:4), and the world is full of defilements (2 Peter 2:20). Probably the most extreme is found in 1 John 2:15–17: "Do not love the world or the things in the world. The love of the Father is not in those who love the world, for all that is in the world—the desire of the flesh, the desire of the eyes, the pride in riches—comes not from the Father but from the world. And the world and its desire are passing away, but those who do the will of God abide forever."

in Scripture and does suggest something important about Christian life.[18] The problem comes when the church-versus-world dynamic defines the church's relation to the world instead of being cast in a larger story about the church *for* the world, the way a loving parent "versus" a child and a best friend "versus" you as you make a bad decision are relationships that are more significantly for the child, for you.[19] When antagonism is not shaped by a more fundamental protagonism, it obscures the messy and complex interactions and connections of the church and world in reality and foments the culture of suspicion and grievance we have seen inflame so much political discourse in the United States.

I didn't read Dreher's book until four years after it came out, after hearing about as many years of conversations about it. To be honest, I found *The Benedict Option* to be, as a whole, more constructive and even gentler than I expected. There are some keen insights in it, including the one that Christians need to divest their hopes from political power, and that they should "prepare to become poorer and more marginalized."[20] But gentleness is not the rule for Dreher's imagination of the world. His blog at the *American Conservative* hosts a series of short essays policing cultural sources and especially universities for their anti-racist, pro-LGBTQ professors and policies and encourages readers to send in their own stories of encounters with such policies so that he can "out" those schools. His last post about my school before he ended that blog was about Baylor "surrendering to aggressive wokeness" through their trans-friendly language. The prior three were titled "Woke Witch Hunt at Baylor," "'Cultural Humility'=Wokeness at Baylor," and "Woking up at Baylor."[21] These essays consistently see a threat to Baylor's Christian identity in its policies, statements, and emails that speak to the most racially and sexually marginalized on campus. That way of speaking and administering is for Dreher the way of the world,

---

18. Another way to put this problem is to say there are certainly scriptural images that suggest an antagonistic relation—for example, the contrast of light and darkness. But so are there myriad others that suggest a protagonistic one, for example, the leaven in the loaf.

19. When the "versus" becomes characteristic of the church's relationship to the world, we have what I am naming an antagonistic ecclesiology, and I think it's important to address because antagonistic ecclesiology has become so popular. Dreher is just one articulation of it. Antagonistic ecclesiology characterizes a popular stream of thought in academic theology as well as wide swaths of the evangelical church in the US and a large section of the Roman Catholic Church in America.

20. Dreher, *Benedict Option*, 192.

21. Rod Dreher, "Woke Witch Hunt at Baylor," The American Conservative, January 26, 2021, https://www.theamericanconservative.com/woke-witch-hunt-at-baylor/; Dreher, "'Cultural Humility'=Wokeness at Baylor," The American Conservative, August 13, 2020, https://www.the americanconservative.com/cultural-humility-wokeness-at-baylor/; Dreher, "Woking up Baylor," The American Conservative, July 28, 2020, https://www.theamericanconservative.com/race-woke -at-baylor-linda-livingstone/.

the way, for Dreher, that has to be battled so that the church does not continue to lose its territory, so that it is not infiltrated by a grace-free zone. Thus, Christian life for Dreher is constantly at war with the world.

THE PROTAGONISM OF NATURE AND CULTURE

So what alternative is there? I believe we can find helpful models and motives for conceptualizing a protagonistic ecclesiology in the recent rethinking of nature and culture. The antagonistic framing of church and world rests upon a dichotomized understanding of them, as if the church and world name distinct territories or spatialities in the world. The church is against the world because the church is separate from the world. The world stands for the territory that has not yielded to church; the church for what is unsoiled by the world. In this way, they formally mimic an understanding of nature and culture that has lately come under criticism, where nature names something apart from culture, something like pristine wilderness that one goes out from culture to be in. And culture, in this understanding, belongs wholly to the realm of artifice, that which transcends nature, for good and ill. It names the realm of human activity, for in this understanding, humans belong to the realm of culture, and all other living beings and their environment, to nature.

This way of conceptualizing nature and culture inevitably frames them competitively, whether it's environmentalists complaining about humans having too many babies or anti-environmentalists chanting, "Drill, baby, drill."[22] Both place nature outside of humans, as something that happens out there and which we either shamefully pollute or bend to our purposes. The very word *environment* suggests its background status, as if it is merely the setting for human action, and that is compounded by the way "nature" often names something that exists apart from human habitation and daily life, something that is found in the wilderness rather than in our

---

22. Matthew Whelan writes in "Creation, Environmentalism, and Catholic Social Teaching," "Notice, for instance, how the developers such conservationists oppose, and to which their conservation efforts respond, presume a similar picture to the conservationists themselves: of humans as fundamentally separate from nature—only nature, in the case of developers, is not to be cared for, but rather, raw material to be developed. Yet for both conservationists and developers alike, the underlying picture of an ontological chasm between humans and nature remains largely the same. Both tend to assume that *all* human use of the world is degrative, which is why conservationists seek to protect pristine places from human use." Matthew Whelan, "Creation, Environmentalism, and Catholic Social Teaching," in *The Wiley Blackwell Companion to Catholicism*, Wiley Blackwell Companions to Religion, ed. Frederick C. Bauerschmidt, James J. Buckley, Jennifer Newsome Martin, and Trent Pomplun (New York: Wiley-Blackwell, forthcoming).

neighborhoods.[23] But a newer paradigm (which is also an older paradigm) has emphasized that nature is not something simply out there to pollute, preserve, or exploit. It is something within us; it *is* us. This is evident from research, for example, on human gut health that shows the way the ecology of our guts mirrors the ecology of what we eat, that our bodies reflect our agricultural practices. And it is evident from our national parks system, a complex set of cultural forms that we use to create for ourselves experiences of "pristine" nature. It is noteworthy that what preceded the setting aside of national parks and wilderness areas in the US was the removal of the prior, indigenous inhabitants of these lands and their relegation to reservations to enact this vision of pristineness.[24] In contrast to that vision, I want to elaborate one that maintains *we* are nature, and nature is constructed, imagined, related to, legislated, represented, cared for, struggled against, and exploited—all through culture.

Bruno Latour, Philippe Descola, Eduardo Viveiros de Castro, Donna Haraway, Isabelle Stengers—these are some of the figures who have been actively dismantling our illusion of a nature-culture dichotomy. They point out that nature and culture are not spatially separate, and they certainly cannot name a meaningful binary, however much we may pretend they do. In his watershed essay *We Have Never Been Modern*, Latour names two ways of relating to nature and culture we have called modern. The first is hybridization, which names the mixtures of nature and culture the modern world continually produces, and Latour has a litany of examples: frozen embryos, expert systems, digital machines, sensor-equipped robots, hybrid corn, data banks, psychotropic drugs, whales outfitted with radar sounding devices, gene synthesizers, audience analyzers.[25] A recent book

---

23. As Matthew Whelan writes, "The picture of humans set apart from nature is not a superficial one. Especially in the West, it has left its impress upon the very language we use, fostering the belief of an essential separation between culture—broadly understood the beliefs, customs, and arts of a people—and nature, the nonhuman world of plants, animals, geology, and natural forces (see Latour, 1993; Descola, 2014). As the American writer, farmer, and activist Wendell Berry has observed, the view that we suffer from an 'environmental crisis' evokes this separation. Insofar as the 'environment' is something that *environs* us, that is, surrounds or encircles us and so essentially separate from us, our words symptomize the very problem we employ them to solve (1993, p. 34). In speaking this way, we misconstrue the kinds of creatures we are, the world we inhabit, and our place within it. For starters, we miss how what environs us is also and at the same time within us. 'We have forgotten that we ourselves are dust of the earth (cf. Gen 2:7),' Pope Francis observes in *Laudato Si'* (2015). 'Our very bodies are made up of her elements, we breathe her air and we receive life and refreshment from her waters' (no. 2)." Whelan, "Creation, Environmentalism, and Catholic Social Teaching."

24. William Cronon, "The Trouble with the Wilderness; or, Getting to the Wrong Nature," in *Uncommon Ground: Rethinking the Human Place in Nature*, ed. William Cronon (New York: Norton, 1995), 69–90.

25. Bruno Latour, *We Have Never Been Modern* (Cambridge, MA: Harvard University Press, 1993), 50.

titled *A Bestiary of the Anthropocene* has come out, which is devoted to drawings and descriptions of creatures that are nature–culture hybrids under the conditions of the Anthropocene. Entries include chicken bones that show in their structure the mark of industrial chicken production and "plastiglomerate" in which hard, molten plastic has melded with natural debris.[26] All of these are hybrids of natural laws and political representations, scientific objects and political ones, part nature and part culture. But the paradox of modernity is that it is characterized both by an intensification of hybrids and by an insistence on purification. This second aspect of modern life generates two ontologically distinct zones: the human and the nonhuman.[27] In Latour's words, the modern constitution "invents a separation between scientific power charged with representing things and the political power charged with representing subjects" that is ill-equipped to grapple with our proliferation of hybrids.[28] And Latour insists that the more we don't allow ourselves to think of hybrids—to think only in terms of purification, in other words, the more hybrids proliferate.[29] It is only once we allow ourselves to consider these hybrids that we find ways of representing them and therefore discerning which hybrids we want to support and which not. I cannot help wondering what ghastly hybrids emerge from church and world, what amalgamations of worldly and spiritual power are wielded, when we think about church and world only in terms of purification. Colonialism seems to me clearly one such ghastly hybrid; Christian nationalism another. Environmental pioneer Rachel Carson said that to destroy nature is to destroy ourselves. And the church bent on defeating or subduing the world inevitably betrays itself by betraying the Crucified One.

But not all hybrids are ghastly, and letting go of the insistence on purification can help us reflect on more salutary hybridizations. The new paradigm for nature and culture helps us to picture the church and world relation as one in which, if the two terms can be said to be separated by any kind of boundary, it is an extremely porous one, a site of constant exchange. And we can enter into this exchange to create with intention. I have learned something about hybrids of nature and culture from my husband's work on agroecology, and I have also learned from that field how nature and culture can be understood in a protagonistic relationship,

---

26. Nicolas Nova and Disnovation.org, ed., *A Bestiary of the Anthropocene: Hybrid Plants, Animals, Minerals, Fungi, and Other Specimens* (Eindhoven, Netherlands: Onomatopoee Projects, 2021).
27. Latour, *We Have Never Been Modern*, 11.
28. Latour, 29.
29. Latour, 11.

where nature need not name a limit on culture but instead names the gift of its origins. Culture needs, draws from, and is implicated in nature—in this way it is not wholly separate from nature—but culture can also name the caretaking of nature as a kind of *telos* and nature as a teacher in this caretaking, this cultivating.[30] Culture, in other words, can name a tilling and keeping of the land that learns from nature how best to till and keep it. Observing nature, we translate those practices into cultural forms that suit our ends of eating and living well together. In this way, agroecology brings into view a protagonistic model for thinking together this dynamic and mutual relation of culture and nature.[31]

If this essay were twice as long, or was, let's be honest, a different essay, I might try to convince you that the old nature-culture binary feeds the imagination of antagonistic ecclesiologies—that they are not just parallel analogous cases but deeply related ones. I might trace the way the nature-culture binary that places nature out there, separate from us and yet legible to us feeds a bad, facile kind of natural law that is used as a bludgeon against the world. Or the way the binary expresses the denial of our embodiment. But instead of staying in abstractions, the grammars of these philosophies, and the structure and sustenance of a binary, I want to venture into the concrete and spend more time unpacking the relation of church and world in the ecclesiology of a different theologian.

ROWAN WILLIAMS: CHURCH FOR THE WORLD

Rowan Williams takes the title for his recent book *Looking East in Winter* from a passage in the *Philokalia*, authored by Diadochos of Photike:

> Looking east in winter we feel the warmth of the sun on our faces, while still sensing an icy chill at our backs. Our divided and distorted

---

30. Nor are humans unique in taking up materials from the natural world into their habitat and making use of them in their common lives together. Bees, for example, have cultural forms that analogize the cultural forms of humans.

31. In the way that culture is always drawing on and interlaced with nature, the church is always drawing on the world—as it drew, for example, on the vocabulary and concepts of Greek philosophy to use words like *ousia*, *hypostasis*, and *Logos* to articulate Trinitarian theology and Christology in the early centuries of Christianity; or the way it adopted from Roman drawing the nimbus and reinterpreted it as a halo that signifies holiness; or the way it drew from the imperial rites its liturgical forms; or the way it drew from the Italian fashion world the expertise to create the vestments of priests, bishops, cardinals, and popes. The 2018 exhibition "Heavenly Bodies: Fashion and the Catholic Imagination" and Met Gala dramatized the sartorial exchanges of church and world, making clear the ways that the church draws on the world and the ways the world in turn receives from and is conceptualized by church, which returned new forms, styles, and imaginaries to the fashion industry.

awareness of the world is not healed instantly. But we are not looking at this phenomenon from a distance: we do not truly sense the sun on our faces; and we have good reason to think that the climate and landscape of our humanity can indeed be warmed and transfigured.[32]

Like Dreher, Williams is a Western Christian. Like Dreher, Williams is concerned about the state of the world. It is for him in a time of winter. And as Dreher retrieves monastic streams in Orthodoxy to address the difficulties of our age, so Williams exhorts us to look east—not only toward a metaphorical sun but also toward the tradition of Eastern Orthodoxy, which can direct us to light and warmth. Moreover, both Williams and Dreher prioritize monastic practice and liturgy as they describe how to live through these difficult times. Dreher interviews monks; Williams opens with the *Philokalia*. And finally, like Dreher, Williams moves from liturgy to politics. The two are, in a way, remarkably similar, which makes the comparison of their ecclesiologies interesting and productive.[33]

Where the two writers majorly diverge is in framing church-world relations, which are not fundamentally antagonistic for Williams but protagonistic. As God sends the Only Begotten into the world to bring to it eternal life, so is the church, for Williams, sent into the world to discover and share that divine life.[34] Like the new nature-culture paradigms (which are actually retrievals of older or suppressed paradigms), Williams's approach suggests an intimacy of church and world, where the two terms under consideration form not a binary but a shingled relation of overlapping objects, a relation of dynamism and exchange.

One of the features of Rowan Williams's protagonistic ecclesiology is

---

32. Rowan Williams, *Looking East in Winter: Contemporary Thought and the Eastern Christian Tradition* (New York: Bloomsbury, 2021), 8.

33. In fact, Rowan Williams himself reviews *The Benedict Option* in an evenhanded, though critical, essay for *The New Statesman*, where he worries that the view does not have ways of engaging in self-criticism: "What is left most worryingly vague is how such groups might maintain a level of self-criticism, and how they would handle issues around authority and management of conflict. Benedict has a fair bit to say about this, and Dreher shows he is aware of it and of the problem of alienating a younger generation by excessive exclusivism. However, more information on how actual communities have discovered and handled (or failed to handle) such matters would help." Rowan Williams, The New Statesman, May 30, 2017, https://www.newstatesman.com /politics/religion/2017/05/benedict-option-new-monasticism-21st-century. Rowan Williams also published, the year before *Looking East*, his own take on the ongoing wisdom of Benedictine monasticism in his book *The Way of St. Benedict* (New York: Bloomsbury, 2020). In that book, he describes himself sympathetic to some of Dreher's *Benedict Option* but "cautious about the radical rejection of social involvement and the focus on a somewhat limited range of supposed social threats to the faith" (8).

34. This is my liberty-taking paraphrase, not a quotation of Williams, though it seems to me quite faithful to his approach.

that "worldiness" becomes a virtue. Explicating the theology of Russian Orthodox theologian Mother Maria Skobtsova, Williams inverts our usual associations of worldliness and unworldliness. The individuals we normally describe as "worldly" are, in Mother Maria's negative sense, the most unworldly. Because they instrumentalize the world for their own gain or agenda, they are alienated from it, unable to truly draw near it.[35] An equally errant religious response can be a kind of pious unworldliness that detaches from the world.[36] The two errors seem opposed but actually mirror one another; both are types of isolation from the world. Instead of instrumentalization or detachment, Christians are called to a true worldliness found in solidarity with the world. The world, after all, is not only beloved of God but "provides the material for Christ's own human self-offering and its sacramental re-presentation." In the incarnation, Christ is united to the world, which means, in Williams's interpretation of Mother Maria, "our communion with the world in Christ simply is communion with God."[37]

Given this view of the world, it may be unsurprising that Mother Maria framed monasticism not as a retreat or "strategic withdrawal" from the world. She popularized instead a worldly monasticism, famously claiming the world as the monk's monastery.[38] The world for her was filled with icons to be venerated, for humans are the "true images of God," impressed with the holiness of the living God.[39] The whole world is church, and the whole world also must be churched: that ecclesialization or Christification of the world, as Mother Maria claimed, is the monastic vocation, a calling that, as Williams puts it, is not an "anxious sacralizing of ordinary life" but the "the habit of recognizing the divine image in the world as it is given to us, 'adorned with icons that should be venerated' (human faces)."[40] The world gives the material for Christ and church. It extends invitations to veneration and so points toward the church and Christ as its own consummation.

To church the world, though, is not to impose my agenda or desires on the world—not even to impose a "Christian" agenda to combat a supposedly secular one. The appropriate worldliness is not making the world more like

---

35. Williams, *Looking East in Winter*, 225.
36. Williams, *Looking East in Winter*, 225–26.
37. Williams, *Looking East in Winter*, 225.
38. "Today there is only one monastery for the monk—the whole world." *Mother Maria Skobtsova: Essential Writings*, trans. Richard Pevear and Larissa Volokhonsky (Maryknoll, NY: Orbis, 2003), 94.
39. Skobtsova, 81.
40. Williams, *Looking East in Winter*, 224. Quoting *Mother Maria Skobtsova: Essential Writings*, 69–70. Theologian Paul Evdokimov takes this one step further when he writes, "If every person is created in the image of God and is a living icon, *earthly culture is the icon of the Kingdom of Heaven.*" Evdokimov, *The Art of the Icon: A Theology of Beauty* (Redondo, CA: Oakwood, 2000), 71.

me but adopting a posture of receptivity to and solidarity with the world. Such a posture requires relinquishing the compulsion to exert control, coercion, or manipulation in the world and stilling my urges to make the world what I want it to be so that I can learn its own self-understanding.[41] It is from that place of stillness and solidarity that church practice flows into politics for Williams. He calls it "a 'contemplative' political practice" that holds space for another's narrative without metabolizing it into my own.[42] The temptation to absorb the other's story is the temptation to a false solidarity, one based on a desire for sameness that makes others into versions of oneself, repeating oneself in one's loves and, paradoxically, increasing the alienation of the self from the other.[43] It is a version of the false spiritual worldliness that in the end names an un-Christlike alienation from the world.

So, if a false solidarity is based upon sameness, what is a true solidarity based upon? It is based simply upon the givenness of creation. It has nothing to do with my choice and therefore does not degenerate into a contest of control.[44] We do not approach the neighbor, Williams emphasizes, with an agenda for them but an openness to them, which entails what Williams calls "'strenuous' imaginative labour" to see from the perspective of the other.[45] Does this mean simply accepting that the neighbor will be how she is, and that is the end of her story? Emphatically no, for Williams, because love aims at transfiguration, which is the hope we hold for every neighbor.[46]

What such solidarity and love look like is evident in Williams's explication of Mother Maria's discussion of neighbor love. To love my neighbor is not an act of the will nor an expression of the essence of Christianity; it is the recognition that Christ is my neighbor, that I am called to bear Christ into the world and so to mother Christ. And in this adoptive motherhood,

---

41. Williams, *Looking East in Winter*, 192.

42. "Only a practice of this sort can ultimately ground a politics that works toward the difficult common ground on which majority and minority can negotiate together: the prevalent pathology of our political life seems to be the idea that majorities obliterate the interest of the minority and that political victory is—while it lasts—licence for a majority to enforce its agenda. And this in turn has a retroactive effect on political campaigning in that it encourages the idea that political disagreement is essentially and invariably a contest of absolute and incompatible loyalties, so that the opponent's victory is the worst outcome imaginable. In other words, the failure to factor in the critical space in which I am able to hear how I am heard and seen becomes a driver of the febrile absolutism of online polemics, and of the corruption of democratic politics into majoritarianism." Williams, *Looking East in Winter*, 192–93. Much here is resonant with agroecology and the forms of industrial agriculture it opposes: agroecology is a form of cultivation that makes room for nature while silencing it with an imposed narrative.

43. Williams, *Looking East in Winter*, 230.

44. Williams, *Looking East in Winter*, 228.

45. Williams, *Looking East in Winter*, 228.

46. Williams, *Looking East in Winter*, 225.

I also adopt the neighbor-Christ's suffering as my own. I find Christ in my neighbor and respond with the intimacy of Mary; I recognize the divine image in the human faces of the world and respond with veneration. I grasp my solidarity with all creation through our givenness by God and appreciate already the deep relation with the world, a relation deepened through human flesh becoming in Christ God's own flesh.

So if at one level Williams through Mother Maria shows the world's affinities, imbrications, and analogies with the church, he also shows that church itself does not name a space free of the world any more than nature names a space free from culture (or vice versa). As culture is made from and co-constructs nature, the church draws from the materiality of the world and also contains the world, which is present within each person. Part of responding to and cultivating our human solidarity is the turn to the "inner world," which one should be "scrutinizing and monitoring . . . for signs of false inwardness, the powerful impulse to protect and quarantine the soul."[47] In other words, inasmuch as the world can name creation that is not intentionally aligned with the kingdom of God, it is not something out there, an external threat of secular agendas and encroaching liberalism. It is something within each of us, part of our own journey as pilgrims who remain on the way to saintliness and Christlikeness. This problematic unworldliness of erecting barriers between ourselves and the world must be uprooted. The habit of keeping the world at bay to protect some notion of spiritual purity constitutes a "false inwardness" signified, Williams claims, by "passionate partisan views and tactics," which express a will to "dominate" the reality of the other.[48] In these passages, Williams evokes the temptations of the culture wars and paints for us an alternative church-world relation that does not so easily give rise to those temptations.

There is a positive side to the inner world, as well, which can be more than a site of resistance to God. For the person who enters the mystery of God's own life becomes a site of the church coming into who and what it is.[49] The church and world are not spatialized realities nor dichotomized territories; both run through the heart of individuals. Williams makes these comments about the church coming to itself in the context of human suffering, and the way he treats that subject points to another important difference with Dreher: though both declare us to be in a sort of winter, Williams does not narrate a declension narrative in which we can look back

---

47. Williams, *Looking East in Winter*, 230.
48. Williams, *Looking East in Winter*, 230.
49. Williams, *Looking East in Winter*, 250.

to and recapture the warmth of spring. No, he looks back to other winters for inspiration and wisdom about how to find warmth and consolation in the cold, guidance about how to live through the winter. Where Dreher's church is a fortress against "grace-free zones," Williams's is the institution that finds itself in going out to where it is not, to the margins of the world, and encountering grace in that journey.

For Williams, church and world are not antagonistic in the way they are for Dreher because of the many ways in which the two commingle, because they exist within each individual—and because both exist inside the liturgy. In liturgy, humanity confesses itself needing "to be drawn from one world to another."[50] Humanity, to put it another way, is the world that needs to be opened, and liturgy performs this passage, representing the world, not as an enemy or an instrument, but as what Williams calls "a vehicle of relations" whose horizon is inexhaustible exchange.[51] In the way that nature is a gift from which culture draws its material sustenance and which culture is given to care for and tend to, so the world provides the church its materiality and is given to the church to love and care for—even, like Christ, giving itself up for the world, even to death. That is the way the church is for the world: not shrinking from the world but passing through the death that is in the world that we might lay hold of the life of Christ.

Williams offers toward the end of his book a picture of a life lived toward this protagonistic ecclesiology. For Mother Maria Skobtsova, the theologian so central to his ecclesiological reflections, was also someone who passed through the cross of Christ—or, as she might put it, who was pierced by the same sword that pierced Mary. She was living as a Russian exile in Paris when the Nazis began rounding up Jews into a stadium. For the next few days, she smuggled food in and children out, putting herself at risk to help her neighbor. When her acts of solidarity were discovered, she was sent with her neighbors to the concentration camp Ravensbrück, where she worked for two years, running discussion groups and encouraging her fellow prisoners before she died. Her life was an icon of the vision of the neighbor love she commended, a way of churching the world that truly venerated her fellow humans as divine images. It is startlingly fitting then that one of her last acts amid the toil and death of Ravensbrück was to write a literal icon of God's love. She loved the world like Christ did, giving her life to it in love.

---

50. Williams, *Looking East in Winter*, 146.
51. Williams, *Looking East in Winter*, 149.

Mother Maria's vision of a church that loves the world and draws materiality from the world, from which it is distinct but not separated, can also help us imagine a type of missions decoupled from colonialist or neo-colonialist impulses. And this imagining is not mere fantasy or wish. Here I want to turn by way of conclusion to two other witnesses of what protagonistic ecclesiology can look like in a life. It has been exemplified, for example, in the life of four missionaries who went to El Salvador in the 1970s—two Maryknoll sisters, an Ursuline sister, and a lay missionary. Americans, they went to El Salvador to serve Christ and found a brutal regime of violence and repression against the *campesinos*. Rather than retreating to the safety of the United States as the situation deteriorated, they lived in solidarity with their new neighbors in El Salvador, for whom they continued to advocate. In 1980, months after Archbishop Oscar Romero was killed, they, too, were killed, numbered among the seventy thousand Salvadorans who died in the civil war. Their voice in life and their witness in death helped draw international attention to the plight of the Salvadoran people. In contrast to antagonistic ecclesiology's colonialist impulses, these missionary women lived out a type of reverse colonialism, or at least exemplified a way of tending the wounds inflicted by colonialism. These women used the power and privilege they had for the sake of the Salvadorans, sharing their fate.

The other witness I want to glimpse takes us back to the new-yet-old nature-culture models, to how the church's togetherness with the world is evoked by nature's togetherness with culture and to how the church is summoned to care for the world as culture is for nature. The interrelations and protagonisms of nature, culture, and church converge in this final exemplar, Dorothy Stang, a nun born American and naturalized Brazilian. Stang spoke out for the poor and the forest, both of whom were exploited by the wealthy. Large companies and wealthy ranchers deforested the Amazon of Brazil that subsistence farmers used to grow their own food. These companies depleted the soil and diminished the rainforest to offer cheap timber and beef to multinational corporations. Known as an environmentalist of the poor who promoted small-scale farmers who integrated care for the forest into their agricultural practices, Stang often wore a T-shirt that read, "The end of our forests is the end of our lives." In 2005, after years of death threats, she was fatally shot by those who opposed her efforts. Today her cause for canonization as a martyr is underway in the Catholic Church.

Stang's life is for us an image of the way culture can be for the nature that gives it life and the way that protagonism can inform a church that is for the world. Through Stang, the missionary women in El Salvador, and

Mother Maria, we see a vision of faithfulness as a calling into risky love for the world rather than into a fortress of protection from it. In this way, they offer a picture of protagonistic ecclesiology that echoes the love of God, who in Christ became vulnerable to the world, to the point of being destroyed by it; but who also nurtures our hope that such love is stronger than death and that the power of this love can be seen precisely in the way it passes all the way through the world's death-dealing forces. This is not a church in a win-lose or even a win-win relationship to the world, because its relationship to the world is not fundamentally competitive nor oppositional. It is a church transcending the boundaries of belonging. It is a church complexly intertwined with the world, caught up in the story of a God who in love draws all creation to Godself.

In the protagonistic ecclesiology these women exemplify, the "versus" of church and world is enfolded into a larger for-ness, and in this way mirrors not only the way culture can be *for* nature but also the way God is *for* the world. There is a kind of against-ness: God did not leave the world to its own deterioration and destruction; God placed God's own body *against* the forces of sin and death. And yet how could this story be told apart from the larger protagonism? How can the picture of ecclesiology to which we are called be painted apart from God's own protagonism, which begins with a God who "so loved the world"? Surely there is no grim, scorekeeping angel watching our battles and entanglements in a heavenly press box. Surely there are only angels rejoicing at the churching of the world embodied in the veneration of Christ in and through the world, as the church answers its summons to imitate Christ by taking God's "so-loving" as its own protagonistic starting point.

CHAPTER 5

EITHER/OR

On the Necessary, but Maverick, Distinction of Church and World

MATT JENSON

FOR MANY REASONS, the distinction between the church and the world seems increasingly implausible. As American churches began to meet after the worst days of the COVID-19 pandemic, many people simply did not come back. In addition to disaffiliation, the relatively thin ecclesial participation of harried and distracted believers, compelling examples of pagan virtue, and repulsive examples of Christian vice all conspire to weaken the *prima facie* reasonableness of a sharp distinction between church and world. In this paper, I defend the distinction, arguing that it is not only plausible but necessary, while also being maverick. I begin with a biblical-theological consideration of the relationship of Israel and the nations. In electing a people for himself, the LORD makes a divine distinction—and surely no ground can be stabler than that! The covenant at Sinai establishes a milieu in which holiness is marked by distinction, and Israel is reminded regularly of her special election, history, and vocation. But as the history of God's people unfolds, it becomes the history of the precipitous "Canaanization of Israel," in Daniel Block's words. Perhaps the distinction between Israel and the nations is suspect after all.

I will then engage Tom Greggs's recent proposal for a "non-binary" ecclesiology, in which he argues that the church is not "a place in which one might think of a binary dividing line from the world."[1] While contemporary

---

1. Tom Greggs, *The Church in a World of Religions: Working Papers in Theology*, ed. J. Thomas Hewitt (New York: T&T Clark, 2022), 134.

experience presses upon us a certain discomfort with triumphalism and the biblical record only underscores the perennial infidelity of God's people, I argue that the very surprising changes in identification of people in Scripture *presuppose and require* the lasting distinction between church and world. If we adopt an ecclesiology in which "non-binary" means "non-discrete," "fluid," or "existing along a continuum of hypothetically infinite options," the biblical reversals lose their punch. The prophetic and apostolic witness in response to Israel's unfaithfulness provides a model for understanding ecclesial unfaithfulness. It suggests the abiding validity of a sharp distinction between church and world, but a distinction that fosters sobriety and hope rather than presumption and despair, in light of the frequent reidentifications peppered throughout the history of God's people.

ISRAEL AND/AS THE NATIONS

In electing a people for himself, the LORD makes a divine distinction and establishes a milieu in the covenant at Sinai in which holiness is marked by this distinction. As he announces the final plague in Egypt, the death of the firstborn, the LORD promises that Israel will remain untouched, "that you may know that the LORD makes a distinction between Egypt and Israel" (Ex. 11:7).[2] The distinction is liberating, life-giving, and absolute. It is also unmerited. On the cusp of the land, Moses reminds the people,

> The LORD your God has chosen you to be a people for his treasured possession, out of all the peoples who are on the face of the earth. It was not because you were more in number than any other people that the LORD set his love on you and chose you, for you were the fewest of all peoples, but it is because the LORD loves you and is keeping the oath that he swore to your fathers, that the LORD has brought you out with a mighty hand and redeemed you from the house of slavery, from the hand of Pharaoh king of Egypt. (Deut. 7:6–8)

To anticipate the words of a Jew who lived hundreds of years later, "Then what becomes of our boasting? It is excluded" (Rom. 3:27). God's distinction between Israel and the nations should not and need not lead to Israel's pride, but to Israel's humility and gratitude, possibly even to her fear.

---

2. All Scripture quotations in this chapter are taken from the English Standard Version (ESV).

After all, the distinction is also demanding. Because the LORD makes a distinction, because "you are a people holy to the LORD your God" (Deut. 7:6), Israel's form of life must be likewise distinct, disciplined by the difference that comes in being chosen by God to be a people for his treasured possession. Covenant faithfulness demands separation—physical, moral, and cultic. For Israel to sin is to transgress the distinction that the LORD makes between Israel and the nations. Of course Israel does just this, committing this sin retrospectively (in longing for Egypt) and prospectively (in their attempt to be like the Canaanites). Almost immediately once the covenant has been made in the wilderness—where Israel has gone to serve the LORD (Ex. 7:16; 8:1, 20; 9:1, 13; 10:3)—Israel becomes Egypt, committing idolatry by worshiping a graven image, and receiving the kind of punishment the LORD has previously reserved for Egypt: "Then the LORD sent a plague on the people, because they made the calf, the one that Aaron made" (Ex. 32:35). Nor is this an isolated occurrence; it is a way of life. Repeatedly in the wilderness, Israel longs for the good old days in Egypt. Upon hearing the pessimistic report from the spies who scout out the land God had promised to them, the "whole congregation" complains, "'Would that we had died in the land of Egypt! Or would that we had died in this wilderness! Why is the LORD bringing us into this land, to fall by the sword? Our wives and our little ones will become a prey. Would it not be better for us to go back to Egypt?' And they said to one another, 'Let us choose a leader and go back to Egypt'" (Num. 14:2–4). This is not merely a moment of wistfulness and cowardice; the people are ready to find someone else to lead them back to Egypt. Implicit here is the belief that it is better *not* to be distinguished by the LORD if this is the life he offers.[3]

The besetting temptation to abandon the distinction and become like the nations seems to motivate the LORD's unflinching command to devote the nations in the land to destruction. The *herem* is put in place as a radical measure to keep Israel from becoming like the Canaanites. "You must devote them to complete destruction" (Deut. 7:2), Moses told the people as they were about to enter the land.

You shall make no covenant with them and show no mercy to them. You shall not intermarry with them, giving your daughters to their sons or taking their daughters for your sons, for they would turn away your

---

3. Also see Numbers 11:4–6, where, dissatisfied with the Lord's miraculous provision of manna, the people wished instead for the food they ate in Egypt.

sons from following me, to serve other gods. Then the anger of the
Lord would be kindled against you, and he would destroy you quickly.
But thus shall you deal with them: you shall break down their altars and
dash in pieces their pillars and chop down their Asherim and burn their
carved images with fire. (Deut. 7:2–5)

In a similar warning in Numbers, the Lord made explicit the peril of
Israel becoming like the nations: "I will do to you as I thought to do to
them" (Num. 33:56). Be careful what you wish for. Being God's covenant
people does not inoculate them from idolatry, nor does it exempt them
suffering his wrath.

Daniel Block writes that "the central theme of the Book of Judges is the
Canaanization of Israel."[4] But Israel's Canaanization is already a foregone
conclusion in Deuteronomy. The Lord doesn't even keep it a secret, telling
Moses, "Behold, you are about to lie down with your fathers. Then this
people will rise and whore after the foreign gods among them in the land
that they are entering, and they will forsake me and break my covenant
that I have made with them" (Deut. 31:16). To belong to Israel is to belong
to God's covenant people who keep covenant with God. But by the time
Israel stands on the threshold of the land, it has become apparent that circumcision of the flesh is no guarantee of covenant faithfulness. Despite
circumcision and the election that it presupposes, despite the exodus and the
law, despite the fact that "this commandment that I command you today is
not too hard for you, neither is it far off. . . . But the word is very near you.
It is in your mouth and in your heart, so that you can do it" (Deut. 30:11,
14)—despite all this, Israel does *not* do it. Why? Because fleshly circumcision is not enough. If the Shema calls Israel to "love the Lord your God
with all your heart and with all your soul and with all your might" (Deut.
6:5), Israel will do so only when God restores her fortunes, regathers her
from exile, and himself circumcises her heart: "And the Lord your God
will circumcise your heart and the heart of your offspring, so that you will
love the Lord your God with all your heart and with all your soul, that
you may live" (Deut. 30:6).

What distinguishes God's faithful Israelites is circumcision of the heart,
and yet the history of Israel is primarily the history of a people of uncircum-
cised heart.[5] This holy people profanes the name of God and becomes like

4. Daniel I. Block, *Judges, Ruth*, NAC 6 (Nashville: Broadman & Holman, 1999), 71.
5. See Deut. 10:16; 30:6; Jer. 9:26. Note that there is no mention of fleshly circumcision in
Deuteronomy.

the nations, with such dire consequences that the LORD can later declare, "You are not my people, and I am not your God" (Hos. 1:9). Thus, not all Israel is Israel.[6]

On the other hand, some that are not Israel *are* Israel. The Old Testament is punctuated by signal examples of those who are not "descended from Israel" joining themselves to Israel. One of the most famous, of course, is Rahab, a Canaanite prostitute who welcomes and hides Israelite spies on her roof. In sharp contrast to the cowardice of the first generation of Israel, Rahab reasoned from the LORD's mighty works in Egypt and beyond the Jordan to the conclusion that "the LORD has given you the land, and that the fear of you has fallen upon us, and that all the inhabitants of the land melt away before you" (Josh. 2:9). The author of Joshua notes that "she has lived in Israel to this day" (6:25), and she is honored among God's people. She is an ancestress of David and Jesus (Matt. 1:5) who is commended for her faith (Heb. 11:31) and for her works (James 2:25) in the New Testament. Isaiah tells of a future in which the nations will not merely be included within Israel like Rahab but stand alongside Israel as God's people: "In that day Israel will be the third with Egypt and Assyria, a blessing in the midst of the earth, whom the LORD of hosts has blessed, saying, 'Blessed be Egypt my people, and Assyria the work of my hands, and Israel my inheritance'" (Isa. 19:24–25).

These dynamics of role reversal lie at the heart of Jesus' ministry. To take one rather striking example, after Jesus healed the man with a withered hand on the Sabbath, the Pharisees "went out and conspired against him, how to destroy him" (Matt. 12:14). These teachers of Israel had become the *nations* (the *goyim*) who rage in Psalm 2, taking counsel "against the LORD and against his Anointed" (v. 2).[7] Just after this, as Jesus continued to heal, the evangelist identified Jesus as the fulfiller of the Isaianic promise that "in [the Servant's] name the Gentiles will hope" (Matt. 12:21). Here is just one representative instance of Israel acting like the nations and the nations being included within and treated as Israel. Not all Israel is Israel, and some that are not Israel are Israel.

---

6. In the ESV's prosaic rendering of Paul's words, "not all who are descended from Israel belong to Israel" (Rom. 9:6)—though one might prefer the punchier "not all Israelites truly belong to Israel" (NRSV) or "they are not all Israel, which are of Israel" (KJV).

7. See Jonathan T. Pennington, *The Sermon on the Mount and Human Flourishing: A Theological Commentary* (Grand Rapids: Baker Academic, 2017), 96, who identifies this theme in Matthew 12:14; 22:15; 26:3–4; 27:1; 28:12. Pennington notes that, in Matthew's gospel, "'gentile' has come to mean any Jewish person or (ethnic) gentile who does not follow Christ; the Jew-gentile distinction still exists, but the lines are now eschatologically drawn based on a faith-response to Jesus rather than ethnicity."

We could proliferate examples of Jesus' shocking inclination toward the unclean, gentiles, women, the poor, imperial oppressors, the sick, those with disabilities. He goes out of his way to extend welcome and access to the kingdom he brings to those who, at least on a cursory read of Israel's history, would seem disqualified from the messianic kingdom. In the temple in Jerusalem, Jesus tells the chief priests and elders of the people, "Truly, I say to you, the tax collectors and the prostitutes go into the kingdom of God before you" (Matt. 21:31). Not only are these outsiders, people who have lived like the nations, allowed into the kingdom of God—which would be scandal enough—but they are given priority admission to the kingdom, ahead of the most esteemed religious leaders. Immediately after this, Jesus tells a parable that is still more ominous, in which the master of the house kills the tenants of his vineyard for their mistreatment of a string of servants and their murder of his son (vv. 33–41). Here the issue seems to be not demotion in the kingdom but exclusion from it entirely. If the religious leaders of Israel according to the flesh are excluded from eschatological Israel, as Jesus' parable suggests (as, too, does their violent antagonism toward the messianic King), then we must at least conclude that the final identity of Israel will surprise many.

Finally, consider Peter's vision, in which a voice commands Peter to kill and eat unclean animals. When Peter protests that he has "never eaten anything that is common or unclean," the voice checks Peter: "What God has made clean, do not call common" (Acts 10:14–15). The vision is disruptive, jarring; and it prepares Peter to tell the gentile Cornelius "that God shows no partiality, but in every nation anyone who fears him and does what is right is acceptable to him" (vv. 34–35). The Spirit falls on these gentiles, who worship God and are baptized on the spot. If Israel's history began with a precipitous tumble into Canaanization, the inclusion of the gentiles represents the latter-day Israelization of Canaan.

Clearly, the distinction between Israel and the nations, between the church and the world, is unstable. Or rather, the identification of each of the parties is unstable, which presses on us the question of whether the distinction itself is abidingly meaningful. We turn now to Tom Greggs's work in ecclesiology in light of his claim that "the categorizing of people into two binary opposed camps does not sit easily with either our tradition or the complexities of scripture."[8]

8. Greggs, *Church in a World of Religions*, 153.

The Critique of Binaries

Over the last fifteen years, Tom Greggs has criticized a binary distinction between church and world. He makes the point most forcefully in his 2011 book *Theology against Religion: Constructive Dialogues with Bonhoeffer and Barth*, calling for a theology that seeks to be "against religion by virtue of" (among other things) "being resolutely *unwilling to engage in articulating binaries*."[9] What is Greggs refusing in his unwillingness to speak in binaries? In what sense does he envision moving "beyond the binary" (as he titles one article)? As applied to ecclesiology, does that imply, for instance, the erasure of a distinction between church and world? Does "non-binary" here mean "non-discrete," "fluid," or "existing along a continuum of hypothetically infinite options"? Or does Greggs object instead to the way the, perhaps still fitting, distinction between church and world is construed, deployed, and navigated?

It will help to set the context for Greggs's concern. This is how he begins the article titled "Beyond the Binary: Forming Evangelical Eschatology":

> Evangelical identity has its origins in strongly particularist senses of Christian self-identity, and has tended to form its own social culture over and against that of the world around (as witnessed to in its puritan and pietist past). While evangelicalism has been happy to assimilate itself to certain cultural phenomena, especially around economic market forces, its desire to be "in the world but not of the world" determines that many evangelical impulses arise from a form of separationism which relies on straightforward binary descriptors of insider – outsider, saved – damned, elect – reject. Strong particularism gives rise to strong separationism, and underpinning this separationism is often a degree of eschatological self-certainty which seeks such utter self-assurance as to push to the outside anyone who seems vaguely other or an outsider to the central issues perceived to be definitive for inclusion in the Kingdom of God.[10]

Greggs rejects binaries in ecclesiology for at least four reasons. First, they are presumptuous. The problematic binary here seems less to be about the distinction of church and world per se than about the way in which that distinction underwrites a presumptuous, self-serving, and judgmental

---

9. Tom Greggs, *Theology against Religion: Constructive Dialogues with Bonhoeffer and Barth* (London: Bloomsbury, 2011), 217, 218.

10. Greggs, *Church in a World of Religions*, 151.

posture on the part of the church. Greggs critiques evangelicalism for its separatist impulses, which are tied to a misplaced confidence about who's in and who's out, both now and at the end.[11] "We" are always the insiders, the saved, the elect; "we" are never on the dark side of the binary. Furthermore, our confidence that we belong inside the camp leads to, perhaps is even sustained by, a confidence that specific others are outside the camp, that they are the outsiders, the damned, the rejected.[12] This is all too obvious and transparent in the minds of the self-assured. But in fact, it is foreign both to the logic of grace and our solidarity as sinners.[13] The use of binaries smacks of the sin of presumption, and it leads to antagonism rather than mission.

Greggs's second reason for rejecting binaries is that they compromise mission. As a priest, Christ was set apart "not *from* the world but *for* the world."[14] The same holds for his priestly people, who exist "for the sake of the world" and to whom he gives sacraments "not to separate the church *from* the world but to demarcate the church as God's church *for* the world."[15] It's a rhetorically effective point, and it rightly names two opposing postures; but as it stands, this is also a false dilemma. For Christ and his people are both separated from the world and set apart for the world.[16] That the one (*from*) is ordered to the other (*for*), that election is for the sake of mission, should not lead to the neglect of the former.[17] Despite his critique of binaries, Greggs does not seem ready to jettison the distinction between church and world. It has a missional function: "The difference between the church and the world is not ever for the sake of the church and its identity," he writes,

---

11. Similarly: "What underlies such binaries is an assurance about who counts as 'us' and who counts as 'them,' whether expressed in terms of personal salvation or ecclesial identity" (Greggs, *Church in a World of Religions*, 60). Also see Tom Greggs, *The Breadth of Salvation: Rediscovering the Fullness of God's Saving Work* (Grand Rapids: Baker Academic, 2020), 69–74.

12. It also suggests we have forgotten Jesus' location outside the camp: "So Jesus also suffered outside the gate in order to sanctify the people through his own blood. Therefore let us go to him outside the camp and bear the reproach he endured" (Heb. 13:12–13).

13. See Greggs, *Church in a World of Religions*, 154, 155.

14. Tom Greggs, *Dogmatic Ecclesiology*, vol. 1, *The Priestly Catholicity of the Church* (Grand Rapids: Baker Academic, 2019), 76.

15. Greggs, *Dogmatic Ecclesiology*, 1:149–50. This is in a subsection titled "Unity with the World, Not Separation from It."

16. Though Scripture can speak of "the world" both neutrally and negatively, Greggs almost exclusively speaks of "the world" neutrally. (A rare exception is *Dogmatic Ecclesiology*, 1:421–22.) He neglects the biblical witness to the world's hostility to God. Because the world has its own god and its own, evil course (2 Cor. 4:4; Eph. 2:2), believers should not be conformed to the world (Rom. 12:2) and must keep themselves unstained from the world (James 1:27). In fact, "friendship with the world is enmity with God" (James 4:4).

17. Greggs puts the point more fittingly elsewhere: "Focus comes to be on the church's differentiation from the world for the sake of ensuring the salvation of the church's members, and not differentiation from the world for the sake of the world." *Dogmatic Ecclesiology*, 1:127.

"but is rather always for the sake of the world and its salvation. The world exists not to be a counterpoint against which the church might be described and measured, but as the purpose for which the church exists. The church is always provisional, proleptic, and anticipatory."[18] In Greggs's mind, binaries reflect the church's diseased concern with self-identification over against an excluded other, rather than the church's Christiform vocation to self-giving love. The church lives for the world, and so "[a] self-interested church is not a church of Jesus Christ."[19] In fact, the distinction between church and world is intended for its own transcendence. Its perpetuation is a sign of partial failure, a sign that the church's witness to the world has been insufficiently successful.

Third, and more briefly, Greggs is concerned that binaries are pneumatologically misleading. "The Spirit who is present extensively in the world dwells intensively with particular communities in time for the service and performance of God's will," he writes. "The church is not, therefore, a place in which one might think of a binary dividing line from the world. It is, instead, the people in which the presence of God, which in God's omnipresence cannot be spatially limited, dwells in intensity by the power of His Spirit in a community in time."[20] The wind of the Spirit blows where it wishes, and God is at work outside the walls of the church (John 3:8). Binaries suggest that the LORD is the special possession of God's people, and they thus misrepresent the biblical and historical witness to the wideness and wildness of divine action.

Finally, binaries are eschatologically invalid. Near the end of the first volume of his ecclesiology, Greggs writes, "This means the church always lives with an eye to its own end, since God is the God of all creation and of the new creation and, therefore, no boundary between church and world can be ultimate."[21] The God who created all there is will make all things new. The church lives with longing for its own end in the new creation, when God will be all in all. So, even amid the world's bleakest antagonism, the church knows that "the difference between the church and the world is not a difference which is absolute, eternal, and oppositional: the Lord who brings life to the church is also the Lord who brings life to all

---

18. Greggs, *Dogmatic Ecclesiology*, 1:366.
19. Greggs, *Dogmatic Ecclesiology*, 1:136.
20. Greggs, *Church in a World of Religions*, 133–34.
21. Greggs, *Dogmatic Ecclesiology*, 1:433. "There is no church in the eschaton because in the eschaton any distinction between church and world will be no more—not in such a way that the world is swallowed up by the church but, quite the contrary, in a way in which the church has fulfilled its purpose of provisionality in the new heaven and the new earth" (131).

creation."[22] A question arises at this point: Is the distinction between church and world eschatologically invalid because the church's mission has ended in the final coming of God's kingdom? Or is it eschatologically invalid because, in the end, the people of God will be composed of all people? We turn now to the question of universal salvation and its bearings on the church-world distinction.

DARE WE HOPE . . . ?

The question of universalism hovers over Greggs's *corpus*. In part, this is due to a sustained polemic against individualism, in which he seeks to change the subject from concern for the eschatological destiny of individuals to the cosmic and corporate victory of God in Christ.[23] He takes a nuanced position that tends toward universalism while stopping short of concluding that each and every individual will be saved in the end.[24] Greggs echoes Hans Urs von Balthasar's insistence that there are two biblical words that must be honored—the threat of separation and the hope of universal salvation.[25] "One cannot simply see separation as the message of scripture and universalism as nonscriptural," he writes. "There is clearly a need to allow both sets of texts to stand side by side, and to seek to interpret one through the other." This is exactly right. A premature harmonization of the passages can easily leave us blind to preconceptions and preferences that keep us from seeing the fullness of biblical teaching. Greggs continues, "Prioritizing the universalist passages, and seeing the passages on hell as contextual imagery related to an existential distance from God for those in the present facing death helps to maintain these two traditions in scripture together."[26] Why, though, ought we prioritize the universalist passages? If the passages on hell have been prioritized in the past, perhaps Greggs seeks to gain a hearing for a neglected biblical theme. Even so, this can only be a temporary strategy.

---

22. Greggs, *Dogmatic Ecclesiology*, 1:412.

23. See Greggs, *Theology against Religion*, 104, 106.

24. See, most extensively, Tom Greggs, *Barth, Origen, and Universal Salvation: Restoring Particularity* (Oxford: Oxford University Press, 2009). In personal correspondence, Greggs writes that "my issue with universalism is that in making a claim about all, we make a claim about each inevitably; and I don't think we can do that." Email correspondence, March 2, 2023. Perhaps it is most apt to speak of hoping for *each* rather than hoping for *all*.

25. See Hans Urs von Balthasar, *Dare We Hope "That All Men Be Saved"? With a Short Discourse on Hell*, trans. David Kipp and Lothar Krauth (San Francisco: Ignatius Press, 1988).

26. Greggs, *Theology against Religion*, 121.

I suspect, though, that Greggs is committed to a programmatic prioritization of the universalist passages, in which case it becomes more difficult to "allow both sets of texts to stand side by side." At the very least, he follows Balthasar in holding out hope for universal salvation.[27] His critique of binary insider-outsider language tends in this direction as well. Greggs commends Origen: "He allows for a picture of God's salvation which is not starkly black and white, and which avoids binary language about salvation in order to escape simple categorization of people as either inside or outside the plan of God. Instead, he recognises that the plan of God is a plan for all."[28] Greggs seems to have gone all in with Barth and Bonhoeffer on the universal election of humanity in Christ.[29] A new humanity is given *de jure*, objectively, and universally in Christ, and given *de facto*, subjectively, in space and time by the Spirit.[30] Much rides on how much weight is given to the two halves of that sentence.[31] While this is a controversial interpretation, it seems to me that Barth and Bonhoeffer tip the scales heavily on the objective side, to the point that the distinction between insiders and outsiders is merely noetic. In his posthumously published *Ethics*, Bonhoeffer wrote, "The church-community is separated from the world only by this: it believes in the reality of being accepted by God—a reality that belongs to the whole world."[32] Some time could be spent in pondering the significance of that "only." A few years later, drawing on Bonhoeffer's language from his recently published *Letters and Papers from Prison*, Barth wrote this:

> Again thinking in terms of the humanity of God, we cannot at all reckon in a serious way with *real* "outsiders," with a "world come of age," but only with a world which *regards* itself as of age (and proves daily that it is precisely not that). Thus the so-called "outsiders" are really only

---

27. "Does, then, this mean universal salvation, a doctrine ostensibly anathematized in 553 CE? It certainly means that one should be open to this, as scripture itself is" (Greggs, *Theology against Religion*, 109). Recently Greggs has described his position as "a more humble and cautious sense that if salvation can even reach me, we might dare to hope for all" (*Breadth of Salvation*, 60–61).

28. Greggs, *Church in a World of Religions*, 191.

29. See Greggs, *Dogmatic Ecclesiology*, 1:84n5, 445n72.

30. See Greggs, *Dogmatic Ecclesiology*, 1:190, 388.

31. John Zizioulas wrote, "The Pentecostal event is an ecclesiologically constitutive event. The one Christ event takes the form of *events* (plural) which *are as primary ontologically* as the one Christ event itself." Zizioulas, *Being as Communion: Studies in Personhood and the Church* (Crestwood, NY: St. Vladimir's Seminary Press, 1985), 132–33, emphasis his.

32. Dietrich Bonhoeffer, *Ethics*, 67–68; cited in Greggs, *Theology against Religion*, 132. Similarly, Greggs writes, "Through the objective justification of humanity in Jesus Christ, the world, too, exists in this ontic condition but is unaware of the reality it has in Christ" (Greggs, *Dogmatic Ecclesiology*, 1:260).

"insiders" who have not yet understood and apprehended themselves as such. On the other hand, even the most persuaded Christian, in the final analysis, must and will recognize himself ever and again as an "outsider." So there must then be no particular language for insiders and outsiders.[33]

For Bonhoeffer, the only distinction between church and world is noetic—the church believes what is already true for the world. Barth agreed, and went so far as to say that therefore there really are no "outsiders." And yet, and here we see his abiding dialectical style and logic, all of us are also "outsiders," those who have been judged and condemned and killed in Christ. Barth was not sentimental about any of this. He took sin with utter seriousness. But he discerned a certain finality to what has occurred in Christ and concluded that "to open up again the abyss closed in Jesus Christ cannot be our task." Certainly, "God does not turn toward [humanity] without uttering in inexorable sharpness a 'No' to his transgression," but this is "the 'No' which Jesus Christ has taken upon Himself for us men, in order that it may no longer affect us and that we may no longer place ourselves under it."[34] Again, we see pride of place given to the objective, *de jure* work of Christ in such a way that there do not seem to be any absolute outsiders. The distinction is merely noetic. Barth did quite a bit with this deflationary form of the church-world distinction. To say it is "merely noetic" is not to say that it is purely imaginary or inoperative. Barth's ecclesiology of witness decenters the church from its mission even as it offers a (resoundingly Johannine) account of the illuminating yet shy witness of a church that points in word and deed to the Judge judged in our place, whose judgment trumps all other words about what the world is and will be.

Nevertheless, and despite its eloquence, I suspect that Barth's christological reduction of eschatological options flattens Scripture's own witness to the present reality of the world, as well as its end. Even if Barth (and Greggs with him) resisted riding the momentum of his argument to the confident conclusion of universal salvation, he would be left with few reasons to do so other than the mysterious freedom of God and an unwillingness to turn the person of Christ into a principle.[35] A lifelong anxiety

---

33. Karl Barth, *The Humanity of God* (Louisville: Westminster John Knox, 1960), 58–59.
34. Barth, *Humanity of God*, 60.
35. See Karl Barth, *Church Dogmatics*, ed. G. W. Bromiley and T. F. Torrance, trans. G. W. Bromiley, G. T. Thomson, et al., 4 vols. In 13 pts. (Edinburgh: T&T Clark, 1936–77), IV/3, 173–80; Greggs, *Barth, Origen, and Universal Salvation*, 207.

about untethering the work of the Spirit from the work of Christ led Barth to leave little for the Spirit to do. Greggs's pneumatological orientation is a significant advance at this point beyond the christological ecclesiologies of Bonhoeffer and Barth. Greggs speaks of the Spirit particularizing the universal reconciling act of God.[36] All the world is justified and sanctified in Christ, but the Spirit works out that justification and sanctification in space and time in the church.[37] "The sanctification in which all humans participate in Christ de jure is also that in which the believer—by an event of the act of the Holy Spirit of God—may participate de facto as she comes to share in Christ's full humanity."[38]

Ah, but there's the rub: *Does* all the world already participate in Christ, even only *de jure*? And if so (or not), what are the implications of that fact? The previous comment comes just after Greggs has been discussing the opening verses of 1 Corinthians. He notes how the opening of 1 Corinthians "holds both of these aspects together—the singular and objective with the temporal and subjective. . . . This condition is an objective reality: they are sanctified in that the grace of God has been given to them (v. 4). But after these unconditional and de jure statements follows a run of statements by Paul that imply growth, enrichment, and strengthening in order that the believer might be 'blameless on the day of our Lord Jesus Christ' (v. 8)."[39] Greggs is right to draw our attention to the need to hold these aspects together, but we need to ask when "the grace of God that was given you in Christ Jesus" (v. 4) was given. Greggs's following comment seems to imply that it was given in the Christ event, but Paul was speaking to Christians here. It seems at least as likely—indeed, much more so, to me—to think that Paul was speaking of the grace given to believers when they hear the good news about Jesus, repent, believe, are baptized, and receive the Spirit. Despite the laudable advance in his pneumatological orientation of ecclesiology, I find Greggs's pneumatology too weak at this point; and I believe he ultimately repeats Barth's and Bonhoeffer's mistake of tilting the balance toward the objective, *de jure* pole, to the neglect of the subjective, *de facto* pole.

---

36. The burden of *Barth, Origen, and Universal Salvation* is "to demonstrate that universal salvation does not remove or lessen the importance of each present particularity, and therefore that it does not stand contrary to Christian faith and decision, but provides the place for genuine Christian faith and decision" (4). Also see Greggs, *Dogmatic Ecclesiology*, 1:21.

37. Greggs, *Dogmatic Ecclesiology*, 1:190.

38. Greggs, *Dogmatic Ecclesiology*, 1:388.

39. Greggs, *Dogmatic Ecclesiology*, 1:387.

Calvin is better here. For Barth (and for Greggs), without the Spirit, we don't know what we have. For Calvin, without the Spirit, we have nothing.

> How do we receive those benefits which the Father bestowed on his only-begotten Son—not for Christ's own private use, but that he might enrich poor and needy men? First, we must understand that as long as Christ remains outside of us, and we are separated from him, all that he has suffered and done for the salvation of the human race remains useless and of no value for us. Therefore, to share with us what he has received from the Father, he had to become ours and to dwell within us. . . . All that he possesses is nothing to us until we grow into one body with him. It is true that we obtain this by faith. Yet since we see that not all indiscriminately embrace that communion with Christ which is offered through the gospel, reason itself teaches us to climb higher and to examine into the secret energy of the Spirit, by which we come to enjoy Christ and all his benefits.[40]

Christ may be for us, but he must be in us to be of any value to us. This is not a crassly utilitarian comment, but reflective of Calvin's high view of union with Christ. The Spirit's work is to unite us to Christ such that he has "become ours" and "dwell[s] within us." The implication here is that, though the eternal Son has taken on flesh, humans do not share in him apart from the Spirit's subsequent work of uniting believers in the church to Christ. Until then, we are not merely ignorant; we are bereft, impoverished, "separated from Christ, alienated from the commonwealth of Israel and strangers to the covenants of promise, having no hope and without God in the world" (Eph. 2:12).

Following Calvin, we can say that "insiders" are those who are indwelt by Christ, while "outsiders" are those for whom Christ remains outside. This is not to foreclose on judgment, nor is it to presume an easy identification of those who are Christ's, nor is it to strictly identify the church militant with the church triumphant. It is, though, to make a sharp distinction between those who are indwelt by the Spirit and united to Christ and those who are not. It is the Spirit, then, who establishes and orders the lasting distinction between church and world. It is the Spirit who makes the people of God gathered around Jesus into a temple in whom the Spirit of

---

40. John Calvin, *Institutes of the Christian Religion*, vol. 2, ed. John T. McNeill, trans. Ford Lewis Battles, Library of Christian Classics (Philadelphia: Westminster, 1960), 3.1.1, 537.

Christ dwells.[41] Greggs regularly speaks of the Spirit's "intensive" presence in the church, as a way to honor his "extensive" presence in the world and not make the mistake of thinking the kingdom of God is coterminous with the church.[42] While his instinct is good, he underplays the qualitative difference that indwelling makes, a difference that sets the church apart from the world even as it sends the church on mission to the world.

But here we return to Greggs's apposite observation about the counterintuitive (to say the least) deployment and population of the categories of church and world in Scripture. "Throughout the gospels," he writes, "we are able to see this undermining of the insider-outsider binary. . . . Jesus is the one who is not only treated as an outsider, but who proclaims the Kingdom of God to be for those we might perceive as outsiders: it is the prostitutes and tax collectors (the perceived outsiders) who will enter the Kingdom of God before those who are perceived to be and perceive themselves to be the insiders (Mt 21.31)."[43] At the very least, the kingdom Jesus brings belongs to those who seem to be outsiders. And even if present-day insiders find a place in it, it is a lesser place than belongs to present-day outsiders. I'm less convinced that this constitutes an undermining of the insider-outsider binary than that it establishes how very confounding membership in each category will be in the eschaton. Greggs points to the universal surprise in the parable of the sheep and the goats ("Lord, when did we see you . . . ?") and concludes that "there is no easy equating of those who in history are seen to be on the inside or outside with those who at the end find themselves on the inside or outside respectively."[44] This seems exactly right to me. The question remains: What should we conclude from this parable, and other, similar parables of Jesus? How are we to interpret the surprise?

The advantage of Greggs's non-binary approach is that it pops the bubble of presumption, reestablishes the solidarity of sinners saved by grace, and

---

41. See Eph. 2:19–22.

42. "As an act of the Holy Spirit, the church is established as a community of the intensive presence of God for active participation in His service and for His purposes. The Spirit who is present extensively in the world dwells intensively with particular communities in time for the service and performance of God's will." Greggs, *Theology against Religion*, 132; Greggs adopts the language of "intensity" and "extensity" from Daniel Hardy's *Finding the Church* (London: SCM, 2001).

43. Greggs, *Church in a World of Religions*, 159. Also: "Jesus' attitude to those who might be perceived to be religious outsiders to the Kingdom of God (sinners, tax collectors, Samaritans and gentiles) presents a situation which is far from easy to summarize in binary terms. . . . Furthermore, while there is no doubt that Jesus speaks at times in clearly separationist tones, it is not always so clear as one might automatically think as to which side of the binary separation we belong." Greggs, *Church in a World of Religions*, 157–58.

44. Greggs, *Church in a World of Religions*, 160.

draws the church out of itself and into the world for whose sake it exists. I am unconvinced, however, that it can bear the weight of the biblical evidence about the threat of separation. In lieu of Greggs's non-binary ecclesiology, then, I propose a return to Augustine's image of two cities being intermingled until the end. Picking up an image from one of Jesus' eschatological parables (see Matt. 13:47–50), Augustine wrote, "In this situation, many reprobates are mingled in the Church with the good, and both sorts are collected as it were in the dragnet of the gospel; and in this world, as in a sea, both kinds swim without separation, enclosed in nets until the shore is reached. There the evil are to be divided from the good; and among the good, as it were in his temple, 'God will be all in all.'"[45]

In the present age, good and bad, elect and reprobate, swim together. They are intermingled, not just in the world, but in the church; and they will not be separated until they reach the shore on the Last Day. One immediate implication of this is that it is both misguided and futile to seek to separate them now, either institutionally or by presuming to be able to transparently identify which is which. Augustine did not find in this cause for anxiety, much less despair; it is rather a reason for humility and hope.[46]

> She [that is, "the pilgrim City of Christ the King"] must bear in mind that among these very enemies are hidden her future citizens; and when confronted with them she must not think it a fruitless task to bear with their hostility until she finds them confessing the faith. In the same way, while the City of God is on pilgrimage in this world, she has in her midst some who are united with her in participation in the sacraments, but who will not join with her in the eternal destiny of the saints. Some of these are hidden; some are well known, for they do not hesitate to murmur against God, whose sacramental sign they bear, even in the company of his acknowledged enemies. At one time they join his enemies in filling the theatres, at another they join with us in filling the churches.
>
> But, such as they are, we have less right to despair of the reformation of some of them, when some predestined friends, as yet unknown even to themselves, are concealed among our most open enemies. In truth, these two cities are interwoven and intermixed in this era, and await separation at the last judgment.[47]

---

45. Augustine, *City of God*, trans. Henry Bettenson (New York: Penguin, 1984), 18.49, 831.
46. Just above the previously quoted passage, Augustine wrote that in the present age, the church is in training, "preparing for future exaltation," and that she "rejoices only in expectation."
47. Augustine, *City of God* 1.35.

This reads like theological commentary on another of Jesus' eschatological parables, the parable of the weeds.[48] Wheat and weeds grow together until the harvest, when they are separately gathered and then stored and burned, respectively. On the one hand, Augustine could not have distinguished between the two cities more sharply.[49] And yet the discernment of the distinction is delayed. The pilgrim city of God knows *that* some in her midst will be exiled at the end, and she knows *that* some of her current enemies will turn out to be her citizens. But it is far from clear in each case (if not all) who is whom.

A certain type of morbid conscience might find in this cause for anxious introspection. Taken wrongly, it could encourage obsessive examination, in the fear that one might have unwittingly disqualified herself from heavenly citizenship. But Augustine drew different implications. For him, the relative opacity of membership in the two cities ought to provoke patience (in "bear[ing] with their hostility"), humility (in the knowledge that not all who are in the church will find themselves in the communion of saints), and hope (in the possible reformation of even those most hostile to the church). Augustine combined as strong a binary as one could imagine with many of the virtues Greggs hopes to foster in Greggs's rejection of binaries.

OUGHT WE FEAR . . . ?

To return to our earlier discussion of the biblical material, and by way of conclusion, let me address a pastoral concern. To draw attention to the reversal of fortunes in Scripture might damage the proper confidence that believers have in the gospel of free, unmerited grace. After all, the peculiar demonstration of God's love occurs in Jesus' death for us "while we were still sinners" (Rom. 5:8). Paul triumphantly claimed that nothing "in all creation . . . will be able to separate us from the love of God in Christ Jesus our Lord," and yet he found himself flummoxed as he considered "my kinsmen according to the flesh," who certainly seemed to be so separated due to their rejection of God's Christ (Rom. 8:39; 9:3). His jubilant assurance immediately gave way to, or at least was complicated by, an unresolved series of questions about Israel according to the flesh. Paul knew of the great reversals in salvation history and seemed perplexed and troubled, at once hopeful and anxious. He insisted that "God has not rejected his people

---

48. See Matt. 13:24–30 and Jesus' explanation of the parable in vv. 36–43.
49. See Augustine, *City of God* 14.28.

whom he foreknew," and spotted a soteriological purpose in Israel being cut off: the inclusion of the gentiles in the people of God (11:2, 11–12). The good news for Israel is that they, "if they do not continue in their unbelief, will be grafted in" (11:23). God is able and eager to reverse his reversal, though we note the condition. Likewise, God is able and willing to reverse his reversal of gentile believers, who have experienced "God's kindness to you, provided you continue in his kindness. Otherwise you too will be cut off" (11:22). Thus, even in an epistle linearly structured to move from the darkness of our sinful past to the light of the church's life in Christ, and amid some of the most joyfully confident declarations of Scripture, Paul espied the possibility of a surprising turn. It would be too much to say this spoils assurance; it would not be too much to say that it introduces a subtle distinction between assurance and presumption. It is vital to see that all of Paul's questions in Romans 9–11 (and the interrogative mood dominates this section), all of the speculation, the warnings, are not mere rhetoric. The hope is real, but so, too, is the threat. "So do not become proud, but fear" (Rom. 11:20).

This is tricky to navigate with pastoral wisdom and due proportion. Too often the wrong passages are applied to the wrong people at the wrong times. A diversity of cures, wisely administered, is required. It behooves us to keep in mind Paul's counsel to the Thessalonians to "admonish the idle, encourage the fainthearted, help the weak, be patient with them all" (1 Thess. 5:14).[50] There is a long history of misapplication of the biblical injunction to fear, but that ought not lead us to neglect fear's place in the life of the church. The very surprising changes in identification of people in Scripture *presuppose and require* the lasting distinction between church and world, and they suggest (to slightly alter Paul's words) that "you too [may] be cut off." If we give up binary language, the biblical reversals lose their punch. An abiding distinction between church and world is both valid and vital, but rightly deployed it is a distinction that fosters sobriety rather than presumption, and hope rather than despair.

---

50. I owe to my dad, Ron Jenson, a sense of the pastoral significance of this verse.

CHAPTER 6

A NEW CREATURE
Holy Branches Grafted into a Single Vine

KIMBERLEY KROLL

JOHN WEBSTER IN "'IN THE SOCIETY OF GOD': Some Principles of Ecclesiology" defined the church as

> a society which moves itself as it is moved by God. Without talk of this divine movement, of the electing, calling, gathering, and sanctifying works of God, an ethnography of the church does not attain its object, misperceiving the motion to which its attention is to be directed, and so [is] inhibited in understanding the creaturely movements of the communion of saints. . . . Dogmatic ecclesiology [he writes] resists this by keeping alive the distinction between and due order of uncreated and created being; by indicating that the phenomena of the church are not irreducible but significative; and by introducing into ecclesiological description and passage of ecclesiological argument direct language about God, Christ, and the Spirit.[1]

Ultimately, the communion of saints—the church—is creature and, like all other created things, must be understood as merely sign. A sign for the Trinitarian God who constitutes such created being via created beings' relation to and participation in the Uncreated One.

Thus, to avoid the possible derailment that Webster warned of, the doctrine of the church, like all other doctrine, must be understood as

---

1. John Webster, "'In the Society of God': Some Principles of Ecclesiology," in *God without Measure: Working Papers in Christian Theology* (London: Bloomsbury T&T Clark, 2016), 193–94.

ontologically dependent on, rooted in, and constrained by the doctrine of God. The difficulty with this is that all doctrine retrospectively reveals that same God for whom those constructing a theology proper seek analogous predication. It is not that there is mutability in God, but there is mutability in creaturely things, including the mediation of God to his creatures. Due to the nature of created being, God's acts appear sequenced, though they are "before the beginning." Thus, the doctrine of the church is formed and being formed at the latter end of the sequence of God's acts in the economy. Specifically, following Bavinck, one could argue that ecclesiology (unlike other doctrine) is uniquely nestled within the doctrine of pneumatology, as ecclesiology might be understood as primarily an investigation into the binding of the church to the third person of the Godhead.[2] And it is for this reason that the focus of this paper will primarily be on the ontological reality of the church bound to God in the third person of the Godhead—holy branches grafted into a single vine.

Proper modes of inquiry regarding a particular reality are dependent on the object under investigation, that is, the object of inquiry determines the manner and scope of inquiry. As this paper seeks to elucidate the Spirit of God's relation to the church (i.e., in its conception) and this relation's effects for the church (primarily, unity with God; secondarily, unity with fellow redeemed creatures; and thirdly, relations between redeemed creatures and not-yet redeemed creation), there needs to be clarification regarding what that relation is and how it might act to unify and yet respect the distinction of being between the Uncreated and created, as well as the distinction within created being (i.e., many creatures constituting a single creature—the church). This unifying relation is understood to be the unique indwelling relation between the Spirit of God and redeemed human creatures.

Relying on a previous model of this indwelling relation, I will make a case that two entities can merge in substantial ways while remaining distinct.[3] Second, if this novel indwelling relation creates a new creature, that is, the church (many creatures united as a single creature in new relation to the Uncreated), that new entity must have novel properties unique to itself. This new creature, the church, participates in and relates to the

2. James Eglinton, *Trinity and Organism: Towards a New Reading of Herman Bavinck's Organic Motif*, T&T Clark Studies in Systematic Theology (New York: Bloomsbury 2021), 184.
3. Kimberley Kroll, "How Might Grafting Elucidate Our Understanding of the Indwelling Relation of the Holy Spirit and the Human Person?" Theological Puzzles no. 4 (2021), https://www.theo-puzzles.ac.uk/2021/11/02/kkroll/.

Godhead anew given the humiliation and exaltation of its Head and the gift of the Holy Presence who remains and dwells "locally." This single creature, nestled within the Spirit of God, I will argue, is the clearest sign of the Trinitarian God due to its (1) participatory holiness, (2) diversity-in-unity, and (3) manifold witness.

In section 1, I introduce the tool of modeling and how it might function to elucidate difficult to comprehend phenomena. In section 2, I make a case for a model of indwelling (i.e., being bound to the Spirit of God through the Spirit's "coming to dwell") given Christ's vine metaphor in John's gospel and the science of molecular transformation. This merger model will provide fodder for understanding the indwelling relation as uniquely intimate, direct, internal, and unifying, such that the creature and Creator remain distinct and yet bound in a novel way. In section 3, I draw out some theological implications of the model regarding the metaphysics of the indwelling relation. In section 4, I extend the model's application to the "new creature"—the church—specifically looking at participatory holiness manifested via diversity-in-unity as novel witness to the Trinitarian God.

1. Intent and Usefulness of Modeling

What constitutes a model and how one should measure a model's value is a point of contention among theologians. Though this is the case among theologians, models continue to be utilized in science to demonstrate and explain unfamiliar and complex phenomena with an appeal to logic (similar to the use of metaphor appealing to shared context). Models, whether mathematical or material, function epistemologically, that is, models are utilized to increase one's depth or range of understanding regarding particular phenomena. The metaphor and model to be elucidated in this paper is the model of the vine presented as metaphor by Jesus in John's gospel. The relations present between the relatum (vine, branches, vinedresser) are the focal point of the biblical metaphor (and not actually the relatum themselves). Therefore, the model is understood as relationally rich. Though the relation of the Holy Spirit to the church is not to be understood as primarily scientific, the construction of a model regarding its nature seems to be the best avenue for understanding its complexity, especially because the model is going to be used to elucidate a given metaphor. Due to the methodological assumption of scientific modeling that there is a causal closure of the physical world, all physical or organic models will be found wanting in their explanatory power regarding theological matters. However, within the creaturely the best we have to work with to understand the metaphysics of relations relies on our understanding of physical causation.

The target relation is the indwelling of the Holy Spirit with the source relation being that which marries the Vine and the branches (i.e., the graft site), which then, consequently, constitutes a new creature.[4] Mary B. Hesse, in *Models and Analogies in Science*, discusses what she calls neutral properties to identify properties that are neither positive (properties of both domains) or negative properties (properties of the source and not the target).[5] Properties of the target domain are not yet known. In analogical models, negative properties are the properties that facilitate predictive interpretations of models. In the case of the vine metaphor, novel properties will be instantiated via the Spirit's indwelling relation. That is, the relation itself is shown to be unique, and the uniqueness of the novel indwelling relation between God and God's people in conceiving a new creature, the church, will make it such that that creature possess and instantiate novel properties. After the ascension of Christ and the decent of the Holy Spirit, Holy Creator is in direct relation with unholy creatures both individually and corporately such that a multitude of redeemed human creatures are said to be both united to and participating in the Son of God as a single creature—the church. Therefore, with limited intellectual tools, we must grapple to understand novel properties of new creation that instantiate because of a new relation between the physical and the nonphysical, the creaturely and the Uncreated, the caused and the Uncaused.

Important in the case of modeling biblical metaphor, is the source of the metaphor itself, i.e., the agent. Janet Soskice, in *The Metaphor and Religious Language*, explains, "Talk based on models will be metaphorical, so model and metaphor, though different categories and not to be—as frequently they are by theologians—equated, are closely linked; the latter is what we have when we speak on the basis of the former."[6] Soskice argues for a tandem understanding of the relation between modeling and metaphor. The latter might be understood to "put flesh" on the former while maintaining some sort of dependency relation. It is the agent responsible for identifying some representing relation between the phenomenon and the model who chooses what dynamic relations present in the model are demonstrative of the phenomenon and how this dynamism might be interpreted. In cases

---

4. See R. I. G. Hughes, "Models and Representation," *Philosophy of Science* (1997): S325–S336.
5. Mary B. Hesse, *Models and Analogies in Science* (Notre Dame, IN: University of Notre Dame Press, 1966), 8–9.
6. Janet Martin Soskice, *The Metaphor and Religious Language* (Oxford: Clarendon, 1987), 55.

like this, it is essentially the agent doing the representing via the model and not the model per se representing. This is especially important in the case of the biblical metaphor of the Vine in John's gospel, because it is Jesus who uttered it, knowing a model could be abstracted from it. That is, in the gospel of John, the author pointed forward and elucidated the work and relation of the third person of the Godhead to the people of God.

2. THE VINE: BOTH METAPHOR AND MODEL
THE METAPHOR

I have made the case elsewhere that the Farewell Discourse in John's gospel (chs. 14–17) should be read pneumatologically.[7] The entirety of this section of the gospel should be understood as preparation for what would occur immediately (historically) and progressively (eschatologically). That is, Christ would be separated from his people through his death, resurrection, and ascension; yet he would remain with them. Somehow Jesus would be in a new relation with them—both present and absent. His Holy Spirit would come and live not only with them (as Christ did) but in them. Christ would leave, but the disciples would rejoice because it was better for them that he ascend to the Father and the Holy Spirit come to indwell them, teaching and revealing truths the disciples could not currently bear—truths primarily regarding the crucified God. And here, sandwiched between these teachings on how the ascended Christ would remain present to and become one with his people via the third person of the Godhead, is Christ's employment of the vine metaphor (John 15:1–8).

Clearly demarcated in the metaphor, the Father tends the vine, the vine is Jesus, the disciples (and by extension those who will also be grafted in) are branches. Yet where is the Spirit of God? It seems quite odd for the author of John's gospel to offer a merely binitarian theology in the middle of an extended exposition of the third person of the Godhead. Thus, the metaphor of the vine needs to be read retrospectively. If, at the time the vine metaphor was first uttered, the sending of the Spirit to indwell and unite the people of God was still a *future* act of the Trinitarian God, it is not surprising that the Holy Spirit is not explicitly mentioned. In contrast to the not-yet-indwelled (very confused) disciples, I assume, Jesus, understood and anticipated the probative force of the metaphor when retrospectively

---

7. Kroll, "Grafting." See also Andrew Byers, *Ecclesiology and Theosis in the Gospel of John* (Cambridge: Cambridge University Press, 2017), 224. See Troels Engberg-Pederson, *John and Philosophy: A New Reading of the Fourth Gospel* (Oxford: Oxford University Press, 2017).

contemplated, reiterated, and expanded by means of the phenomena itself, that is, the not-yet instantiation of the indwelling presence of the Spirit of God in the human creature acting as interpretive guide and teacher (John 16:12–15). The biblical metaphor functions not only to communicate truth but, I believe, to make its hearers/readers curious regarding how this might be the case, raising questions regarding how the vine and its grafted branches can be representative of God and his people:[8]

1. How should one understand the merging of two entities (branch and vine) into one entity (single chimeric plant), while also maintaining distinction between the two?
2. What effects does this merging have on the relatum?

THE MODEL

The act of grafting is the natural or controlled merger of plant parts, resulting in a composite plant that functions and appears as a singular organism. Grafting consists of combining the upper part of a plant (scion) with the lower part of another plant (the rootstock), which can be of a differing species or genetically modified; the former contributes stems, leaves, fruits, and so on, while the latter provides the root system and lower end of the trunk. The entirety of the plant, rootstock and scion, is considered a chimeric-graft. However, each plant part remains intact and genetically distinct, retaining its individual identity with the ability to be separated.

At the point of contact between the scion and rootstock, that is, the graft union, molecular transformation occurs by way of cambium contact and regeneration of cells in the wounded plant parts. In other words, at the graft union, cells of both the rootstock and scion begin to divide, regenerate, and differentiate, causing them to naturally bump up against one another and begin to share and/or transfer proteins and MRNA with one another. This is often referred to as "communication" between cells. Understanding how healing and union occurs by way of contact is not clear.[9] One way is that the injury to the plant produces an asymmetry at the wound site, changing the transport dynamics. The second is that, due to injury, hormonal and mechanical cues trigger a regeneration response in the plant. The former

---

8. It is worth noting that Paul's use of the body metaphor for the church would raise very similar questions to that gospel writer (see 1 Cor. 12:12–27). The similarities/differences between the metaphors' possible metaphysical implications is an area for further study.

9. I began reading on grafting over five years ago; there has been no overtly helpful developments in recent years regarding what is happening at the unification sight of a graft or how "materials" are transported, though there has been an explosion of literature.

theory of healing might be thought of as a literal restructuring of the plant; the latter theory of healing would occur through the activation of potential properties already existent yet dormant (and unseen) in the scion, which require the interpenetration relation with a given set of "alien" cells to catalyze their potential and affect the manifestation of properties. It seems the latter is more probable due to the genotype being maintained in the scion. That is, when scions are grafted into the rootstock, becoming a singular plant, both scions and rootstock retain their own unique genomes, and change evidenced in the scions is merely a change in the phenotype expression, that is, property expression.

The scientific data regarding molecular transformation offers evidence that two distinct subjects with varying degrees of similarity can come together and interpenetrate without being identified as a new fused entity or blurring the lines of identity between the subjects involved. Molecular transformation, normally performed in a lab, can be observed naturally at the site of the graft union of every individual scion. In the case of induced molecular transformation, the modified cell (X), though now composite in that it has received and thus been changed by external RNA from another living cell (Y), retains its identity as (X). The merged cell (X) can manifest properties of varied quality impossible without the merging of the two subjects.

3. The Vine: Theology Proper

When applying the model to the relationship of Christ and his disciples/believers, it seems that Christ can be united to human creatures in a real and substantial way through the Spirit's uniting the two subjects via indwelling relation. The story: (1) the Father places the human creature in contact with Christ; and in this case, Christ might be understood as a uniquely modified subject in that he is a single person with both divine and human natures, each nature being essential to his identity; (2) this unique identity of Christ allows for him to be united to other persons with one or both of these natures; and (3) via the Spirit's indwelling, particular properties of Christ, upon union, can be shared with other persons (either of divine or human nature) with whom Christ is united. And so we return to the two questions posed earlier:

1. How should one understand the merging of two entities (branch and vine) into one entity (single chimeric plant) while also maintaining distinction between the two?
2. What effects does this merging have on the relatum?

Regarding question 1, simply put, just as the rootstock and scion become one and yet do not share genetic material, remaining distinct entities, so, too, can the believer become one with Christ while maintaining the Creator/creature distinction. The Holy Spirit, represented in the model as the union site, is able somehow, in his person, to maintain the abiding relation in a state of dynamic re-creation and transformation while initiating and allowing for the sharing of properties by way of his indwelling the human creature and his perichoretic relation to the Son; these relations remain asymmetric. The Holy Spirit acts to both unite the person of Jesus and the human creature, and to maintain the distinction between the Son and the human person; he alone hypostasizes the union as divine being. Just as God the Son remains Creator when he assumes a creaturely nature thus being modified to take on the form of human creatures, so, too, the Spirit of God, condescending to dwell among human creatures in new indwelling relation, confirms he is Creator conceiving of a new creature—the church—by way of being united to and uniting to one another redeemed creatures. The Holy Spirit acts to resurrect what is dead in fallen yet reconciled human creatures, not by merely taking a single concrete particular of humanity into his own person through assumption, as is the case with the Son, but by way of gifting himself to multiple concrete particulars of redeemed humanity because Christ has made a way for human creatures to properly relate to God via his condescension, life, death, resurrection, and ascension.

What occurs at the site of union, that is, the Spirit's indwelling presence, allows for transformation and transference of divine properties into that which the human creature can instantiate (and express) without a change in nature.[10] This occurs through the Spirit's condescension to indwell human creatures just as the Son had condescended to indwell the creation. The Spirit does not take on his own flesh; he enters the flesh of other human creatures through interpenetration, participating in their progressive sanctification. The Holy Spirit maintains the relation in Himself, just as Christ maintained the hypostases of natures within himself in union yet distinction.[11] When sent by the Father and the Son, the Holy Spirit merges with human creatures who are brought into union with

---

10. I am thinking particularly of the property of participatory holiness, which I will discuss in the next section.

11. This is not a hypostasis between the human person and the divine person of the Spirit; this is a hypostasis of natures within the Holy Spirit that allows for the indwelling relation of the Holy Spirit in the human person.

the Son through the revelatory grace of the Father putting them in direct contact. Transfiguration of relations, shifting of what appear to be essential properties of human creatures, and the metaphysical structures of a subject can all occur, and that subject retains its identity and distinction. This is because the apparent change occurs (similar to the union of natures in the Son) within the Holy Spirit himself, at the site of union.

4. The Vine: Ecclesiology

In this final section, I will turn to the new creature and the second question raised by the vine metaphor: what effects does this merging have on the relatum? That is, given the church is a single creature—many branches bound in new relation to a single rootstock (Christ) and one another, via the presence of the Spirit of God—what should we expect this creation to look like, that is, what unique properties does it express, and how are these properties unique in their signification of the Trinitarian God?

Webster wrote, "The *res* of ecclesiology is no more available, no less difficult to access, no less reserved from us than the Christian doctrine of God, for the simple reason that it is an extension of the doctrine of God."[12] The concept of participatory holiness is directly tied to the technical metaphysical question that attempts to explicate how it is that God accomplishes his acts in the world given our understanding of metaphysical constraints for action in the creaturely order. Holiness is a unique attribute of God. Instinctively, it seems incommunicable, as it is not shared with the creaturely in the beginning.[13] We see that God does pronounce different objects as holy throughout Scripture. And this holiness seems to be twofold: (1) pure gift, (2) reflective of the participatory holy one's being put in proper relation to the Holy himself. The church is the unblemished bride of Christ, full of "holy ones," and that which is made holy participates in a new form of expression or sign of its God due to its being in proper relation.

Of all the things that have been put in proper relation to God, that is, all holy things, it is only human creatures who can *willfully* participate in the *extension* of God's holiness. Reconciliation through the person of Christ creates an ontological space enabling creatures to be transformed through new relation to God, which consequently puts them in new relation to all that is creaturely. And this relation is binding in that it is not

---

12. Webster, "'In the Society of God,'" 178.
13. The creation is very good, but the creation is not holy (see Gen. 1:31).

merely one of creatureliness or dependence, but it is one of supererogatory power due to its life being from and maintained by the life of the Vine, that is, the Spirit himself. God's acts in creation are necessarily generative. This relation makes it possible for indwelt persons to assume a derivative participatory holiness that is revelatory regarding the glory of God acting within the creation as the new creature actively participates in this derivative holiness. This is not an act of necessity but an act that confirms the generosity that is God's glory. Webster commented, "In his goodness, out of his own fullness and free determination, God bestows life upon a reality other than himself. . . . He does not replicate or communicate himself; creaturely being does not partake in divine being but rather has its own identity and integrity at the hands of God."[14] We belittle the creature if we seek to understand the creature as separate from God. Understanding the ontology of the church—what it is—is inexplicable, for we cannot grasp how it is that the Holy makes himself known through that which in itself is unholy. But, oh, he does!

Second, diversity-in-unity. The church is one creation though many creatures. The author of John's gospel, immediately preceding his discourse on the Spirit, wrote, "A new commandment I give to you, that you love one another: just as I have loved you, you also are to love one another. By this all people will know that you are my disciples, if you have love for one another" (John 13:34–35 ESV). A novel unity occurs in creatures redeemed by Christ through the indwelt Spirit. The way in which redeemed creature loves redeemed creature is to be distinct from the broken atomistic nature of the world and revelatory of the Trinitarian God who is love and loves perfectly and maximally within himself.[15] For a creature's love of another creature is just, in its purest and most revelatory form, love of God and love from God—a sign of the unique Trinitarian God who is one and yet three.

My friends, we are to grow together toward a single end—knowledge of God—and strive together toward a single end—consummated union with the Beloved. Just as a well-tended vine should be predictable and the pruning that takes place be not merely for a single branch but for the abundance of the whole, so, too, the church should have a predictability

---

14. Webster, "'In the Society of God,'" 182.

15. The redeemed creatures united as single creature have the same life of the Spirit that acts as witness. The new creature is able to love all that is creaturely in a new holy way, yet there is a qualitative difference between the love of the Spirit of God manifesting in another creature and the redeemed creature loving that which God is not actively indwelling and transforming via the life of the Spirit of God.

about it—a diverse set of creatures bending, supporting, energizing, and tending toward a singular end—abundant and revelatory glory—glory so extensive that it cannot be attained with infinite instantiations because of the creatures' inability to ever exhaust the God for whom it is a sign.

Third, manifold witness—outward-reaching effects. C. S. Lewis wrote in the preface to *The Great Divorce*, "Even on the biological level life is not like a river but like a tree. It does not move towards unity but away from it and the creatures grow further apart as they increase in perfection. Good, as it ripens, becomes continually more different not only from evil but from other good."[16]

Goodness, manifest through the Spirit and in individual creatures, though more closely resembling and highlighting the Good himself, increases in its particularity. For the goodness of God can never be exhausted in its creaturely mediation. Thus, increasingly varied and tended fruit, becoming sweeter and fuller of nutrition proper to its being and its telos, buds. The holy ones having their quality modified, express participatory holiness in the fruit produced finding life in the Christ who modifies them and the Spirit who enlivens them. This holy fruit is not for the sake of the Vine, which has its needs fully supplied by the divine, but for those not grafted in, the not yet redeemed. For the life of the new creature—the church—is not its own, but an extension of the life of divine being that comes from outside the created—always ripening, always generating, always pointing, ever more growing in its abundance, ever reaching, with the tended and guided tendrils of the Vine extending to every corner of the earth.[17]

The people of God witness to him, blessing those who benefit from the holy fruit he produces through them, multiplying and making manifest his Trinitarian nature in a creaturely and finite mode. Each branch is unique, and though the fruit of the Spirit remains the same, its quality has been made holy, and so we can assume that each fruit is unique in its beauty having particular purpose determined and constituted by its Vinedresser. The church—indwelt by the Holy Spirit, sharing in the life of the Son, maintained and sustained by the Father—continues to grow, to be formed and shaped, not merely for the sake of itself but as witness and sign, so that the not yet reconciled creation might see and be drawn to the Beautiful One, coming to know their hunger through the love that manifests within and extends out of the single diverse creature made holy in grace—Christ's

---

16. C. S. Lewis, *The Great Divorce* (New York: HarperOne, 2001), viii.
17. Webster wrote, "The church is not finished, it learns over time, it does not possess itself wholly, because its source of life is in the infinity of God." Webster, "'In the Society of God,'" 191.

beloved, the church. And so the hope is that the people will come and feast on the fruit of his Spirit manifested through his redeemed.

The metaphor, and the model it elucidates, is clearly uniquely revelatory of a perichoretic triune God—the Father as tender, Christ as root, Spirit as life, and the church branching out as extension. Beautifully, this model of the vine shows how it is that creatures put in proper relation to this triune God are enveloped and participate in this abiding relation while remaining distinct from his being. We, church, are holy branches grafted in by grace, indwelt by the Spirit of God, producing a multiplicity of distinct, diverse, and holy fruit unique to each particular branch yet modified by the same life to manifest the abundance of the Creator and the abundance possible of the creaturely when in proper relation to him.

CHAPTER 7

THE CHURCH IN A POSTMODERN AGE

Millard Erickson

TRAVELING IN A FOREIGN COUNTRY can be a bewildering experience. The language may be unintelligible. Nonverbal communication can be misleading or worse. For example, in Brazil, one should avoid giving the A-OK sign. It's an obscene gesture there. Street signs are not where an American expects them to be. Even words that look familiar may mean something other than expected. An English speaker may be pleased to see the word "gift," but in Swedish it means "married" and in German it means "poison."

Today the Western church finds itself in a strange country culturally. Large numbers of younger people are classified as "nones"—persons who don't identify with any organized religion.[1] Major denominations find their numbers declining as their congregations age. Many people find that much of the church's traditional message does not make sense to them or contradicts what they feel intuitively is the case. There are many aspects to this, but in part, welcome to postmodernity.

The goal of this paper is to ask how the church can best be the church in a world where a large force of intellectual beliefs is postmodernism and culture is postmodernity. The plan of this paper is as follows: to describe an analytical model; to relate it to certain aspects of ecclesiology; and to apply it to certain functions of the church.

---

1. "The Age Gap in Religion around the World," Pew Research Center, June 13, 2018, https://www.pewresearch.org/religion/2018/06/13/the-age-gap-in-religion-around-the-world/. Later research projects indicate continuation of this trend.

I am a strong believer in self-criticism. One of my heroes is the late Nobel Prize–winning economist Milton Friedman, who said, "You cannot be sure that you are right unless you know the arguments against your view better than your opponents do."[2] Among my criticisms of my own paper is that it is more an instance of practical theology than systematic theology, but I note that the title of this conference series does not add a modifier to the word "theology." I would also argue that this is what is needed at this point in time. While appearing to be based extensively on anecdotal evidence, it should be judged by paradigm evaluation.[3] Rather than responding extensively to this and several other criticisms, I would simply suggest that we draw on a comment of one of the thinkers whose thought we will be examining, Richard Rorty, "Let's try looking at it this way and see how it works out," in other words, whether it illumines our problem helpfully.[4]

I also want to acknowledge that this paper draws heavily on nonbiblical sources. I am treating them as general revelation, what I term "judicial authority," which rules on the meaning and truth of assertions, rather than as "legislative authority," which gives us the content of doctrine.[5]

Please note that this discussion deals primarily with what is usually referred to as the local church, the empirical church, or the congregation, as contrasted with the universal or invisible church. The discussion is primarily applicable to western Europe, Canada, and the United States rather than what used to be called the "third world."

ANALYTICAL TOOL: THE THREE-TIERED MODEL

The specific analytical tool employed here will be the three-tiered model, utilized in a number of disciplines but applied here to the doctrine of the church. I first encountered this in ethical theory, but it is applicable to many disciplines.[6] It can be illustrated with art, and specifically, painting.

LEVEL ONE: PAINTERS

On the first level are the painters. They are at work actually producing works of art. They are the doers, whether they be masters or novices.

---

2. Mary Ruth Yoe, "Market Force," *University of Chicago Magazine* 99, no. 3 (January–February 2007): 30.

3. See, e.g., Robert C. Rowland, "Standards for Paradigm Evaluation," *Journal of the American Forensic Association* 18, no. 3 (1982): 133–40, and the ensuing responses.

4. Richard Rorty, *Contingency, Irony, and Solidarity* (Cambridge: Cambridge University Press, 1989), 8–9.

5. Millard Erickson, *Christian Theology*, 3rd ed. (Grand Rapids: Baker, 2013), 225–26.

6. Bernard Mayo, *Ethics and the Moral Life* (London: Macmillan, 1958), 9–12.

The results of their activity are concrete productions on canvas. They are not engaged in debating theories of art; theirs is the doing of art or making art. While they may have relatively sophisticated theories underlying their work, these are frequently implicitly held.

LEVEL TWO: ART TEACHERS AND ART CRITICS

On the next level are the art critics and art teachers. They are attempting to teach theory and practice that will improve the work being done by those on the first level and are evaluating that work.

LEVEL THREE: AESTHETICIANS

The third level is that of the aestheticians, the philosophers or theoreticians of art. They are asking what is the nature of beauty, whether it is in the eye of the beholder and similar issues. Their tradition goes far back in philosophy.

ECCLESIOLOGY ANALYZED USING THE THREE-TIERED MODEL

This schema can be applied to the discipline of theology, and specifically to the doctrine of the church.[7]

On the first level are Christians who are "doing church." They are worshiping, fellowshiping, praying, evangelizing, doing social ministry, and so on.

On the second level are pastors and teachers of theology. They are evaluating the activities of those on the first level and teaching and guiding them to better be the church.

On the third level are what I would call theoreticians of theology or philosophers of theology. They are asking what the church is, and beyond this, what doctrine is, and even what truth is. While this may seem to conservatives to be an issue settled once for all, these persons are concerned with what the essence of church is and how that could faithfully be embodied in different settings. Even more basic, they are examining the philosophical and sociological conditions in which the church is situated. The ultimate instances of these are the super-theologians, who lead the church into new forms of theology, such as Augustine, Aquinas, Calvin, Schleiermacher, and Barth.

---

7. More than fifty years ago, Francis Schaeffer pointed out the progression of ideological concepts from philosophy through art, music, general culture, and finally to theology. Francis Schaeffer, *The God Who Is There* (Downers Grove, IL: InterVarsity), 13–14.

The terminology of levels deserves some clarification. Higher and lower tend to carry evaluative connotations, so that the higher level is superior to or more valuable than the lower. It can also function conversely, so that those producing paintings criticize the aestheticians as unable to create an acceptable painting. Since there currently is sensitivity to any suggestion of superiority of any individuals or groups to others of the same kind, it might be helpful instead to label these in terms of their functions:

Performative/productive: those actually engaged in this type of activity.

Instructional/evaluative: those teaching or critically assessing the preceding.

Reflective/analytical: those reflecting on the nature and content of the activity and its concepts.

Of course, listing one before or, alternatively, after the other may be construed as superiority. Let us simply agree that no such distinction should be considered part of this model.

APPLICATION OF THE THREE-TIERED MODEL TO THE CHURCH
REFLECTIVE/ANALYTICAL

Starting on the reflective/analytical level, I note that theology is done in an intellectual environment. One of the primary elements in today's milieu is the movement referred to as postmodernism (the conceptual dimension) or postmodernity (the cultural phenomena). I am referring here primarily to the Western church. It is not my aim to undertake a complete discussion of postmodernism. That would require an entire book, one that I have already written.[8] Rather, I will examine three themes of postmodernism and ask how the church can effectively express itself while still remaining the church in this culture. I am not asking whether the church should totally accept or totally reject postmodernism. Postmodernism simply is here, and must be taken into account. The parallel is to speaking doctrine in a particular language. How do we discuss the church in postmodern categories or

---

8. Millard J. Erickson, *Truth or Consequences: The Promise and Perils of Postmodernism* (Downers Grove, IL: InterVarsity, 2001). See also, Erickson, *The Postmodern World: Discovering the Times and the Spirit of Our Age* (Wheaton, IL: Crossway, 2002); and Erickson, *Postmodernizing the Faith: Evangelical Responses to the Challenge of Postmodernism* (Grand Rapids: Baker, 1998).

conceptual language? It appears to me that for about the past twenty years a countertrend has been emerging in academic circles.[9] There also are now organizations devoted to opposing some of the features of postmodernism, like FIRE (the Foundation for Individual Rights and Expression) and the Academic Freedom Alliance.

Developments in areas such as virtual reality and artificial intelligence are stretching scientific thinking. In fact, Henry Kissinger, Eric Schmidt, and Daniel Huttenlocher say in a recent article, "Generative artificial intelligence presents a philosophical and practical challenge on a scale not experienced since the beginning of the Enlightenment."[10] These concerns are major obstacles to postmodern thinking. They also imply that the church has some major tasks ahead of it. On the popular level, however, postmodernity is still widespread.

I make several assumptions here. One is that the Christian church makes certain truth claims and that part of its mission is the communication of those truths to those outside the church, whatever form that communication may take. The second is that we are not considering whether the tenets of traditional Christianity and those of postmodernism are compatible or incompatible, whether the church should attempt to refute postmodernism or rather to become postmodern. I am aware that I should not make the assumption that a noted evangelical leader did when he spoke on postmodernism to the student body of which one of my former students was a part at the time. My student said of that speaker, "He was like a leader of the Ku Klux Klan attempting to recruit members at a meeting of the NAACP." Neither am I suggesting that the church is to become thoroughly postmodern. I am rather raising the question of how the church can engage in dialogue in a culture where postmodernism is a major feature of the ideology.

Many churches are attempting on a sort of intuitive basis to relate their ministry to what they perceive the contemporary culture to be. This is usually done somewhat as follows. Two types of worship services are offered, termed respectively *traditional* and *contemporary*. The difference is primarily in the style of music and to some extent the attire of the attendees. There are

---

9. Patricia Cohen, "Digital Keys for Unlocking the Humanities' Riches," *New Times*, November 16, 2010, C1; Patricia Cohen, "Analyzing Literature by Words and Numbers," *New York Times*, December 3, 2010, C1; Patricia Cohen, "In 500 Billion Words, New Window on Culture," *New York Times*, December 10, 2010, C1; Elizabeth Blackwell, "The Data Renaisance," *Weinberg Magazine*, Fall/Winter 2016.

10. Henry Kissinger, Eric Schmidt, and Daniel Huttenlocher, "ChatGPT Heralds an Intellectual Revolution," *Wall Street Journal*, February 25–26, 2023, A13, 15.

two problems with the typical array, however. The music is often not contemporary, but rather what was contemporary thirty years ago. I have not been in a service featuring hip-hop music. I have heard only one rap sermon, although it was well done. Often the preacher delivers the identical message at both services, wearing the same attire. Sometimes the cognitive dissonance breaks through. At a predominantly black congregation eleven blocks from George Floyd Square, one Sunday morning several years before Floyd's death, the white preacher remarked that if he was there long enough he would attempt to preach a rap sermon. The Blacks present responded with thunderous applause. One midtwenties Black man told the speaker after the service, "You let me know when you are going to preach that rap sermon and I'll bring all my friends." One congregation, after planting a Hispanic congregation, dissolved and the following Sunday reopened as a second-generation Hispanic congregation for young Hispanics who wanted to preserve the Hispanic culture but not use the Spanish language. These are good starts but often insufficiently based on analytics.

On closer examination, I note several postmodern motifs. All of these stem from a more basic conception: the rejection of essences. Earlier thought had considered the characteristics of things to exist independently of anyone knowing them. There were real qualities, whether anyone knew or believed them. In the premodern period, these qualities or essences were derived from something beyond the physical world, whether deity, as in religious views, or some supersensual reality, such as Plato's ideas. In the modern period, such essences were considered inherent in nature.[11]

A postmodernist such as Jacques Derrida, however, rejected this concept, which he termed "logocentrism." On that model, reality is independent of anyone knowing it. The world is like a statue, with an independent existence and characteristics.[12] On Derrida's view, however, reality is like Play-Doh. It is what one makes it to be. Many postmodernists claim that what they term "modernism" is based on classic foundationalism, in which propositions are justified by being based on certain foundational propositions that are indubitable.[13] Note, however, that recent forms of foundationalism are

---

11. Postmodernists often characterize the position they oppose as basically originating with the Enlightenment. I prefer to refer to "prepostmodernism," because on this crucial issue both premodernism and modernism agree, while differing on the basis.

12. Jacques Derrida, *On Grammatology* (Baltimore: Johns Hopkins University Press, 1976), 14–15.

13. E.g., Stanley J. Grenz and John R. Franke, *Beyond Foundationalism: Shaping Theology in a Postmodern Context* (Louisville: John Knox, 2001).

specifically designed to avoid this criticism, and that there is a compatibility and even an overlap of foundationalism and coherentism.[14]

On a simpler level, this is the fact that we all come to physical reality and experience from different perspectives. Just as two persons viewing a building from different sides would judge its color to be different if those two sides were of different colors, so different people see things differently because of their different backgrounds and experiences.

Postmodernism is more than this, however. The building does not really have color. The color seen depends on the one seeing it. The knower creates the quality. The distinction here is like the old story of the three baseball umpires discussing the calling of balls and strikes. One says, "I call them as they are." That is the epistemological absolutist, who believes not only in the existence of reality independently of any knower, but also that he perceives it just as it is.[15] The second umpire says, "I call them as I see them." He is an objective relativist, who believes that reality exists independently, but that he has limitations on his perception of that reality. The third umpire declares, "They ain't neither balls nor strikes until I call them." That is the viewpoint Derrida was expressing.[16]

This view has implications for many areas. One of these is the concept of justice. A more traditional view holds that justice exists independently, and the task of the judge is to discover what is the just position, and rule accordingly. To the postmodernist, however, justice does not exist prior to and independently of judgment. The judge, by her decision, brings justice into existence.[17]

In the thought of Michel Foucault, power has a significant place. The traditional view was that knowledge was power. Whoever had greater knowledge of a situation therefore was able to exercise control or at least greater influence than someone of less knowledge, by persuading others of the truth. Foucault, however, reversed this relationship: power is knowledge. Teachers have the authority to decide what is "true" by selecting what the students will and will not be required to read. Those who hold

---

14. Tim Triplett, "Recent Work on Foundationalism," *America Philosophical Quarterly* 27, no 2 (April 1990): 93–116. Grenz and Franke seem unaware of this article and writings of philosophers such as William Alston and Roderick Chisholm.

15. The masculine pronoun is used here because as of the start of the 2023 season, no female umpire has ever officiated a regular season Major League Baseball game.

16. Paradoxically, as of the 2023 Major League season, a ball or strike may be called without a pitch being thrown.

17. Derrida, in John Caputo, *Deconstruction in a Nutshell: A Conversation with Jacques Derrida* (New York: Fordham University Press, 1997), 6.

political power in terms of possession of larger numbers of powerful offices pass the laws and make the rules that govern human behavior.[18]

This power may be exercised in varying ways. One that has become popular of late is by the writing of history. William Dean described this in a very aptly titled book, *History Making History*.[19] In what Dean called the new historiography, the historian does not so much discover and describe what has happened in the past, as to create, by his writing, the conception of what happened, which then comes to be believed and functionally is what did happen.

One implication of what we have been describing is that there will be varying opinions about what is the case, on a variety of issues. This results in what is termed "perspectivalism." You and I see this issue differently. The reason, however, is because we approach the issue from different perspectives. I see it this way. If, however, I viewed it from your perspective, I would see it quite differently.

A second manifestation is community. Perspectivalism could result in a subjectivism, in which there are as many truths or rights as there are individuals. One way for this to be handled is by power, so that those who possess power make their ideas and values normative. The other possible solution, generally more acceptable, is that the group of which an individual is part establishes what is true and right. On this model, community is the guard against subjectivism, in which there are as many truths as there are individuals.[20] What gives objectivity is that the community agrees on what is right and true. Thus, for political conservatives, political conservatism is true. For Muslims, Islam is true.

A final manifestation is narrative. A consequence of the foregoing is that there are no metanarratives, no all-inclusive explanations of everything. What purport to be that are actually the narratives of a given community, or petit narratives. And since there is no "God's-eye view," no universally accepted data, it is not possible to convert others to one's position by appealing to rational arguments.[21]

Expression of a viewpoint will not be by means of propositional truth.

---

18. Michel Foucault, "Truth and Power," in *Power/Knowledge*, ed. Colin Gordon (New York: Pantheon, 1980), 131.

19. William Dean, *History Making History: The New Historicism in American Religious Thought* (Albany: State University of New York Press, 1988).

20. Stanley Fish, *Is There a Text in This Class? The Authority of Interpretive Communities* (Cambridge, MA: Harvard University Press, 1980).

21. Fish rejects the use of "demonstration," which appeals to objective facts, preferring "persuasion," which requires assuming the same perspective as the teacher. Fish, *Is There a Text in This Class?*, 365.

There will not be syllogistic proofs, in which premises are established and arranged to form syllogisms. Inductive logic, in which evidence is compiled and the view supported by the preponderance of the evidence followed, is also rejected. The preferred form of expression is not the rational propositional argument. Rather, it is the story, the narrative, that is respected.[22] While metanarratives, or universal accounts, are not possible and therefore not acceptable, petit narratives, or individual stories, are to be utilized.

As we move forward to the other two levels, we will select these three themes—perspectivalism, community, and narrative—as the focus of our discussion. These should be understood as representative of our endeavor, not exhaustive.

INSTRUCTIONAL/EVALUATIVE

What would the insights we have observed about postmodernism suggest as to the nature and function of the church, as viewed on the second level? First, the church should emphasize the perspectival. Traditionally, the church has been characterized by proclamation. It has had certain beliefs that it believed to be objectively true and universally applicable, so that everyone, inside and outside the church, needed to hear them. Its expression would take a form somewhat like, "Here is the truth; listen to it and accept it." The use of "Four Things God Wants You to Know," "The Romans Road," and "The Four Spiritual Laws" illustrates this well. When expressed to a postmodernist, however, the response would be something like, "That's how you see it," or "That's your opinion," or "It's fine that what you say works for you, but that's not for me."

I would suggest that the better approach may be somewhat different when dealing with postmoderns. If what is asserted to be different is considered to be different perspectives, then the church will need to try to assume the perspective of the postmodern. To put it differently, the approach will be more successful if it is dialogical.

There are two qualifications on this suggestion. The first is that this assumes that we are dealing with soft, rather than hard, postmodernists. The former are willing to engage in conversation, to allow the expression of divergent viewpoints, even if they believe them to be mistaken. Hard postmodernists on the other hand do not believe that contrary viewpoints should even be allowed to be expressed. These are the advocates of cancel

---

22. Although not postmodern, many African societies prefer narrative to propositional presentation.

culture and similar practices. There may be little hope, at least for the time being, of communicating with them.[23]

The second type of qualification is the contention that since there is no neutral zone, no possibility of a universal "God's-eye view," theoretically there really cannot be any communication between advocates of competitive views. Here some have attempted a rational proof of one viewpoint and refutation of another. The response, however, is "That's just how you see it." Without completely rejecting such an approach, I suggest, however, that there is a practical response that holds more promise. Most postmoderns do expect that they can express their viewpoint and have it understood, and actually attempt to do so. They do not live by their theory.[24]

Two rather dramatic examples bear examination here. The first case involved Derrida. The philosopher John Searle wrote an eleven-page criticism of Derrida's thought.[25] In response, Derrida wrote a ninety-four-page article, in which he repeatedly asserted that Searle had misunderstood what he, Derrida, was saying.[26] The second was the criticisms of the Duke University English literature department as not encouraging the expression of differing opinions. In response, Stanley Fish, who at the time had been a member of that department, asserted, "I am prepared to back up that statement with massive documentation."[27] Massive documentation? That sounds rather non-postmodern to me. Perhaps the best response here is Rorty's: "Let's try it out and see how it works."

A second suggestion here is that the theme of community be emphasized. If that is the locus within which truth claims are to be evaluated, then the church would be wise to utilize that avenue. Here would seem to be a particularly efficacious area given the nature of the church.

A third suggestion is that the church particularly utilize narrative as its initial approach to dialogue. Traditionally, Christianity has often begun

---

23. A recent instance took place at Stanford University Law School, where a federal judge was to give a public talk. Because he had made a ruling with which many of the more liberal law students disagreed, they created such a disturbance that he could not be heard. The law school's associate dean for diversity, equity, and inclusion intervened, basically blaming the judge for the disturbance. The president of the university later apologized to the judge.

24. Once on a panel of postmodernists and non-postmodernists, I raised the question of the status of our discourse: was it modern, postmodern, or what? A postmodernist on the panel responded, "I don't understand the question." I concluded internally that we would not be functioning on the top level of the three-tiered model that day.

25. John Searle, "Reiterating the Differences: A Reply to Derrida," in *Glyph* (Baltimore: Johns Hopkins University Press, 1977), 1:198–208.

26. Jacques Derrida, "Limited Inc, abc . . . ," in *Glyph* (Baltimore: Johns Hopkins University Press, 1977), 2:162–254.

27. Stanley Fish, *There's No Such Thing as Free Speech, and It's a Good Thing, Too* (New York: Oxford University Press, 1994), 63–64.

with its metanarrative, its big story, and moved to petit narratives, particular historical accounts, or particular elements of the story, to elucidate and validate its message.

PERFORMATIVE/PRODUCTIVE

But what of the performative/productive level? If the middle level is the level of strategy, then this would be the area of tactics, of practice. What are some examples of this that we might emulate?

Regarding the concept of perspectivalism, one suggestion is that the church and its individual members emphasize listening over talking. To some this may seem like compromise. After all, if we have the truth, we should announce it to anyone. However, rather than just being expressed, the aim is for the message to be heard. Perhaps we here face a form of the old tree in the forest conundrum: if a tree falls in the forest and there is no one there to hear it, was there any sound? In this case, if the church announces the gospel and no one is listening, has there been any proclamation?

Here we suggest that the church might try to bridge the gap initially not by trying to get the non-Christian to view the issue from the Christian perspective but by first trying to view it from the postmodernist's perspective.

This involves such a simple and common practice as listening before speaking. As a college sophomore, I took a three-quarter sequence in psychology. The first two quarters were general psychology and the third quarter was practical psychology. While I assume I learned quite a lot in that latter course, I remember just one suggestion vividly: "Do more asking and listening than talking and you will be considered a brilliant conversationalist." The revised edition of Dale Carnegie's *How to Win Friends and Influence People* makes the same point.[28] Carnegie was once approached by a man who declared, "You're not Dale Carnegie." Rather than pulling out his driver's license or other form of identification, which would have terminated the conversation, Carnegie simply responded, "You may be right."

The basic approach is not telling but asking. This is of more general application than just this specific technique. Questions, if posed correctly, are less threatening and thus less likely to provoke defensiveness than assertions. By correctly, I mean doing so in such a way as to value the other's opinion, rather than making the person feel obligated to respond. It also avoids conveying the impression that the questioner has all the answers.

---

28. Dale Carnegie, *How to Win Friends and Influence People: Updated for the Next Generation of Leaders* (New York: Simon and Schuster, 2022), 96.

One might begin by asking the other person to explain what she believes, and even why. One would hope that after doing so, the dialogue partner would then respond by saying, "And please share your thoughts on the subject with me," but realistically there are some persons who are not really listeners. Enough are, however, that dialogue will ensue. Beyond that, really understanding the other person's view will make us more effective in relating to him or her.

This has been an emphasis in homiletics for some time as well. One of the earliest applications of modern communications theory was a book titled *The Preacher and His Audience* by Webb Garrison.[29] Most textbooks on homiletics had emphasized the former pole of the communication process: the content and delivery of the message.[30] Books like Garrison's emphasized the mind of the recipient: What is the hearer thinking? What questions are on his or her mind, and how might the message be structured to relate to those questions? This was an echo of Paul Tillich's concept of "answering theology."[31] To listen is to pay one's dialogue partner the compliment of saying in effect, "What you are thinking is important."

A more specific suggestion is that the church will want to attempt to go to where the nonbelievers are, rather than asking them to enter its physical and conceptual walls. Let me illustrate with two congregations and their practice.

Both are suburban congregations with two campuses each. Congregation A conducted a major event off campus. They held a worship service at the Mall of America, the largest shopping center in the United States, with none of their services meeting Sunday morning at their main campus. Their members were encouraged to invite persons at the mall who were not from their congregation to join them for lunch after the service. The pastor preached from Acts 17 on "The Unknown God of the Mall." Remarkably, a speech professor at a state university requested a copy of the manuscript of the message and assigned it as required reading in his course on public address.

Congregation B presents concerts and drama outdoors in the local park. It also works with the local police department, supplying them with gift cards to give to needy persons. It cooperates with a group known as

29. Webb B. Garrison, *The Preacher and His Audience* (Westwood, NJ: Revell, 1964).

30. E.g., John A. Broadus, *A Treatise on the Preparation and Delivery of Sermons* (Philadelphia: Smith, English and Company, 1871); Andrew W. Blackwood, *The Preparation of Sermons* (New York: Abingdon-Cokesbury, 1948).

31. Paul Tillich, *Systematic Theology* (Chicago: University of Chicago Press, 1956), 1:1–8.

"Cops' Church." When the next adjacent suburb had a weekend event, the church conducted an outdoor service to which it encouraged its members to attend as well. Located quite close to the state fairgrounds, it provides parking and transportation to the fair for a fee.

Yet another congregation chose to emphasize reaching high schoolers. Although there was adequate meeting space on the church's campus, the church rented space at a local school, not the one where the students attended. They offered a religion discussion class in a neutral setting, and a number of teenagers from outside the congregation attended.

On an individual level, this suggests finding ways to engage persons outside of religious circles. One of my former students is a missionary in Sofia, Bulgaria. She quickly found that many Bulgarians were reluctant to engage in conversation with strangers, not uncommon with older persons in formerly communist countries. Sara, however, has owned a series of dachshunds. She found that if she took her friendly dog, Edna, on a leash and strolled through the local park, Bulgarians there who would not otherwise respond to attempted conversation were glad to relate to Edna, and then to Sara.

This principle carries over to other areas as well. One Japanese pastor was also a golf professional. He offered free golf lessons on Sunday afternoons. Taking advantage of a growing Japanese interest in golf, he established relationships with a large and growing number of Japanese men and eventually women as well. The most common version of this practice in foreign countries has been the teaching of English as a second language. Application of this principle to domestic settings will come to mind: sewing clubs, flying clubs, book clubs, and other special interest groups are among them.[32]

A second theme that may offer guidance to today's church is that of community. One dimension of that is to make the entrance to the church as open as possible, at least figuratively. If we have successfully entered into the non-Christian's sphere, then we may be able to invite him or her into the church's.

This involves enabling persons to see the benefits of being part of the community called the church, and that they are not immediately confronted with the necessity of accepting all of the beliefs and practices of the community. By that I do not mean that anyone should be able to

---

32. David Clark, *Dialogical Apologetics: A Person-Centered Approach to Christian Defense* (Grand Rapids: Baker, 1993).

become a member of the church regardless of beliefs and practices, but that nonbelievers should be made to feel at home within the community on a noncommittal basis. It is a somewhat threatening experience for a visitor to enter a church building or an official function of a local church. Three principles seem to follow: to make the community of the church as warm, welcoming, accepting, and affirming as possible; to find nonreligious activities to sponsor in the church building; and, as already noted, to find ways to extend some aspects of the church's community beyond the traditional boundaries of the church.

To address the first of these, let me offer a contrast. Twice, once in Germany and once in California, I and my family visited churches where, during the worship service, visitors were asked to stand and identify themselves, which I did. In each case, when the service concluded, not one person approached us and spoke to us. The feeling of not being part of the community was powerful. The other was a church in Albuquerque, New Mexico. When we entered, we were warmly greeted at the door by a gentleman who asked us our names and introduced us to several other worshipers. At one point in the service, the worshipers were encouraged to greet one another. Of the approximately one hundred persons present in the service, at least half came over and spoke with us. We learned that the church has a class on greeting for the constituents. As we left, the gentlemen who had greeted us when we entered bid us a good week and addressed us by name. We definitely felt ourselves a part of the community although we had never been within the building before.

The very design of the church building is important. While many older buildings resemble fortresses for the preservation of the faith, newer buildings can be designed to show the activities within. This was especially suited to evening services, when churches still had them. One congregation built a new sanctuary with a lobby that could be viewed through the outer doors and windows. It featured a fireplace, around which young people in particular gathered to talk. To someone looking in, this was an appealing sight. Another church had a room with movable seating behind the sanctuary, separated by a folding door. This area served as the chapel and an overflow room with glass across the outside exposure. Across the street was a large and growing hospital. On Sundays the folding door was thrown open so that visitors going to and from the hospital could look in and see happy worshipers.

Location of church buildings is important. In many cases, established churches are locked into their locations, which may have been selected as the least expensive, rather than the most strategic. One director of church planting put it this way: "When you see a sign that says, 'Church X four blocks this way,' you know the sign is where the church building should have been." Churches seeking locations for their building may find that although a more strategic and visible location costs considerably more than a prosaic one, that cost is more than offset by the marketing costs saved. Renting space rather than owning buildings may alleviate the problem somewhat.

A third suggestion relates to the postmodern preference for narrative. This suggests that the use of narrative may be more effective than the more propositional approach. Jesus' frequent use of parables is instructive for us. This is a more indirect form of communication.

Narrative lets the postmodern discover the truth or draw his or her own conclusion. One effective form of this is what I term "sneaking up on someone with the truth." Although the events reported in the Bible did not take place in postmodern times, we find clear and powerful examples of this method in the Bible.

Perhaps the most dramatic instance is found in 2 Samuel 12:1–15. The prophet Nathan was sent by God to King David to confront him with the awful sin he had committed. If Nathan had made a direct approach to the issue, he would have accused David of committing adultery and then murder in order to conceal the former. Had he done so, the king would likely have become defensive, seeking to excuse what he had done. Each man might have lost his head, the king figuratively and the prophet literally. Rather, the prophet told the king a story about a rich man who had many sheep, but instead of taking one of his own sheep to feed his guest, he took the one little pet lamb belonging to his neighbor. David saw the injustice of this and was furious: "The man who has done this deserves to die!" (v. 5). He had condemned himself. Only then did the prophet apply the parable to the king. He had enabled David to see the essential injustice in his own act without realizing he was doing so. That was his truth, not Nathan's. It was a discovery, a truth that came from within, rather than from outside.

Jesus frequently used the same method. On one occasion he was invited to the home of a Pharisee for a meal (Luke 7:36–50). While they were reclining for the meal, a known sinful woman came into the room, approached Jesus from the rear, and began to wash Jesus' feet and wipe them with her hair. The Pharisee was privately critical of Jesus for allowing the woman to do this. Jesus did not rebuke the Pharisee directly. Rather, he told a story of two men, one of whom was forgiven a small amount of money and the other a large amount, and asked the Pharisee which of these two men would love the master more. Only when the Pharisee indicated that he supposed it would be the one who had been forgiven a larger debt, did Jesus proceed to apply the parable to the present situation. The Pharisee had judged himself by intuitively recognizing the truth in the situation.

Notice the procedure followed in both of these instances. First, the speaker relates a short narrative. Then he asks the listener what he thinks or, in the first case, simply lets his dialogue partner express himself. Only then does the speaker apply that truth to the listener.

A final suggestion relates to the postmodern aversion to metanarratives. The reality is that for Christianity to be true to what it has historically been, it must express itself as universally true and applicable. Somehow one must induce one's dialogue partner to think about ultimate questions, questions of eternity. This is not easily done in a world of instant communication and of messages of one or a few words. The practical concern will be to try to find ways to get postmoderns to think beyond the immediate concerns. This is not a uniquely postmodern endeavor. Four centuries ago, Blaise Pascal posed his famous wager. One is either wagering that God is or that he is not. If one wagers that God is not and he is, one has lost infinitely. If, however, one wagers that God is and he is, one has gained infinitely.

I have found that human psychology often emerges quite clearly through the study of behavioral economics. Perhaps this is because money plays such an important place in human life. I have often wondered why God created the world in such a way that economics is so important, but I suspect the key may be found in the story of the rich young man in Mark 10:17–22. There Jesus' aim was to create a tension, making the choice of God a real test. He provides, however, a guide to our messaging.

One phenomenon that has been highlighted in behavioral economics but also appears elsewhere is FOMO, the fear of missing out.[33] This might be utilized in two senses. One is the aversion many non-Christians as well as some Christians have to the idea of hell, or an eternal separation from God. While not proposing the abandonment of the concept of hell, I am suggesting that emphasizing the wonders of heaven as eternal personal existence beyond this earthly life may have greater potential for appeal to a postmodern. The emphasis could be on the emotion of joy, rather than the furnishings of heaven. This could be combined with a sort of neo-Pascalian

---

33. Mayank Gupta and Aditya Shanka, "Fear of Missing Out: A Brief View of Origin, Theoretical Underpinnings and Relationship with Mental Health," *World Journal of Clinical Cases* 6, no. 9 (July 2019): 4881–89, https://doi.org.10.12998/wjcc.v9.i19.4881.

presentation. The other would be more concrete and combined with an actual demonstration of the benefits of Christian community.

One who utilized a form of thought provocation was Ben Haden. An atheist until becoming a Christian at age nineteen, he became a lawyer and practiced law for several years before becoming a pastor. On his radio program, *Changed Lives*, he told one time of traveling on a flight and engaging in a conversation with the passenger seated next to him. The man was returning from interviewing for a job, which he had been offered and accepted. It represented a major promotion for him, and he was excited. Haden asked what he would do, and the man replied that he would move his family to the new city. "Then what will you do?" Haden asked. "I'll buy a larger house than we now have." "What then?" "I'll send my children to the best private schools." "What will you do then?" "I'll probably move to a more prestigious neighborhood." What will you do then?" "I'll probably be promoted to higher positions, maybe even to CEO." "What will you do then?" "Eventually I'll retire." "What will you do then?" "I'll play a lot of golf and do a lot of travelling." "What will you do then?" "I'll move to a retirement home." "What will you do then?" "I suppose I may be moved to a nursing home." "What will you do then?" "Eventually I'll die." "And what will you do then?" asked Haden.

CONCLUSION

This is a different world, culturally, from the one in which I grew up and initially ministered. Many of the procedures that were effective in that day do not suffice today. Because, however, Jesus said that he was sending his church into all the world and for all ages (Matt. 28:18–20; Acts 1:6–8), we can expect that the church can be the church today, still being true to its nature and task.

CHAPTER 8

THE COMMUNITY OF THE APOSTLES AND THE SPIRITUAL NATURE OF CHRISTIAN UNITY

Steven Nemes

WHAT EXACTLY IS THE CHURCH? This is a question to which many possible answers can be given. Avery Dulles lists a few models of the church, each of which might be thought to have some basis in the New Testament texts: the church as institution, as mystical communion, as sacrament, as herald, and as servant.[1] Everett Ferguson likewise mentions a number of images for the church to be found in the earliest apostolic and postapostolic sources: body of Christ, bride of Christ, a mother, a temple, the people of God, and a boat or ark.[2] Joshua Cockayne writes in a more analytic and technically precise manner that "the Church is a social body, composed of many individual members, united through the work of the Holy Spirit to be the body of Christ."[3] I am presently concerned with the question of the "ontology" of the church, that is, the question of what the church is at its most fundamental and essential level.

On the one hand, the church can be understood as an institution with a certain intrinsic hierarchy and differentiation of roles. On the other hand,

---

1. Avery Dulles, *Models of the Church*, rev. ed. (New York: Image, 2002).
2. Everett Ferguson, ed., *Understandings of the Church* (Minneapolis: Fortress, 2016), 1–21.
3. Joshua Cockayne, *Explorations in Analytic Ecclesiology: That They May be One* (New York: Oxford University Press, 2022), xi.

146

the church can be understood as a "spiritual" community in the sense that it is a grouping that arises out of a shared experience among many persons. To be more precise, the church can be understood as a "spiritual" community of which its invisible principle of unity is a certain shared experience held in common by many persons, though it only becomes visibly or manifestly one or unified once its members recognize one another as having this experience in common. These two ideas are of course not mutually exclusive. It is certainly possible for the members of an institutional community to share a common experience, and it is likewise possible for a spiritual community to institutionalize for whatever reason. The question to be asked here is only whether one of these dimensions of the church is more fundamental and essential than the other. I will argue against the institutional and in favor of the spiritual understanding of the community of the church. The church is fundamentally *only* a spiritual community in the sense of being a group that arises out of a shared experience of many persons. Its institutionalization is accidental to it and contingent.

One might initially object that this thesis is too obviously true to be worth arguing for. Henry Chadwick wrote, "The first Christians were Jews differentiated from their fellow-countrymen by their faith that in Jesus of Nazareth the Messiah of the nation's expectation had now come."[4] What differentiated these early Christians from other Jews was precisely a shared experience of faith in Jesus and commitment to him. There was presumably no significant institutionalization of the church at this stage. It must therefore follow that the essence of the church is spiritual in nature, being founded upon a shared experience. It can exist even apart from any institutionalization at all. But there are also New Testament passages that have been taken as suggesting that there is an institutional structure to the community of Jesus' followers. The apostles specifically might be thought to have been set apart as unique leaders and guides of the group. A person could refer also to Jesus' remarks to Peter at Matthew 16:17–19 or to the Eleven at Luke 22:28–30 as justifying this conclusion. It is also possible to argue that the church may not have been institutional from the beginning, but it is irrevocably so now. I address these points at some length in my *Theological Authority in the Church*.[5] I will only mention here that the rejection of the idea of an institutional essence of the church is a matter of theological controversy. I am here trying to make a further contribution to an ongoing discussion about this issue.

---

4. Henry Chadwick, *The Early Church* (Baltimore: Penguin, 1967), 9.
5. Steven Nemes, *Theological Authority in the Church: Reconsidering Traditionalism and Hierarchy* (Eugene, OR: Cascade Books, 2023).

The argument here will unfold in three stages. First, I will argue that the apostles thought of themselves as independent messengers of the gospel of Jesus, each having the right to engage in his task freely of the consultation, intervention, and management of the others. There is evidence for this to be found as much in the New Testament as also in the immediate postapostolic period. But a collection of independent workers certainly does not make up an institution. This means that the unity of their group fundamentally is not institutional but rather spiritual in nature. It is a unity arising out of their shared experience of commitment to Jesus Christ and to the sort of life with God that his teachings make possible.

Second, I will argue that this same principle of spiritual unity ought to be applied to the church as a whole. Just as the apostles themselves are one group because they have a shared experience, so also the church as a whole is principally a spiritual and egalitarian community rather than an institutional or hierarchical one. This conception of things can be found in the works of Christian theologians whose relationship with the "catholic" tradition is tenuous, specifically Huldrych Zwingli, Adolf von Harnack, and Michel Henry.

Third, this notion of the church as a spiritual community makes it possible to sketch in broad strokes the contours of an "immanent Christianity." Such an understanding of the faith calls for a reprioritization of the ethical, spiritual, and practical dimension over the dogmatic and metaphysical, a scheme that makes it possible to achieve the unity of the church insofar as the disputable points that differentiate the Christian communities from each other and provoke their disunity are subordinated and relativized as matters of opinion and academic curiosities.

THE COMMUNITY OF THE APOSTLES

My first claim is that the apostles thought of themselves as independent messengers of the gospel of Jesus, each having the right to engage in his task freely of the consultation, intervention, and management of the others. There are a number of lines of evidence in favor of this thesis coming as much from the New Testament texts themselves as also from the postapostolic period immediately afterward.

I will begin with the New Testament evidence. The first consideration is the way that Paul speaks in his epistles. In his letter to the Romans, for example, he says that he does not make it his habit to preach the gospel "where Christ has already been named, so that I do not build on someone else's foundation" (Rom. 15:20). Michael Gorman comments, "[Paul] does not wish to add to the work of other architects of Christian community."[6] In the epistle to the Galatians, Paul wrote about Peter, James, and John, the pillars of the community at Jerusalem, that it "makes no difference" to him who they are because "God shows no partiality" (Gal. 2:6). And as for himself, Paul insisted that he was an apostle sent by Jesus himself rather than by any merely human authorities (1:1). He had no problem criticizing Peter while he was at Antioch, in Paul's own home territory, for refusing to sit with the gentiles at the table and thus leading Barnabas astray (2:11–14). J. Louis Martyn wrote, "Bearing the ultimate message from God to human beings, he is a man whose identity is determined by the God who sent him and by the message God gave him to preach. To other human beings (sometimes including ones in the church—2:4, 14), he is himself a stranger, a person who, in a profound sense, 'comes from somewhere else.'"[7] And in response to the divisions among the Corinthians along the lines of each person's preferred teacher, Paul insisted that he, Apollos, and Cephas alike were but "servants of Christ and stewards of God's mysteries" (1 Cor. 4:1). He flattened any distinctions between them as teachers and pointed to Christ, who died for the Corinthians and into whom they were baptized (1:13). He did not care if anyone judged him; nor did he even bother to judge himself, since it is the Lord who judges (4:4).

Luke portrayed Paul and Timothy as communicating the decisions reached at the so-called council of Jerusalem as they went from place to place (Acts 16:4). But as Luke Timothy Johnson notes, one finds no clear mention of this council in any of Paul's epistles.[8] Neither does he ever repeat or recommend the rules that James established, even when it would be relevant to his subject matter, for example in the discussion of food offered to idols at 1 Corinthians 8, the question of obedience to the law in the epistles to the Galatians and Romans, the matter of food restrictions in Colossians, and so on. Dale Martin notes that the chronological presentation of Paul's early activities as a Christian in Galatians and Acts cannot be reconciled.[9] If this council did happen in anything like the way that Luke presents it,

---

6. Michael J. Gorman, *Romans: A Theological and Pastoral Commentary* (Grand Rapids: Eerdmans, 2022), 287.

7. J. Louis Martyn, *Galatians: A New Translation with Introduction and Commentary* (New Haven, CT: Yale University Press, 1997), 95.

8. Luke Timothy Johnson, *The Acts of the Apostles* (Collegeville, MN: Liturgical Press, 1992), 269–70.

9. Dale B. Martin, *New Testament History and Literature* (New Haven, CT: Yale University Press, 2012), ch. 5.

it seems that it had very little significance for or impact on Paul's own thinking and writing. In all these ways, then, the apostle to the gentiles gives the impression of thinking of himself as an independent messenger of the gospel of Christ, by rights free of the control and intervention of the others, responsible to the Father and to Jesus alone for his work.

Second, there is evidence from the New Testament itself that the apostles generally operated independently of one another and without frequent consultation. For example, there is no explicit mention of most of the Twelve after Pentecost. One would expect their names to appear more often if they were regularly in close contact with one another. Luke mentioned their names in his gospel but said nothing about what most of them ended up doing after the resurrection. Going further, there are clear differences in the reception of the message of Jesus as expressed in the New Testament documents, another indicator that their authors were not in close contact with one another. Otherwise, they would have spoken in the same way and made use of the same formulas, just as one can discern similarities of "dialect" and expression among Thomists, Lutherans, Roman Catholics, phenomenologists, analytic philosophers, and so on. People who are always talking with one another, spending time in close quarters, and concentrating on the same things end up speaking the same way. But Pauline literature emphasizes justification and the death of Christ as the principles of unity of a new humanity; Johannine literature emphasizes the intimate fellowship between Father and Son and the commandment to brotherly love; James puts the accent on the practical consequences of a life lived in Christ; and so on. Of course they all share the material emphasis on the life with God made possible by faith in Jesus. But one does not find in the New Testament the same formal similarities of speech and of emphasis as in later catholic orthodoxy. Finally, the apostolic authors do not shy away from critiquing one another. Matthew's depiction of Peter in his gospel is almost uniformly negative, becoming increasingly so from the episode with "Thou art Peter" (Matt. 16:18 KJV), the last mention of Peter by name being his curse and triple denial of Jesus in the hour of his trial (Matt. 26:75). By the time of the "Great Commission," Peter has disappeared into the crowd of the Eleven, not being explicitly named, nor is any reconciliation with Jesus narrated (Matt. 28:16–20). Robert Gundry goes so far as to argue that Matthew considered Peter to be an apostate and false disciple,[10] although the opinion

---

10. Robert H. Gundry, *Peter: False Disciple and Apostate according to St. Matthew*, 2nd ed. (Eugene, OR: Wipf & Stock, 2015).

of Craig Blomberg may be more palatable: "Matthew paints a consistently negative or at least ambiguous portrait of Peter, which may make it more probable that he was trying to temper an already overexalted view of that apostle."[11] Chrys Caragounis summarizes the point: "Peter is presented by Matthew as confused, cowardly, without understanding, disliking suffering, giving with a view to future gain, impetuous, impulsive and unstable, stingy in forgiving, overestimating his ability, and denying his Master miserably."[12] Matthew likewise related some of Jesus' most egalitarian statements about his disciples. For example, Jesus said in Matthew 23:8–10 that all his disciples are to think of themselves as brothers and equally children of God the Father and students of the Messiah. Gundry thus comments that all of Jesus' disciples are in a position of "equality of subjection to Jesus' didactic authority."[13] And James likewise critiqued a typically Pauline formula about justification very openly and without the sorts of qualifications one would expect him to make out of respect for Paul or politeness or for precision's sake (James 2:14). The point is not that James necessarily disagreed with Paul's theology but that he wrote in such a way as to suggest that it would make no difference to him if he did. These facts sooner paint a picture of the apostles as individuals who share a common purpose and orientation but who generally operate freely and independently of one another.

Third, there is also evidence from the postapostolic period. *First Clement* contains the advice of the Roman Christian community to the community at Corinth in light of the removal of certain bishops from their position. This letter was written at the behest of the Corinthian church itself, as its opening suggests. But why should the Corinthians have written to Rome in the first place? This letter is generally dated within the limits of the first century, either just before the destruction of Jerusalem or else around the year 90.[14] In either case, however, John the Elder would have been alive in Ephesus, which is closer than Rome. Robert Eno noted that some people make much of this and think it points to evidence of a consciousness of Roman primacy in the early church.[15] But there is another and more plausible explanation at hand. Both the Roman and Corinthian churches

---

11. Craig L. Blomberg, *Matthew* (Nashville: Broadman, 1992), 255.

12. Chrys Caragounis, *Peter and the Rock* (New York: de Gruyter, 1990), 99.

13. Robert H. Gundry, *Matthew: A Commentary on His Literary and Theological Art* (Grand Rapids: Eerdmans, 1982), 457.

14. See Jonathan Bernier, *Rethinking the Dates of the New Testament: The Evidence for Early Composition* (Grand Rapids: Baker Academic, 2022).

15. Robert Eno, *The Rise of the Papacy* (Wilmington, DE: Michael Glazier, 1990), 36–37. Cf. Editors of Encyclopedia Britannica, "St. Clement I," *Encyclopedia Britannica*, August 17, 2022, https://www.britannica.com/biography/Saint-Clement-I.

were Pauline-Petrine communities. Paul's letters to the Corinthians provide evidence that Peter had some connection with these congregations, since some there were saying, "I belong to Cephas" (1 Cor. 1:12). *First Clement* 5 sets forth only Peter and Paul as apostolic examples to be followed. It apparently does not know anything about the others. And in *Against Heresies* 3.3.2, Irenaeus related the tradition that both Peter and Paul played a role in organizing the nascent congregations in Rome before their martyrdom.[16] One can therefore propose that the Corinthians appealed to postapostolic Rome and not to John the Elder in Ephesus, not because of some intuition of Roman primacy, but rather because the churches in both cities "belonged" to the same apostles. The apostles and major leaders of early Christianity operated independently of one another in caring for their churches and perhaps even expected freedom from the intervention of others. The Corinthians knew Peter and Paul but did not know this John.

Fourth, the Quartodeciman controversy gives strong evidence that the apostles operated freely and independently of one another without frequent consultation. The churches in Asia Minor celebrated the resurrection of Christ on 14 Nisan, whatever day of the week this might have fallen on. The habit in most of the other churches was otherwise, namely, to celebrate the resurrection only on Sunday. Brian Schmisek hypothesizes that they did this as a celebration of Jesus' glorification in his crucifixion as the Passover lamb.[17] Eusebius's *Ecclesiastical History* recounts how Polycrates composed a letter on behalf of the bishops in Asia in defense of this practice, citing the authority of the apostle Philip who died in Hierapolis and the elder John in Ephesus.[18] Although Victor, the bishop of Rome at the time, hastily wanted to cut the Quartodeciman churches in Rome from the fellowship of the other congregations,[19] Irenaeus convinced him not to, since even his predecessor Anicetus could not convince Polycarp of Smyrna to do otherwise than he had learned from John the Elder.[20] This curious episode in the early history of the church thus provides some significant evidence that the apostles and significant leaders of Jesus' followers did not regularly consult with one another, in this way considering themselves at

16. In Alexander Roberts, James Donaldson, and A. Cleveland Coxe, eds., *Ante-Nicene Fathers*, vol. 1 (Buffalo, NY: Christian Literature Publishing Co., 1885), 315–567.

17. Brian Schmisek, "The Quartodeciman Question: Johannine Roots of a Christian Controversy," *Biblical Theology Bulletin* 52, no. 4 (2022): 253–61.

18. Eusebius, *Ecclesiastical History* 5.24.2–3, in Philip Schaff and Henry Wace, eds., *Nicene and Post-Nicene Fathers*, Second Series, vol. 1 (Buffalo, NY: Christian Literature, 1890), 81–404.

19. See John Behr, *Irenaeus of Lyons: Identifying Christianity* (New York: Oxford University Press, 2013), 57.

20. Eusebius, *Ecclesiastical History* 5.24.9, 16–17.

liberty to tend to their churches and to propagate the gospel of Jesus freely of the consultation, intervention, and management of the others.

Therefore, on the basis of the evidence drawn from the epistles of Paul, from the rest of the New Testament, from the incident at Corinth to which *1 Clement* is a response, and from the Quartodeciman controversy in the second century, one can draw the conclusion that the apostles and leaders of early Christianity thought of themselves as independent messengers of the gospel of Jesus. They considered that they each had the right to propagate the message and care for their churches free from the consultation, intervention, and management of the others. This further means that their unity was not fundamentally institutional in nature. There is no such thing as an "institution" whose principal agents hardly if ever consult with one another. Put another way, the independence the apostles and early Christian leaders presumed relative to one another is indicative of the fact that they did not consider themselves to be constituting a formal institution. Still less was their unity a matter of common submission to a single leader among them, such as Peter, since it appears that Philip and John did not consult with Peter about the celebration of the resurrection in their own churches, and their own followers refused to do other than what Philip and John had taught them. Not being institutional, their unity must rather have been spiritual in nature. What united them was a shared experience of commitment to Jesus and to the life with God that his teachings make possible. It is these teachings and this life that mattered most of all. Naturally, their individual appropriations of these teachings and this life differed from person to person, but what made them all to be Christians in unity with one another is the condition of their hearts in orientation toward Christ. Such is my first claim.

THE CHURCH AS SPIRITUAL COMMUNION

My second claim is that this conception of things should be applied to the church as a whole. What is sauce for the apostolic goose is sauce for the ecclesial gander: the church is not an institutional but rather spiritual communion. The apostles did not understand themselves as constituting a formal institution, so contemporary Christians should not think in these terms either. What makes the church to be one is rather that it is the community of persons who share a commitment to Jesus and to the life with God that his teachings make possible. It is a community whose principle of unity is a condition of the heart.

It is true that a more institutional conception of the church comes to dominate in history as the "catholic" tradition develops. The word "catholic" here refers not to Roman Catholicism per se but to that mainstream tradition that first distinguished itself from various forms of Gnosticism in the second century as genuinely apostolic by episcopal succession and later came to codify and enforce its dogmatic commitments through the assistance of the secular powers in the so-called ecumenical councils. "Catholic" thus means episcopal-conciliar. The bishops of the "catholic" churches, spurred on and also assisted by the secular powers that be, come to claim for themselves the right to make definitive and binding declarations of dogma in the face of seemingly intractable disagreement and disputation, to make pronouncements to be accepted simply on their own authority, to exclude dissidents from their communities, and to set Christian theology on a particular theoretical trajectory without the foreseen possibility of reversal or course correction. Hence arises a conception of the faith as a matter of submission to authoritative testimony, while theology itself comes to function principally on the foundation of appeal to testimony rather than by free reasoned argument. This is how Henry Chadwick would characterize the difference between Berengarius and Lanfranc of Bec in the Middle Ages.[21] Something like this idea is also found in Vincent of Lérins's *Commonitorium* 2.5–6, where the "catholic" faith is discerned by appeal, not principally to Scripture, which is ambiguous and multiply interpretable, but rather to what is believed by "everyone," more specifically as determined by the well-known teachings of the "holy fathers and ancestors," in accordance with their interpretation in all or at least most "priests" and "doctors."[22] The truth itself is not easy to get at, so it must be received from those who have the proper standing and authority within the hierarchy of the church to bear witness to it. The appeal to authority becomes the foundational method in catholic theology.

It is therefore not surprising that those persons who insist upon the spiritual nature of the communion of the church tend also to stand in a tenuous relation to the "catholic" tradition and its institutional ecclesiology. The examples mentioned here will be Huldrych Zwingli, Adolf von Harnack, and Michel Henry.

---

21. Henry Chadwick, "Ego Berengarius," *Journal of Theological Studies* 40, no. 2 (1989): 415–45, here p. 427.

22. Vincent of Lérins, *Commonitorium*, trans. C. A. Heurtley, in *Nicene and Post-Nicene Fathers*, ed. Philip Schaff and Henry Wace, 2nd ser., vol. 11 (Buffalo, NY: Christian Literature Publishing Co., 1894), 123–59, here p. 132.

In his "Exposition of the Sixty-Seven Articles," Zwingli insisted that the gospel has authority from itself and not from its endorsement by the authorities of the church. Thus, this gospel can be brought in critique of these authorities if they should depart from it (art. 1). The unity of the church is not a matter of its submission to, say, the testimony of the Fathers as authorities, but rather of its acceptance of the one word of God (art. 8).[23] And God's commandments, prohibitions, and promises for human beings, such as these are revealed in Christ (art. 2)[24] and are made not intelligible but rather desirable to human beings whose hearts are changed by the Holy Spirit (art. 16).[25] The *ecclesia catholica* of the creed is, in Zwingli's words, "the communion of all godly, believing Christians"[26] with whom the teachings of Jesus resonate internally. He wrote, "Here everyone may discover for himself whether he is in the church or not. For if he has all confidence, hope and comfort in God through Jesus Christ, he is in the church, i.e. in the communion of all the saints."[27] At this point, the nature of the church as spiritual, as founded in a shared experience, becomes explicit.

So also, in *What Is Christianity?* Harnack found the essence of Jesus' preaching to concern the fatherhood of God, the forgiveness of sins, trust in God's providence, and purity of life in the fellowship of the brethren.[28] It is in brief a message about a certain form of life with God that is possible here and now. The "catholic" tradition erred by prioritizing its metaphysical speculations to the point of putting a well-defined Christology before the gospel message, making God inaccessible apart from a purportedly correct understanding of the ontology of Christ. In Harnack's opinion, this stemmed from the historically contingent but significant identification of Jesus with the notion of "Logos" of Greek philosophy.[29] Harnack insisted that the "catholic" tradition is not Christianity *tout court* but rather a historically contingent reception and development of the gospel message that took a certain shape in time. Christian faith for him was not principally a matter of belonging to a well-defined institution but rather something "inward": "trust in God, unaffected humility, the assurance of redemption,

23. Huldrych Zwingli, "The Exposition of the Sixty-Seven Articles," p. 46, in *Huldrych Zwingli Writings*, vol. 1, *The Defense of the Reformed Faith*, trans. H. Wayne Pipkin (Eugene, OR: Pickwick, 1984).

24. Zwingli, "Exposition of the Sixty-Seven Articles," 14.

25. Zwingli, "Exposition of the Sixty-Seven Articles," 62–68.

26. Zwingli, "Exposition of the Sixty-Seven Articles," 45.

27. Zwingli, "Exposition of the Sixty-Seven Articles," 45.

28. Adolf von Harnack, *What Is Christianity?*, trans. Thomas Bailey Saunders (New York: Putnam, 1902), 284.

29. Harnack, 202–3.

the devotion of one's life to the service of one's brethren."[30] And the church is "held together by the Holy Ghost and by faith" as "a spiritual community of brothers and sisters."[31] It is a "'societas fidei' which has members everywhere, even among Greeks and Romans."[32]

Finally, the phenomenologist Henry distinguished sharply between two dimensions of reality. There is the image or representation that is cast out by each thing into the "world," this common sphere of manifestation in which things show themselves to the intentional gaze of consciousness, and then there is the experience that each living person has of himself or herself in the domain of "life," the experience of being something that can experience itself in diverse modes: joy, suffering, desire, repulsion, and the rest.[33] There is what is seen in the "public" sphere of the world, and then there is what I experience myself to be on the "inside." For Henry, subjectivity, or the "inside," is the more fundamental reality. The public phenomenon is derivative precisely as a representation and image of the private inner reality. Thus, the unity of a group of persons does not arise out of external conditions that become manifest in the "world" but rather out of a harmonization or consonance of their subjective experience. It is the sameness of feeling that makes them to be one.[34] And the essence of Christ's teaching is that each person is a son of God, the absolute Life immanent in each finite life, which every finite life feels as its source and in which each living being feels himself or herself to live.[35] The community of Christians is therefore the community of those who know this truth about themselves—that they are sons of the Father, finite lives continuously being engendered in the absolute Life of God—and who in loving others love the absolute Life that lives in them.

As I said earlier, these three figures stand in a tenuous relation to the "catholic" tradition. Zwingli, for example, subordinated all ecclesial hierarchs, all fathers, and all traditions to the gospel of Christ as communicated in Scripture. Although in the matter of the Eucharist he made appeals to Augustine and Tertullian,[36] Zwingli felt no qualms about contradicting

30. Harnack, 266.
31. Harnack, 285.
32. Harnack, 277.
33. Michel Henry, *I Am the Truth: Toward a Philosophy of Christianity*, trans. Susan Emanuel (Stanford, CA: Stanford University Press, 2003), 14–15, 34; Henry, *Incarnation: A Philosophy of Flesh*, trans. Karl Hefty (Evanston, IL: Northwestern University Press, 2015), 151.
34. Henry, *Incarnation*, 244–45.
35. Michel Henry, *Words of Christ*, trans. Christina M. Gschwandtner (Grand Rapids: Eerdmans, 2012), 119.
36. E.g., Zwingli, "On the Lord's Supper," 219.

what he took to be a patristic consensus on baptismal regeneration when he was convinced that the biblical teaching and plain facts of experience suggest otherwise.[37] Harnack's analysis in *What Is Christianity?* relativizes the "catholic" tradition and its dogmatic priorities as a contingent historical appropriation of Christian faith with (in some cases) very little basis in Jesus' actual teachings as they are related in the New Testament. And more or less all of Henry's theological critics—James Hart, Emmanuel Falque, Joseph Rivera, Amber Bowen, and others—effectively complain that his conception of things cannot be squared with certain dogmatic commitments of the "catholic" tradition that they take for granted as belonging to Christianity as such, for example, ideas about God's relation to the created order, the inspiration of Scripture, and the nature of Christian faith.[38] But what these authors have in common is the idea of the spiritual nature of the unity of the church. What makes Christians to be a single body is not a matter of shared institutional belonging but rather of shared spiritual experience, more specifically a shared sense of themselves as belonging to God, this self-conception being opened up to them by their subjective resonance with the teachings of Jesus.

IMMANENT CHRISTIANITY

My first claim was that the apostles thought of themselves as equal, independent messengers of the gospel with the right to operate generally freely of the intervention and consultation of the others. This means that their unity is fundamentally not institutional but rather spiritual in nature. My second claim was that this same understanding of things should be applied to the church as a whole. It is a spiritual communion of persons who have a shared loyalty to Jesus and to the life with God that his teachings make possible. This is also the understanding of things one can find in theologians like Huldrych Zwingli, Adolf von Harnack, and Michel Henry, who not coincidentally stand in a tenuous relation to the "catholic" tradition and its more "institutional" conception of the unity of the church. The final claim to make here is that this understanding of the church as a spiritual communion makes it possible to exposit in broad strokes the basic shape of an "immanent Christianity" as a promising alternative to the more

---

37. Ulrich Zwingli, "Of Baptism," in *Zwingli and Bullinger*, ed. G. W. Bromiley (Louisville: Westminster John Knox, 1953), 130; see 129–75.

38. See Steven Nemes, "The Life-Idealism of Michel Henry," *Journal of French and Francophone Philosophy* 29, nos. 1–2 (2021): 87–108.

"metaphysical" variety proposed by the "catholic" tradition for achieving Christian unity.

What is "immanent Christianity"? It can be found in varying degrees in the thinkers I mentioned earlier, and I have tried to develop my own version of it in a recent work titled *Theology of the Manifest.*[39] In brief, it is committed to the following theses:

1. Salvation is the reharmonization of human life with the intentions of God, understood formally as the source of one's life and of the being of all things.
2. This reharmonization is mediated by Jesus Christ and his teachings in the preaching of the gospel.
3. This salvation makes it possible for human beings to live a different sort of life in the world, specifically in their interactions with themselves, with others, and with the whole created order.
4. This entire process takes place within the sphere of the manifest, in the immanence of each person's subjectivity. Put another way, becoming and being a Christian is a matter of experiencing oneself and all things differently.
5. The work of the Holy Spirit is not "epistemological," that is, he does not make possible knowledge of realities antecedently inaccessible to human beings by nature, but rather "affective," in that he changes the interior disposition of the human being to be in harmony with God and with what Jesus teaches.

"Immanent Christianity" therefore means a Christianity of experience and of action. It is not principally preoccupied with matters of metaphysics, which is to say that it does not concern itself with purely noumenal realities lying beyond the manifest sphere of experience, such as the intratrinitarian relations, the nature of the hypostatic union, the purported transformation of the elements in the Eucharist, and so on. It does not necessarily deny any of these things, but neither is it preoccupied with them, nor does it define itself through them. It is rather a matter of being reconciled with God, with oneself, and with others in one's heart.

What does this amount to? Being reconciled with God means loving and accepting the fact that you have been brought into life by God and

---

39. Steven Nemes, *Theology of the Manifest: Christianity without Metaphysics* (Lanham, MD: Lexington Books / Fortress Academic, 2023).

trusting in God's intention to do good to you thereby rather than evil, especially as evidenced by the life and death of Jesus himself. Being reconciled with oneself means accepting one's life and value as an individual brought into life by God himself as his son or daughter, subordinate to no one else per se and owing no one else anything except love (cf. Rom. 13:8). Being reconciled with others means seeking their good and trying to live according to the law of love of neighbor, seeing them also as God's children who have been brought into life to be the beneficiaries of his goodness, rather than thinking of the world as being the means for one's own personal satisfaction. Thus, Zwingli said that the whole of Christian life can be summed up as follows: "In Jesus Christ God has provided us with the remission of sins and everything else, and . . . we are to show forth and imitate Jesus Christ in our lives."[40] Harnack said that "religion is not only a state of the heart; it is a deed as well; it is faith active in love and in the sanctification of life."[41] And Henry's interpretation of the Christian faith seamlessly transitions from the "second birth" as the recognition of oneself as a son of God, engendered in the absolute Life of the Father, to the life of a son expressed through the works of mercy.[42] Here are therefore where the emphases of an "immanent Christianity" lie: in matters of ethics, spirituality, and practice, rather than in metaphysical speculation and dogmatics.

My final claim is thus that "immanent Christianity" serves a better chance of achieving Christian unity than does the metaphysically preoccupied "catholic" variety. Why is that? Because its concerns are with the things Christians actually have in common, things Jesus teaches about clearly: how to live a human life in the world as children of God. The metaphysical preoccupations and doctrines of the "catholic" tradition, precisely because they are preoccupations with matters of "metaphysics," that is, matters lying beyond the sphere of the manifest, are by its own admission not easily proven from Scripture (hence Vincent's rule), nor are they the sorts of things one can demonstrate by means of the appeal to experience or rational argumentation (hence Thomas's insistence in *Summa theologiae* I, q. 1, art. 1, that sacred doctrine goes beyond the "philosophical disciplines"). Therefore, these doctrines must be accepted simply by appeal to the authorized testimony of ecclesial hierarchs who came to be convinced that they are essential to the faith per se and by imperial assistance who

---

40. Zwingli, "Of Baptism," 145.
41. Harnack, *What Is Christianity?*, 287.
42. Henry, *I Am the Truth*, ch. 10.

won widespread agreement with their views, which authorities we must assume to have been granted a special insight into a supernatural reality by the Holy Spirit, since only thus would they be deserving of the sort of irreversible commitment that they demand of us. In theology obscure points of metaphysics, institutional hierarchy, and special theological epistemology go hand in hand. And yet I think there is ample evidence in the history of the church to the present day that the Holy Spirit has been given even to persons who disagree radically in their dogmatic commitments. The Spirit of Jesus plainly exceeds all confessional and ecclesial borders. It may well be, then, that the "catholic" form of Christianity ought to be reconsidered as a particular instantiation of the church, rather than simply the church itself, just as the giving of the Spirit to the gentiles taught the earliest disciples that the messianic community of Jesus extended beyond the borders of law-observant Judaism (Acts 10–15). The church is instead the spiritual communion of all persons loyal to Jesus and who by his teachings come to understand themselves to be and live as God's children in the world, whatever particular differences of appropriation of this message there might be among them. And "immanent Christianity" draws the attention of the church away from the things that distinguish Christians from each other to the things they all have in common.

CHAPTER 9

EXILIC ECCLESIOLOGY
Suffering and Apostolicity in Early Modern Reformed Theology

JENNIFER POWELL MCNUTT

THE EARLY-MODERN CRISIS OF APOSTOLICITY

On the brink of the Reformation, the idea of "apostle" had become so wedded to the notion of papal "succession" that it was feared that apostolicity was in danger of losing its inceptive meaning and purpose in the confession of the church. The affirmation of "apostolic succession" has been foundational to the thriving of Christianity since its earliest days, conveyed by 1 John 1 and formalized by Irenaeus of Lyon, as a means of verifying the validity of its faith claims. An unbroken chain that linked all the way back to Christ, gave assurance to the truth of the gospel and the model of discipleship during and after the time the apostolic fathers lived. But was the succession of Christ a seat of wealth and power or one of suffering and the cross? What should apostolicity look like?

The concern to "re-Christianize"—to borrow a phrase from Reformation scholar Scott Hendrix[1]—particularly apostolicity was shared by more than the "Morning Star of the Reformation," Englishman and cleric John Wyclif. Well before Luther ever came on the scene, some of the most important voices of medieval scholasticism, and through a framework of nominalism, worried that Christlike apostolicity had become a mental construct devoid of true meaning in the universal experience of the church.

---

1. Scott Hendrix, "Rerooting the Faith: The Reformation as Re-Christianization," *Church History* 69 (2000): 558–77.

Well-documented practices of hedonism and avarice shocked onlookers of the papacies from Sixtus IV to Innocent VIII to Alexander VI to Julius II to Leo X, the last of which notoriously excommunicated Martin Luther from the Roman Catholic Church. But the array of critics was more diverse and wider ranging than is sometimes recognized.

As Wyclif decried the fact that apostolicity had lost sight of the poverty of Christ and the rule of the apostle over food and clothing,[2] so, too, did the father of Renaissance humanism, Francis Petrarch, critique the corrupt lifestyle of the papacy while growing up in the city of Avignon during a time that he described as the "second Babylon," which came to be known as the Babylonian Captivity of the Church.[3] If the Italian Dominican friar Savonarola is received as a prophetic voice in challenging the Medici stranglehold on Italian politics and papacy,[4] so, too, might Dante be heard in attributing the root of the simoniac papacy on Constantine's supposed donation.[5]

The role that Luther's school of scholasticism, the *via moderna*, played in this conversation should not be overlooked. After all, the Franciscan William of Ockham (c. 1288–1347) was himself in trouble with the papacy and summoned to the papal court in 1324 to answer for charges of heresy.[6] This was the Avignon papacy, and Pope John XXII did not look kindly on Franciscans who claimed that apostolicity was tied to poverty as the truest imitation of Christ. In his bull *Cum inter nonnullos* (1323), Pope John XXII denied that Jesus and the apostles owned nothing either individually or as a group; lest any irony be lost in this statement, it is worth noting that this was declared from the grandeur of the Palais de Papes in Avignon, France, for the purpose of undercutting the validity of the Franciscan order and the mendicants, or begging orders.[7]

Over the course of the tug-of-war that took hold between them, Ockham declared the pope a heretic and in breach of office. He fled to

---

2. John Wyclif, "The Pastoral Office," in *Advocates of Reform: From Wyclif to Erasmus*, ed. Matthew Spinka, Library of Christian Classics (Westminster John Knox, 1953), 43.

3. Peter Hainsworth, ed. and trans., *The Essential Petrarch* (Indianapolis: Hackett, 2010), xiv, 31, 210, 238.

4. John C. Olin, *The Catholic Reformation: Savonarola to Ignatius Loyola* (Harper & Row, 1969), 1–15.

5. Dante mentioned the simoniac popes: Dante Alighieri, *Inferno*, trans. Robert and Jean Hollander (New York: Doubleday, 2000), 321, 19:117. The Donation of Constantine was deemed a forgery in 1440 by Lorenzo Valla.

6. For a brief biographical account, see Paul Vincent Spade, ed., *The Cambridge Companion to Ockham* (Cambridge: Cambridge University Press, 1999).

7. This analysis benefits from John Kilcullen, "The Political Writings," in *The Cambridge Companion to Ockham*, 302–25, here at 306.

Munich to live out the rest of his life under the protection of the Holy
Roman emperor Ludwig of Bavaria (who had also been excommunicated).
In Ockham's final writings, including *Eight Questions on the Power of the
Pope* (1340–41),[8] he maintained that the practice of voluntary poverty was
the truest imitation of Christ. For him, Scripture taught that Jesus chose
lowliness and poverty. He pointed out that Jesus' instructions to the Seventy
or Seventy-two to take nothing with them in their ministry were perennial
instructions for the leadership of the church.[9] In fact, the mendicant practice
of renouncing ownership was, in his mind, a return to the precedent set
by God in the garden of Eden, a place he described as free from claims of
property.[10] By that reasoning, the Franciscans were the true successors of
the apostles because of their commitment to poverty.

The restoration of Ockham's position never came (although he also never
sought reconciliation), and he died excommunicated in 1347.[11] Scholar John
Kilcullen's work on Ockham points out what might easily be overlooked
in this dramatic showdown, namely, how moderated Ockham was for his
time. He claimed limits and exceptions to the fullness of papal power, not
the complete denial of power and papal office. While he made distinctions
between papal power and Christ's power,[12] he never went as far as contemporary Marsilius of Padua in rejecting the idea that Jesus appointed Peter as
head of the church in Matthew 16.[13] On the contrary, Ockham defended
the divine establishment of the papacy.[14] Not that it mattered in the end
for him, but this moderated approach toward papal reform informed the
next generation as well.

After Ockham's time, more and more ripples began to disrupt the ecclesiological pond of the West, particularly when the conciliarists surfaced.
In the first place, conciliarists grappled with papal infallibility in light of
the papal schism that rocked Europe in 1378 by insisting that a general
council held more authority than the papacy. Henry of Langenstein, in a

---

8. William of Ockham, *Octo quaestiones de potestate papae*, in OP I, ed. J. G. Sikes (Manchester:
Manchester University Press, 1940), 1–221. For an English translation, see "William Ockham:
An Excerpt from Eight Questions on the Power of the Pope," in *A Scholastic Miscellany: Anselm to
Ockham*, ed. and trans. Eugene R. Fairweather, Library of Christian Classics (Philadelphia: West-
minster, 1956), 437–42.

9. Kilcullen, "Political Writings," 303.

10. Kilcullen, 309.

11. This part of his story should give insight into the complexity of Ockham's reception history
in contrast with someone like Thomas Aquinas, who would win over the court of ecclesiastical
opinion in the coming generations.

12. Kilcullen, "Political Writings," 311–12.

13. Francesco Maiolo, *Medieval Sovereignty: Marsilius of Padua and Bartolus of Saxoferrato* (Delft,
Netherlands: Eburon Academic, 2007), 161–216.

14. Kilcullen, "Political Writings," 314.

pointed critique of the pope and the college of cardinals in 1381, asked, was it not the case that even Peter himself denied Christ three times and all the disciples abandoned him?[15] Rather than apostolicity, "apostasy rules supreme."[16] Thirty years later, a twofold papal divide had compounded into a threefold papal divide. Conciliarist Dietrich of Niem described a crisis of apostolic visibility, leadership, and presence. Who were the true apostles of Christ?

From Niem's standpoint, apostolicity had become detrimentally conflated with the papal court, a place he described as one of open robbery and public violence worse than any secular court.[17] Niem bemoaned, "Today there is . . . a disappearance, nay, a complete abandonment of good moral practices, for simony, avarice, the sale of benefices, tyranny, and cruelty hold sway, approved as it were by wont amongst the ecclesiastics."[18] It was no small matter to declare—and boldly at that—that the pope was just a man who could sin and should be corrected and judged since the seat of the papacy could not purify a person.[19] The state of the crisis was dire, particularly as he likened popes such as John XXIII to Judas, saying, "Judas did, indeed, once sell Christ for thirty pieces of silver, but they [our ecclesiastical superiors] every day sell Christ and his Church a thousand times not merely for thirty pieces of silver but for hundreds and for thousands."[20] Drawing from Ockham's application of the Aristotelian distinctions between genus and species to the doctrine of ecclesiology, Niem championed the distinction between the universal church—under the headship of Christ without error, division, or end—in contrast with the apostolic church or Roman Church, which was prone to error, deception, schism, heresy, and even failure, in his mind.[21] In his estimation, this deterioration of the papacy correlated with the unwillingness to convene general councils whose authority represented the universal church and could act as a curb to the potential failures of the papal office.[22] True apostolicity was marked by the preaching of poverty, the forbidding of avarice, and the

---

15. Henry of Langenstein, "A Letter on Behalf of a Council of Peace (1381)," in *Advocates of Reform: From Wyclif to Erasmus*, ed. Matthew Spinka, Library of Christian Classics (Westminster John Knox, 2006), 118.

16. Henry of Langenstein, 108.

17. Dietrich of Niem, "Ways of Uniting and Reforming the Church (1410)," in *Advocates of Reform: From Wyclif to Erasmus*, ed. Matthew Spinka, Library of Christian Classics (Westminster John Knox, 2006), 168–71.

18. Dietrich of Niem, 153.

19. Dietrich of Niem, 155–56.

20. Dietrich of Niem, 172.

21. Dietrich of Niem, 150–51.

22. Dietrich of Niem, 170.

advocacy of chastity, said Niem, which was a far cry from what was being practiced and preached at Avignon by all accounts.[23]

Conciliarism proved to be the means of resolving the papal schism at the Council of Constance, but that did not entail that conciliarists were treated kindly, as Wyclif's desecrated bones and Jan Hus's scattered ashes can attest. These were the children of the Avignon papacy and the Great Papal Schism, and they could not unsee the failures of the church that they witnessed and experienced. As it turned out, to demote the fullness of papal power was a crucial step toward untethering "apostolicity" from Petrine supremacy in the West, which became an open door and an open question for ecclesiology in the context of the Reformation. In what way had the church received the keys from Christ, according to Matthew 16? Could the Reformers still confess the apostolicity of the church and bypass Petrine supremacy?

This chapter will explore the ways in which Reformed ecclesiology came to identify with apostolic suffering to quell accusations of ecclesiastical innovation and to confirm its standing as a true legacy of the one, holy, catholic, and apostolic church. Reformed martyrologies, French Bibles, and a close reading of John Calvin's dedication to the *Institutes of the Christian Religion* offer insight into the formation of what I am describing as an "exilic ecclesiology" that was shaped and confirmed by the early modern refugee crisis.[24] To confess the true church was to embrace the realities of dislocation and suffering as exiled pilgrims seeking first and foremost the heavenly kingdom.

CLAIMING APOSTOLICITY THROUGH SUFFERING

During a time when Reformed theology, practice, and ecclesial identity were gaining form in the context of the refugee crisis of the mid-sixteenth century, the French Reformed tradition walked through the open door of conciliarism. As the Reformation untethered the one, holy, catholic, and apostolic church from Petrine supremacy and from the standards of monastic Christianity (namely, poverty and chastity as apostolicity), the French Reformed tradition came to identify apostolicity with the suffering of exile and persecution due to the right preaching of the Word. What that

---

23. Dietrich of Niem, 149.

24. For more on the early modern refugee crisis, see Nicholas Terpstra, *Religious Refugees in the Early Modern World: An Alternative History of the Reformation* (Cambridge: Cambridge University Press, 2015).

meant is that the *ad fontes* of Renaissance humanism was not *merely* a cry of methodology, to return to the fount of apostolic Scripture, but of apostolic ecclesiology and the dynamics of a pre-Constantinian era. In that regard, the writings of John Calvin give insight into the way that early French Reformed ecclesiology confirmed its authority through the shared experience of suffering, exile, and persecution with the apostles as an assurance of salvation in Christ and in a way that functioned like a supporting mark of the true church.

APOSTOLICITY IN JOHN CALVIN'S DEDICATION

Calvin claimed apostolicity for French Protestants from the first moments of his writing ministry on the pages of his dedication of the *Institutes of the Christian Religion* to the king of France, Francis I.[25] The dedication was written in the context of the royal persecution that erupted from the Placard Affair of 1534 as well as the severe persecution of the Vaudois, who are also known as the Waldensians. Significantly, Calvin never removed the dedication from the *Institutes*, though the king never read it. Even so, over the years, Calvin edited the dedication and added other prefaces to later editions to reflect the evolving circumstances of his ministry and purposes of the *Institutes*. The persistence of the original dedication is a reminder that the conditions of persecution persisted in France until limited toleration was introduced by the Edict of Nantes in 1598, though persecution continued to trouble French Protestants with the revocation of that Edict in 1685 until the Napoleonic era. Consequently, the dedication was relevant for three centuries.

In his appeal to the king of France, Calvin addressed several accusations raised against Protestants in France, including that of innovation, an effective way to slander someone in the Renaissance. The Bible must be unfamiliar to his accusers, wrote Calvin with pointed humor.[26] It was a jab that reflected the heart of the reforming zeal to go back to the fount (*ad fontes*), namely, Jesus and the Bible. For Calvin, denying innovation also entailed rejecting the need to prove their apostolicity through miracles. The miracles of Christ and of the apostles are ours, claimed Calvin, and the cessationist view was born. The claim to apostolicity would be proven not by miracles but suffering.

25. See vol. 1 of *Ioannis Calvini opera quae supersunt omnia*, ed. Wilhelm Baum, Eduard Cunitz, and Eduard Reuss, 59 vols., Corpus Reformatorum, vols. 29–87 (Brunswick, Germany: C. A. Schwetschke and Son [M. Bruhn]), 1863–1900. For translation see John Calvin, *Institutes of the Christian Religion*, 2 vols., ed. John T. McNeill, trans. Ford Lewis Battles, Library of Christian Classics (Philadelphia: Westminster, 1960).
26. McNeil, 16.

Although, starting with Martin Luther, the Reformers went beyond conciliarist ecclesiology in their reform of the church, it was nevertheless the very existence of the conciliarist option that provided Calvin with valid opportunity for contesting the visible church without breaking from the "church," since the church under the reign of Christ exists even when it is not visible.[27] Conciliarist ecclesiology gave Calvin space to question the visible clerical succession of the Roman Church in so far as it manifested in "the parade of popes, cardinals, bishops, abbots, and priests."[28] To make his point, Calvin went beyond conciliarist ecclesiology, through a similar tactic to Luther's at the Leipzig Disputation, by drawing out the implications of the Council of Basel's failure to depose Pope Eugenius IV. A mini papal schism followed from that gathering in 1431 with the counterelection of Felix V (or Amadeus), who could not hold on to his new office and eventually accepted the consolation prize of a cardinal's hat, which Calvin described as like "a barking dog" to a morsel.[29]

By highlighting the failure of the Council of Basel, a legitimate general council that could not follow through with its own judgment in the face of political power plays, Calvin undercut conciliarist ecclesiology as the ultimate answer to the problem of church reform. The fact that Eugenius was reinstated as pope against the wishes of the Council of Basel was a visible breach of true apostolic succession, by his estimation. The papacy was no longer furthering the succession of apostles but conversely, in his words, a succession of heretics: "From these rebellious and obstinate heretics have come forth all future popes, cardinals, bishops, abbots, and priests."[30] In response to accusations of schism, Calvin's claim to apostolic succession benefited from conciliarism without having to ascribe to it. Indeed, rather than appeal to an authority rooted in councils, Calvin appealed to authority validated through suffering from persecution for Christ.

Right out of the gate, Calvin painted a bleak picture of his persecuted brethren: "shackled with irons, some beaten with rods, some led about as laughingstocks, some proscribed, some most savagely tortured, some forced to flee. All of us are oppressed by poverty, cursed with dire execrations, wounded by slanders and treated in most shameful ways."[31] He described

---

27. McNeil, 24: "But they stray very far from the truth when they do not recognize the church unless they see it with their very eyes, and try to keep it within limits to which it cannot at all be confined" (25). Calvin explored the theme of the hidden church further.
28. McNeil, 27.
29. McNeil, 27.
30. McNeil, 27.
31. McNeil, 14.

them as a flock scattered by violence and exile, destroyed and buried by hate (they were, in fact, buried alive at points), and hidden as well as silenced by fear.[32] If Francis continued to entertain slander against them, Calvin feared that prison, scourging, racking, maiming, and burning would persist.[33]

Calvin's account of persecution is verified by a variety of outside sources. One can quickly see resonance with early Christian, pre-Constantinian persecution in so far as Huguenots came to be accused of sodomy, infanticide, and even cannibalism.[34] The Edict of Nantes, which passed in 1598, sought to end a practice of kidnapping Protestant children from their families to be raised in convents as a means of forcing conversions.[35] Suffering was multifaceted, but it was in every way a displacement or exile: displacement from legal standing, which implicated criminal proceedings, displacement from the legality of one's marriage, and displacement from the guardianship of one's biological children. The losses compounded from livelihood and property to inheritance, and most grievously, the right to live at all. Calvin accordingly described the true church as hidden and scattered. It was only visibly known by the pure preaching of God's Word and the right administration of sacraments,[36] actions in his time that were met with suffering, exile, and persecution. In this way, human suffering for Christ did not rival the two marks; it confirmed them.

To go further, Calvin directly equated the experience of persecution among the Protestants of France with the experience of the apostles to confess the validity of his church. He declared, "Let them, however, know that the apostles in their day experienced the same things that are now happening to us."[37] Calvin pointed out that, like the apostles who were charged in Acts 14:5 with "stirring up the people," so, too, were the Protestants of France blamed for creating tumults and disturbances and any conflict that emerged around them.[38] Just as the apostle Paul was slandered and his teachings distorted, they, too, were maligned with Paul over teachings of the gospel as justification by faith alone.[39] These opponents not

---

32. McNeil, 11.
33. McNeil, 31.
34. Mark Greengrass, "Hidden Transcripts: Secret Histories and Personal Testimonies of Religious Violence in the French Wars of Religion," in *The Massacre in History*, ed. Mark Levene and Penny Roberts (New York: Berghahn Books, 1999), 83–84.
35. See Henri IV, "The Edict of Nantes," in Barbara B. Diefendorf, *The Saint Bartholomew's Day Massacre: A Brief History with Documents* (Boston: Bedford/St. Martins, 2009), 144–47.
36. McNeil, 24.
37. McNeil, 29.
38. He also noted that Elijah and Jesus faced these same accusations. McNeil, 28.
39. Calvin did not explicitly mention the doctrine of justification but implied it by the fact

only acted as "false prophets"; in Calvin's words, they were actually "false apostles."[40] For Calvin, suffering that results from the right preaching of the Word is in fact a mark of true apostolicity since the teachings of the prophets and the apostles provide the foundation of the church (Calvin explored this in more depth in the 1539 edition of the *Institutes* in reference to Eph. 2:20)[41]—not because those teachings point to the apostles but because they point to Christ.

Calvin then asked rhetorically, "What were the apostles to do here? Ought they not to have dissembled for a time, or, rather, laid aside that gospel and deserted it because they saw that it was a seedbed of so many quarrels, the source of so many dangers, the occasion of so many scandals?" The answer is an implied "no," and here again, Calvin equated the circumstances of the apostles to the circumstances of French Protestants. But the answer was no to Calvin because the cause of the disturbances should not be attributed to French Protestants but to the "rock." However, Calvin was purposefully *not* talking here about "Cephas," or Peter, as the rock and Matthew 16, though one would expect him to do so. On the contrary, he intentionally skipped over that most obvious and central issue of ecclesiological dispute in the progression of this portion to supplant Petrine supremacy with Christ. Christ was the Rock that was causing the disturbances, and Calvin referenced Romans 9:33; 1 Peter 2:8; and Isaiah 8:14 in support to essentially say, "But what can you do about that?"[42] In a word, it is better to stumble over the rock of Peter than to stumble over the rock of Christ.[43] Calvin described this as an "assurance" that not only helped the apostles to withstand the dangers of their time when they faced persecution but could sustain the French Protestants' community in their time.[44] In his words, to be involved in disturbances over Christ is "a unique assurance of salvation."[45]

The dedication closes with a final claim to apostolicity through suffering for Christ, and this time by citing Hebrews 11:36–37.[46] Again, the shared experience of imprisonment, torture, and execution led not to doubt but to

---

that there is a struggle over the license to sin, which was a most common critique of the Protestant understanding of the doctrine. McNeil, 29.

40. McNeil, 29.

41. Calvin, *Institutes*, 1.7.2.

42. These Scripture passages are also cited in Calvin's *Institutes*, 1.13.11.

43. Calvin pointed out the slippery slope of reasoning "Christ and all the prophets of God schismatics; Satan's ministers, conversely, the organs of the Holy Spirit." McNeil, 26.

44. McNeil, 29.

45. McNeil, 30.

46. McNeil, 31.

the assurance of salvation. After all, like the French Protestants, the church's fathers were also tortured (11:35–37). Calvin's commentary on Hebrews in 1549 unpacked the parallels further. Like the French Protestants, the patriarchs also pleased God by faith alone.[47] Like the patriarchs, they, too, "wandered in deserts and mountains and in caves and holes in the ground."[48] For Calvin, a flipped paradigm was at work; while it may seem like wandering is a sign of unworthiness for the world (here we can see the shame that was felt in exile), it is actually that the world was not worthy of them to settle since they brought God's blessings with them. It's clear how the commonalities of treatment and circumstance between the patriarchs and matriarchs and French Protestants offered encouragement and strength for Calvin's community in times of adversity. He wrote,

> For we ought not to refuse the Lord's favour of being connected with so many holy men, whom we know to have been exercised and tried by many sufferings. Here indeed are recorded, not the sufferings of a few individuals, but the common persecutions of the Church, and those not for one or two years, but such as continued sometimes from grandfathers even to their grandchildren. No wonder, then, *if it should please God to prove our faith at this day by similar trials;* nor ought we to think that we are forsaken by him, who, we know, cared for the holy fathers who suffered the same before us.[49]

To identify with the same suffering as the patriarchs and matriarchs was to embrace a valid place in the succession of the apostles. After all, as Calvin added to the *Institutes* in 1539, the "covenant" God established with them was so similar in substance and reality that the two were, in fact, the same.[50] This means of confessing the church would also frame the most significant Reformed martyrology of the day.

APOSTOLICITY AND MARTYROLOGY

The claim to apostolicity through the experience of suffering and exile for faith in Christ was reinforced by Reformed martyrology being published

---

47. John Calvin, *Commentaries on the Epistle of Paul the Apostle to the Hebrews*, trans. John Owen (Grand Rapids: Baker, 2009), 11.4., p. 266–68.

48. Calvin did not directly engage with this passage, but the connection is implied in his discussion of verse 38.

49. Calvin, *Hebrews*, 11:37, p. 307, emphasis mine.

50. Calvin, *Institutes*, II.10.2.

in Calvin's Geneva. As a genre, martyrologies have functioned to form communal cohesion and identity, in this case, among a group facing displacement and *diaspora*. Remembrance of those who had been martyred for their Reformed faith served as a means of mobilization and resistance that was all at once social, political, and religious. The importance of remembering Reformed suffering finds deeper layers of meaning when drawing out the political context and the fact that mention of the massacres of French Protestants were intentionally left out of official records. In fact, the Royal Edict of Pacification of 1563 demanded the erasure of all and any mention of sectarian violence from court records.[51] But it is even more complicated than that.

Reformation scholar Mark Greengrass's work has shown how recorded accounts of sectarian violence had a legal function that allowed families to seek restitution or recompense. These accounts nonetheless are hard to come by for a variety of reasons, including the experience of amnesia among survivors after violent trauma as well as the resistance to recording or reporting their experiences. Shame was also at work in these events, and it was also felt on all sides in the aftermath. Survivor shame came to the forefront as communities asked, how did that person survive? Abjuration was very often suspected. While attackers feared being named, victims feared naming attackers, and onlookers feared getting involved, which ensured that silence was the response of choice. The account of Anne de Bourg is instructive here. De Bourg was a member of the Parlement de Paris, the highest court in France, but when he protested the persecution of Protestants in France, he was burned at the stake in 1559; he was an onlooker. The psychology at work in these incidents should illumine the significance of publishing a martyrology, which was in fact a dangerous and complex enterprise to pursue let alone realize. But this is where the city of Geneva, the city of refuge, comes into play.

It became customary for eyewitnesses of sectarian violence to flee to the city or even send written accounts of persecution in hopes of advocacy.[52] Advocacy took many forms, including through the publication of a martyrology. Geneva's printing industry was crucial to the resistance, persistence, and growth of Protestantism in France,[53] even though its

---

51. Greengrass, "Hidden Transcripts," 81–82.

52. I want to express my gratitude to two research TAs who gathered data on this topic for me: Jonathan Liversedge and Katherine Goodwin.

53. Geneva was cited numerous times in the Edict of Chateaubriand for its disruptive publishing. Navigating censorship was a complex endeavor for printers: see Jennifer Powell McNutt, "Partnering

"intrusions" in French church affairs were not always welcome.[54] Whether psalm books, French Bibles, Bible commentaries, or theological treatises, printing Protestant literature from Geneva found shared purpose and natural alliance with the publication of French martyrology. Methodologically speaking, Alexandre Ganoczy's "hermeneutical circle" could be expanded to include the latter for how much these sources intersect and mutually confirm one another.[55]

Our brief focus will be on the Dutch Protestant Jean Crespin, who found refuge in Geneva in 1538 after forced separation from his pregnant wife and loss of livelihood. Once there, he turned from the law profession to the printing industry, though both were a profession of advocacy in their day and age. In 1554 he published two of his most important works,[56] his *History of the Martyrs, Persecuted and Put to Death for the Truth of the Gospel, Since the Times of the Apostles until the Present*[57] and a reissue of his French Bible, one of many vernacular Bibles being published by refugee printers. Unsurprisingly, given the title, Crespin's martyrology played a key role in advancing the connection that the true apostle is not the one who inflicts suffering on others but the one who suffers at the hands of others for the purity of their faith in Christ.

The apostolic link is strong in not only the content of the book but its material culture. Intentionally, Crespin begins the story of French Protestant persecution with the New Testament church and the persecution experienced by the apostles under Nero. The first volume extends to John Wyclif, and then it pivots into a new age. The denial of innovation is implicit; they are not a branch without a root and trunk. The very first page of the first book includes in the margins Tertullian's famous words to set the stage: "The blood of the martyrs is the seed of the church."[58]

Like Calvin before him, Crespin flips the paradigm of tribulation on its head from the first words. The "worldly" (*les mondains*) are those who consider

---

with Pastors: How Early Modern Printers Advanced the Reformation" in *Technē: Christian Visions of Technology*, ed. Gerald Hiestand and Todd A. Wilson (Eugene, OR: Cascade, 2022), 221–36.

54. Michael W. Bruening, *Refusing to Kiss the Slipper: Opposition to Calvinism in the Francophone Reformation*, Oxford Studies in Historical Theology (Oxford: Oxford University Press, 2021).

55. Citing Alexandre Ganoczy in David Steinmetz, *Calvin in Context* (Oxford: Oxford University Press, 2010), 64.

56. Jennifer Powell McNutt, "The Bible for Refugees in Calvin's Geneva," in *Global Migration and Christian Faith*, ed. M. Daniel Carroll R. and Vincent Bacote (Eugene, OR: Wipf & Stock, 2021), 18–36.

57. No critical edition or translation exists today in either modern French or English.

58. Jean Crespin, *Histoire des martyrs persecutez et mis à mort pour la verité de l'evangile, depuis le temps des apostres jusques à present (1619)*, Histoire Ecclesiastique et Actes des Martyr (Toulouse: Société des Livres Religieux, 1885), bk. 1, 1.

their lives and works as pleasing to God because they are *not* visited by chastisements and the mocking of other Christians compared to those leaving behind family, inheritance, life, and sacrificing body and soul for Christ. Crespin interprets this reasoning through the lens of 1 Corinthians 1:18 and 23, meaning that those of the world see the cross of Christ as folly and scandal rather than Christian obligation. The worldly honor the flesh, earthly honor, and the kindness of the world over eternal life and the glory promised there. Again, like Calvin (though written from the safety of Geneva), the persecuted are in a sense greatly blessed by God since, in his words, "affliction can serve as confirmation of the faith."[59] This observation finds important resonance for those sixteenth-century martyrs whom Crespin recounts as arrested for preaching the gospel, reading the Bible, owning a Bible, or printing and selling the Bible. Their stories include the reciting of Scripture at court and the singing of psalms from prison to execution. In Crespin's account, their boldness comes from rootedness in God's Word. Examples abound of this prominent theological accent at work in early Reformed ecclesiology and as it developed within a context of exile, persecution, and diaspora. As the interior plate of French printer Christophe Plantin's 1577 Dutch Bible further confirmed, "Apostles will be Persecuted."[60]

EXPLORING EXILIC ECCLESIOLOGY

"Exilic ecclesiology," as I am developing here to represent early modern Reformed ecclesiology in theology and praxis, claims apostolicity through the shared experience of suffering and persecution due to the right preaching of the Word. Because the status of apostolicity is able to bypass Petrine supremacy postconciliarism, and according to the reasoning of the Reformers, the church body requires no tether of place, institution, or person apart from Christ as revealed through God's Word, which is the teaching of the prophets and apostles and the foundation of the church (Eph. 2:20) in so far as it points to Christ the stumbling stone. By this reasoning, Reformed suffering is not an experience apart from Christ but *because* of Christ. Importantly, in their reading, Reformed suffering is not the cause of salvation—since only Christ's suffering is the cause—but a *sign of* salvation. And so suffering is a paradoxical comfort because it offers assurance.

---

59. Crespin, "Preface monstrant une conformité des persecutions et des martyr de ces dernier temps a ceux de la premier eglise," xxxvii.

60. Bart A. Rosier, *The Bible in Print: Netherlandish Bible Illustration in the Sixteenth Century*, trans. Chris F. Weterings, vol. 1 (Leiden: Foleor, 1997), 51, #319.

Exilic ecclesiology meanwhile mirrors the early apostolic church in terms of a church on the move, unbound by place but always tethered to Christ in apostolicity. It is why French Protestants could worship God in the meadow under cover of night, in the cave, or in the streambed under duress. It is why French Protestants favored patriarchal stories of exile and migration and even the Apocrypha's 1 and 2 Maccabees but especially the Psalms, which Calvin believed gave voice to the very soul of the Christian life, particularly in the worship context.[61] French Protestant behavior reflects a fundamental shift in medieval thinking about access to God. Whereas the medieval church rooted access to God through the mediation of the priest (and of course, in a pre–printing press era this makes sense), the Reformed clasped an increasingly accessible although censored Bible. It is why smuggling and hiding French Protestant Bibles became so precious, like early Christians unwilling to become *traditores* by refusing to hand over the scrolls of Scripture under threat of execution.

The understanding here is that anywhere the Bible is, access to God and the hearing of the good news of Jesus Christ through the working of the Holy Spirit is possible. Where the Bible goes, so goes the promise of Christian freedom. Calvin's preface to the 1546 French Bible describes it as the keys to the kingdom.[62] Beza's preface to the 1588 French Bible describes it as the "Temple, the Tabernacle, the Ark."[63] To encounter the Bible is to enter the presence of God—but not just any Bible. Apostolicity was further identified with the use of common language. That is, to preach in the common language so that the gospel could be understood was to preach as the apostles intended. This thinking is evident in other Protestant traditions facing persecution as well. William Tyndale's *The Obedience of a Christian Man* (1528) was published two years after the burning of his New Testament. In the letter to the reader, he made this case, stating, "All that the apostles preached were no doubt preached in the mother tongue."[64]

Preaching in the common tongue among common people was a claim to apostolic succession.[65] Lest it be forgotten, the right to preach was extended

---

61. Karin Maag, *Lifting Hearts to the Lord: Worship with John Calvin in Sixteenth-Century Geneva* (Grand Rapids: Eerdmans, 2016).

62. John Calvin, "Si je voulois icy," *La Bible* (Geneve: Jehan Girard, 1546): "C'est la clef qui nous ouvre le royaume de Dieu pour nous y introduire."

63. Theodore Beza, "A tous vrais amateurs de la verité de Dieu," *La Bible Qvi est Tovte la Saincte Escritvre dv Vieil & du Nouueau Testament* (Geneve: [Jeremie des Planches], 1588), 5.

64. David Daniell, *William Tyndale: A Biography* (New Haven, CT: Yale University Press, 1994), 229.

65. This, too, found its inception among the Waldensians: Euan Cameron, *The Reformation of the Heretics: The Waldenses of the Alps, 1480–1580* (Oxford: Clarendon, 1984), 121–25.

beyond male clergy alone among the Waldensians back in the twelfth and thirteenth century, and their group joined the Reformed Church certainly by 1555 (although it was already happening in 1532). Did not Christ's commission at the ascension to go and preach to all the world include them too, they asked in response to being named heretical? In praxis, exilic ecclesiology allowed for unusual circumstances for the sake of the gospel, and this shaped the institutional functioning of a church in crisis and under duress. Consider that Geneva's academy trained pastors and then immediately ordained them even before they had a calling from a church, so that wherever they ended up they would be ready to serve.[66] It was a mobilization of the clerical force to be equipped and adept for mobility and locality. Exilic ecclesiology allowed (though exceptionally) temporary suspension of polity for women to preach out of necessity and emergency as Reformation scholar John Thompson has shown.[67] The needs of the church could, at times, outweigh the decorum and right order of early modern sensibilities; after all, women's silence was a matter of *adiaphora* according to Calvin's commentary on 1 Corinthians 14:34–40.

In summary, the early modern French Reformed mindset regarded the experience of persecution for faith in Christ as treatment befitting an apostle, and the prophets and patriarchs before them. Importantly, this exilic perspective on ecclesiology did not equate human suffering with the *cause* of salvation but as the *indication* of salvation secured through Christ, which is the direct result of right belief and right preaching of the Word (i.e., the stumbling stone of Christ). For this reason, suffering does not rival the marks of the church but confirms them so that interpreting suffering as salvific assurance works in tandem with Christ and the Bible in the confession of the church. Exilic ecclesiology recognizes that there is no hope in the face of suffering apart from a God who sees and advocates for the sufferer. In this way, exilic ecclesiology wholly hinges on the freedom of a benevolent God to enact God's will as God wills. To a community that is not free, a sovereign God is the only promise of freedom.

Consider again Calvin's dedication of the *Institutes*. There he explored the idea of the hidden nature of the true church. Late medieval conciliarism

---

66. Karin Maag, *Seminary or University? The Genevan Academy and Reformed Higher Education, 1560–1620* (Aldershot, UK: Scolar, 1995).

67. John L. Thompson, "Polity as *Adiaphora* in John Calvin: The Strange Case of Women's Silence in Church," presented at the Sixteenth Century Studies Conference in Philadelphia, October 1991. Thompson engages with Jane Dempsey Douglass's works, namely, "Christian Freedom: What Calvin Learned at the School of Women," *Church History* 53 (1984): 155–73; and *Women, Freedom, and Calvin* (Philadelphia: Westminster, 1985).

allowed him to explore the visible and invisible sides of ecclesiology without having to accept the accusation of schismatic or innovator; from his standpoint, apostolic succession was not in jeopardy. In reference to Daniel 3, Calvin noted that God preserves true believers, even in Babylon.[68] He declared, "God preserves his own children from extinction."[69]

As Calvin wrote these words, he had also just penned another piece— this one for the first French Bible translated from original languages. The Bible was the vision of the Waldensians or Vaudois who joined the Reformed cause in 1532. A new, complete French translation was commissioned that year to be completed by Calvin's cousin, Pierre-Robert Olivétan. The 1535 Olivétan Bible was printed in June at the Vaudois's expense in Neuchâtel.[70] Calvin contributed to it by writing three prefaces, two of which were only published in Wingle's 1535 edition and Calvin's preface to Olivetan's French New Testament, which gained prominence beyond the 1535 Bible to be discussed here. Calvin's preface to the New Testament provides the first glimpse into his newly emerging and largely self-taught theology.[71] The seeds of the first draft of his *Institutes* were already present, though underdeveloped since he was working on both pieces at the same time.[72]

Calvin's preface offers an ambitious summary of the entire story of salvation, spanning from the point of creation to the fall to the coming of the "Mediator" Jesus Christ.[73] Importantly, there is really no part of the preface that does not speak to an audience facing oppression and exile. For them, Calvin stressed allusions of Paul's affirmation in Romans 8 that no crisis of suffering and evil could separate believers from the love of God. He highlighted that Christ's own experience of suffering should remind believers that earthly prosperity was not promised. For them, Calvin taught to expect and accept "banishments, proscriptions, privation from good

---

68. Calvin, "Dedication," ed., McNeil, *Institutes*, 26.

69. Calvin, "Dedication," ed., McNeil, 25.

70. "Au Lecteur de la Bible," in *La Bible Qui est toute la Saincte escripture* . . . (Neuchâtel: Pierre de Wingle, 1535): "Les Vaudois, peuple évangélique, Ont mis ce thrésor en publique."

71. *Ioannis Calvini opera quae supersunt omnia*, 9:791; John Calvin, "Preface to Olivétan's New Testament," *Calvin Commentaries*, vol. 23, Library of Christian Classics, ed. and trans. Joseph Haroutunian (Philadelphia: Westminster, 2009), 58–73.

72. I first delivered this research for the inaugural lecture of my Franklin S. Dyrness Chair on April 13, 2022, at Wheaton College. For more about my work on Reformation Bibles, see McNutt, "Bible for Refugees in Calvin's Geneva," 18–36.

73. The piece was well suited to move from introducing the New Testament to introducing the complete Bible from 1543. The preface is identified by several titles: "Preface Showing How Christ Is the End of the Law" and "To All Those Who Love Christ." It begins with the phrase "God the Creator / Dieu le Créature . . ." The title "Epistle to the Faithful Showing That Christ Is the End of the Law" was added to the 1534 preface after 1543.

and riches" as the consequence of authentically following Jesus body, heart, and soul. Calvin wrote,

> But we know that if we shall be banished from one country, the whole earth is the Lord's, and if we be thrown out of the earth itself, nonetheless we shall not be outside of his Kingdom. [We know] that when we are despoiled and impoverished, we have a Father who is rich enough to nourish us; even that Jesus Christ was made poor, so that we might follow him in his poverty. Will there be afflictions, prisons, tortures, torments? But we know by the example of Jesus Christ that this is the way to arrive at glory. Finally, will there be death? But death does not do away with a life that is worth having.[74]

In this way, Calvin shaped an *expectation* of persecution, suffering, banishment, and even death. Repeating the famous words of early church father Tertullian, that "the blood of the martyrs is the seed of the church,"[75] Calvin taught that suffering was expected for those following in the footsteps of Christ and of the apostolic Christians. And yet a journey of this nature could not be undertaken apart from God's active, sustaining, and restorative activity. Calvin viewed the salvation story through Exodus and the flight from Egypt.

For God to liberate Israel from an oppressive king was a welcome promise to French Protestants facing the oppression of their king. Calvin wrote, "[God] drew them away from the subjection to Pharaoh the king of Egypt, under whom they were held down and oppressed, to deliver them and set them at liberty."[76] He stressed how God did not desert his people in their journey but ensured their well-being by joining their flight from day to night. The goodness of God was shown in the way he provided food for them (i.e., manna) and led them to a better home in fulfillment of his promise, all traits that Calvin identified with God's fatherhood. Moreover, God's commitment to show solidarity to his people rendered God himself "a fugitive in their midst."[77]

God not only stood on the side of the displaced, but he became one of them in order to fulfill his promise to give them an eternal home.[78]

---

74. Calvin, "Preface to Olivétan's New Testament," 67–68.
75. Calvin, "Preface to Olivétan's New Testament," 68.
76. Calvin, "Preface to Olivétan's New Testament," 60.
77. Calvin, "Preface to Olivétan's New Testament," 60. See Heiko Oberman, *John Calvin and the Reformation of the Refugees* (Geneva: Droz, 2009).
78. Calvin, "Preface to Olivétan's New Testament," 64.

The exilic outlook is clear—modeled by God's own faithfulness and intended for Calvin's congregation, but the mindset is also meant for more than Calvin's congregation. For him, the Christian life for all believers is likened to an exilic journey—displaced in this world and seeking the true home. Calvin taught an exilic mindset for the Christ follower when he declared in the *Institutes*, "If heaven is our homeland, what else is the earth but our place of exile."[79] The declaration comes in chapter 9 of book 3, a chapter dedicated to meditating on the future life, which was added to the *Institutes* in 1539 during Calvin's second experience of exile. Fascinatingly, the Protestant assurance afforded by the doctrine of justification is on full display here; Calvin actually looked forward to the last judgment when Christ will return and the resurrection take place: "If believers' eyes are turned to the power of the resurrection, in their hearts the cross of Christ will at last triumph over the devil, flesh, sin, and wicked men."[80] With uncommon confidence, Calvin exhibited no dread at the thought of coming face-to-face with God as Judge since, as he explained in the preface to the French New Testament, God is on the side of the displaced who are his true apostles on earth. The suffering experienced from following and proclaiming Christ is redeemed by a God who frees his people from bondage. Suffering for Christ is assurance of salvation.

WEIGHING EXILIC ECCLESIOLOGY

This paper has sought to show how confessing the apostolicity of the church became central to the early modern Reformed tradition as it navigated faith and ministry unmoored from the acceptance and recognition of both the Roman Church and the French monarchy (with the most notable exception of King Henri IV). To be bound to the universality of Christ's church required the claim of apostolicity, which became located in the experience of suffering because of the gospel, or the right preaching of the Word, which Calvin adopted in his dedication as the first mark of the true church. Suffering proved to be a locus of continuity with the experience of the apostolic church and, through a covenantal lens, to the patriarchs of the Old Testament.

But there is an elephant in the room, and it is Anabaptists. They, too, regarded suffering as confirmation of apostolicity; the Dutch Anabaptist

79. Calvin, *Institutes*, ed. McNeil: 3.9.4.
80. Calvin, *Institutes*, ed. McNeil: 3.9.5–6.

Martyr's Mirror is an excellent parallel and counterexample to the Dutch Reformed *History of the Martyrs*.[81] Both featured their communities in line to inherit the apostolic succession through suffering for the gospel by beginning their martyrologies with the New Testament church. Both claimed that suffering, exile, persecution, and martyrdom can provide confirmation of their right teaching as the true followers of Christ. Both navigated *diaspora*, though surely it is worth considering that the Anabaptists faced displacement without a mother church while French Protestants benefited immensely from the city of Geneva.[82] In both cases, suffering shaped their confession of the church, and in the French Reformed tradition, as has been shown here, suffering functioned early on to confirm the marks of the church.

With this comparison, the limits of exilic ecclesiology can be recognized in so far as it is highly dependent on the social circumstances of one's position. In fact, the church has been in this position before. One day in 313, suffering and martyrdom was the highest expression of piety that early Christians could offer God, and the next day, with the passing of the Edict of Milan, it was no longer possible to receive capital punishment for faith in Christ. Were they more assured Christians the day before? The early church struggled to work this out, and the Desert Fathers and Mothers of the hermitic movement bore witness to that complexity. Similarly, if the suffering of a Christian is a discernible means of evaluating one's assurance of salvation and relationship with the true church, then who is the victim in the story of the Reformation? As Jesse Spohnholz's work has shown, every group in the Reformation experienced some level of dislocation due to how the Reformation intersected with and exacerbated the early modern refugee crisis (though again, the Anabaptists and the Reformed bore the brunt of displacement).[83] It is not easy to work out the answer given the shifting power differentials, borders, and lines of succession,[84] which no doubt gets at the heart of the fury that has so often been directed at Calvin for his part in the execution of Michael Servetus.

French Reformed exilic ecclesiology faced other challenges, and one of

---

81. Thieleman J. van Braght, *The Bloody Theater or Martyrs Mirror of the Defenseless Christians*, trans. Joseph F. Sohm, 2nd ed. (Eng. repr., Scottdale, PA: Herald, 1938). The Waldensian book was called *Book of the Elect*. Cameron, *Reformation of the Heretics*, 120.

82. The Moravian princes offered only a temporary location for Anabaptist refuge.

83. Jesse Spohnholz, "Refugees," in *Calvin in Context*, ed. R. Ward Holder (Cambridge: Cambridge University Press, 2019), 150.

84. Further complicated by the Peace of Augsburg's policy of *cuius religio eius regio* ("whose realm, their religion").

the most difficult ones was a tendency toward passivity, which is also evident in the historical record.[85] Consider Calvin's dedication in the *Institutes* again. At the close, he talked about awaiting "the strong hand of the Lord, which will surely appear in due season, coming forth armed to deliver the poor from their affliction and also to punish their despisers, who now exult with such great assurance."[86] I will make two points regarding this:

French Reformed theology is left with the quandary of discerning suffering, if even possible. The inability to discern the will of God in the context of disastrous events leads to questions about God's relationship with evil, an issue that Calvin dealt with on many occasions. Did God will this? Is this God's discipline for my sin? Alternatively, is this a sign that I am somehow favored (which is the answer that both Calvin and Crespin gave in different settings)? Even survival becomes part of God's secret providence, which can limit activism and potentially allow the persistence of victimization.[87] Pointing to suffering as a mark of apostolicity must reckon with God's intentions in the circumstances of the time, which even by Calvin's estimation is mysterious since suffering can have many different purposes in the life of the believer as discipline, testing, and even judgment.

The French Reformed tradition became caught in the tension between accepting suffering (as possibly God's will) and resisting suffering, which certainly plays out in the wars of religion and response to the St. Bartholomew's Day Massacre (1572). This ambivalence is not as present in the Anabaptist tradition after the debacle at Münster in 1534 and through the legacy of Menno Simons, which turned to nonresistance and maintains a separatist, pure-church ecclesiology that the Reformed tradition eschews. Meanwhile, the French Reformed tradition navigated the following questions: How can a church in exile embrace exile without elevating monastic withdrawal (Anabaptists were accused, meanwhile, of doing that)? How does a church in exile avoid a gnostic regard for the suffering body, which is destined for bodily resurrection (another objection that Calvin raised against Anabaptism)? How can one maintain an eschatological outlook that also waits patiently for Christ's return rather than seeking to cause it (another concern with Anabaptism)? How can the exilic church appreciate that while hope is found in the next life, where one's citizenship lies, yet God still calls the church to work in this life for his glory and purpose? All of these questions and dynamics were at work in the rich and complex shaping of

---

85. Greengrass, "Hidden Transcripts," 83.
86. Calvin, "Dedication," ed. McNeil, 31.
87. Greengrass explores the trauma of survival as well. Greengrass, "Hidden Transcripts," 81.

the early modern French Reformed Church and in Calvin's theology as it sought to dodge the challenges of fatalism (i.e., there is no justice here) and the dangers of Gnosticism (i.e., the suffering of our bodies does not matter).

But another challenge came as suffering was eventually mitigated over time (though not until the Napoleonic era). French Reformed ecclesiology had to understand its apostolic identity apart from the experience of what could be described as social and political suffering, thereby mirroring the patterns and complexities of the post-Constantinian church. Under Calvin, the Reformed church was taught faithful suffering by accepting one's allotted circumstances and waiting patiently on God's intercession. This so permeated the Reformed understanding of the time that it is echoed in the writing of Geneva's early Reformer Marie Dentière to the patron queen and theologian Marguerite of Navarre:[88] "The true pastors and ministers of Jesus are persecuted, banished, and exiled."[89] Indeed, this is how she validated Calvin's legitimacy since it was he who had recently been exiled by civic leaders in Geneva. The greatest challenge came with shifting power dynamics and the need to then advocate for justice and work toward the end of suffering for others. It is an uncontested fact that Calvin and Geneva worked tirelessly as advocates to end the suffering of French Protestants in France (though not without internal contention),[90] but more baffling are the cases in which Reformed churches moved from positions of persecuted minority to persecutor, as evident in the treatment of Anabaptists and later in the support and activity of the slave trade, slave ownership, and reaching all the way to apartheid.[91]

In closing, in Matthew 5, the Beatitudes of the Sermon on the Mount,

---

88. For an overview of Marguerite of Navarre's contribution, see Jennifer Powell McNutt's "In Her Own Words and Actions: Marguerite of Navarre (1492–1549), as a Theologian and Patron of Evangelicals," in *Women Reformers: Protestant Voices in Early Modern Europe*, ed. Kirsi Stjerna (Minneapolis: Fortress, 2022), 153–61.

89. Marie Dentière, *Epistre tres utile faicte et composée par une femme Chrestienne de Tornay, Envoyée à la Royne de Navarre seur du Roy de France, Contre Les Turcz, Iuifz, Infideles, Faulx Chretiens, Anabaptistes, et Lutheriens* (Geneve: Jean Gérard, 1539). She was referring to Calvin and Guillaume Farel here: Marie Dentière, "Epistle to Marguerite de Navarre," in Epistle to Marguerite de Navarre and Preface to a Sermon by John Calvin, ed. and trans. Mary B. McKinley (Chicago: University of Chicago, 2004), 87.

90. See Esther Chung-Kim, "Aid for Refugees: Religion, Migration, and Poor Relief in Sixteenth-Century Geneva," *Reformation & Renaissance Review* 20, no. 1 (2018): 4–17. During the twentieth century, French Protestants at Le Chambon showed courageous support of the Jews during the Holocaust by hiding many thousands of Jews fleeing Nazi occupation. It is often reasoned that their compassion for the suffering of the Jews came from their own experiences of genocide for significant periods in French history.

91. John de Gruchy, "Calvin(ism) and Apartheid in South Africa in the Twentieth Century: The Making and Unmaking of Racial Ideology," in *Calvin and His Influence, 1509–2009*, ed. Irena Backus and Philip Benedict (Oxford: Oxford University Press, 2011), 306–18.

Jesus declared blessing for those who are persecuted for his sake, and this blessing would be a source of comfort for French Reformed Protestants facing exile and persecution, and it is indeed a comfort for all who suffer for Christ today. But the search for assurance of salvation is not resolved by the sometimes fleeting or temporary experiences of suffering, though suffering for the faith should be expected at some level and perhaps in different seasons of the Christian life. Like the mobility of its people, an exilic ecclesiology, too, must adapt to shifting circumstances, especially in those moments when the community is no longer in the social and political position of the victim but in the position of power, so that they can act as a Christlike neighbor to friend and enemy alike. Followers of Jesus Christ should expect to suffer even as they also remember that assurance is found not in the suffering of the believer but in Jesus Christ, the one who suffered on behalf of the believer. As Calvin wrote later in his *Harmony of the Gospels* (1555), the foundation of the Christian faith rests in God's Word, but assurance is only fully sealed by the Holy Spirit no matter the circumstances that are faced.[92]

---

92. Calvin, *Commentary on a Harmony of the Evangelists, Matthew, Mark, and Luke*, trans. William Pringle (Grand Rapids: Baker, 1981), 5.

CHAPTER 10

BOUND TOGETHER IN THE HOLY FIRE

The Holiness of the Church and Ecclesial Sin

DANIEL LEE HILL

INTRODUCTION

The Christian Scriptures, creeds, and tradition consistently affirm that the church is a holy people set apart by the holy God and called to a life of holiness. The Apostles' and Nicene Creeds both affirm faith in this distinctive mark of the church, underscoring its importance to the earliest Christian communities. So much so that in earlier eras the moral purity of the Christian community and willingness of those selfsame Christians to die for their faith were viewed as an authentication of the gospel message. Ephraim Radner summarizes the disposition of many of the early apologists aptly: "The critical test for [the validity of Christianity] lay in the manner in which Christians actually exhibited the holiness that they claimed was gained from them by God's Word come in Jesus. . . . Christians, [the apologists] asserted, are demonstrably better, holier, more righteous, and more loving people than non-Christians."[1]

Yet to the ears of modern readers, such a claim rings strange and somewhat hollow. In recent years, theologians and ecumenists alike have realized

---

1. Ephraim Radner, *Hope among the Fragments: The Broken Church and Its Engagement of Scripture* (Grand Rapids: Brazos, 2004), 166. E.g., see Athenagoras of Athens, *A Plea for the Christians*, trans. B. P. Pratten, in *The Ante-Nicene Fathers*, ed. Alexander Roberts, James Donaldson, and A. Cleveland Coxe, vol. 2 (Buffalo: Christian Literature Company, 1885), 146.

that the ecclesial community's claim to holiness is difficult to square with the sins that mark its life. Berkouwer highlighted this tension exactly, asking, "Can this unmistakable claim be proved? Is it not flagrantly contradicted by countless facts?"[2] Karl Rahner was even more pointed:

> Christianity has always declared, "I believe in the holy Church." Again and again in the course of history the question has arisen where this church is to be found which so confidently declares itself to be a holy Church. . . . Again and again, on the basis of this article of the creed, the concrete Church has been rejected as sinful; again and again some new church has been founded as the true and holy one, and declared to be the true Church of God and of his Christ.[3]

The question of the church's holiness is all the more pressing when held up against the concrete reality of the sins that litter the church's life in the world. Indeed, the church has frequently shown herself to be a morally compromised community. Whether it is her participation in the horrors of the Shoah, the Rwandan genocide, the tyranny of Pinochet, the erasure of indigenous populations in the Americas, or the trans-Atlantic and Pacific slave trades, it seems that the church has often failed to display any semblance of moral or ethical distinctiveness over against her nonbelieving neighbors.[4] What then does it mean to confess faith in the church's holiness in light of her participation in the "sins of the world"? In this paper, I will articulate the grammar of the Christian confession of faith in the church's holiness with special attention to how the church's holiness pertains to the

2. G. C. Berkouwer, *The Church*, Studies in Dogmatics, trans. James E. Davison (Grand Rapids: Eerdmans, 1976), 313.

3. Karl Rahner, "The Church of Sinners," in *Concerning Vatican Council II*, vol. 6 of *Theological Investigations*, trans. Boniface Kruger (Baltimore: Helicon, 1969), 253.

4. On the church's responsibility vis-à-vis the Rwandan genocide, see Ephraim Radner, *A Brutal Unity: The Spiritual Politics of the Christian Church* (Waco, TX: Baylor University Press, 2012), 29–50. On the church's involvement in the Shoah, see Mary M. Solberg, ed. and trans., *A Church Undone: Documents from the German Christian Faith Movement, 1932–1940* (Minneapolis: Fortress, 2015). On the church's complicity in Pinochet's regime, see William T. Cavanaugh, *Torture and Eucharist: Theology, Politics, and the Body of Christ*, Challenges in Contemporary Theology (repr., Malden, MA: Wiley Blackwell, 2002). On the church's participation in the erasure of indigenous peoples in the US, see George E. Tinker, *Missionary Conquest: The Gospel and Native American Cultural Genocide* (Minneapolis: Fortress, 1993); Shaun Retallick, "Christological Ecclesiology and Reconciliation: A Way Forward for the Catholic Church," *Journal of the Council for Research on Religion* 4, no. 1 (2022): 1–11. On the church's participation in the trans-Atlantic slave trade, see Willie James Jennings, *The Christian Imagination: Theology and the Origins of Race* (New Haven, CT: Yale University Press, 2010). On the church's participation in the lesser-known trans-Pacific slave trade, see Tatiana Seijas, *Asian Slaves in Colonial Mexico: From Chinos to Indians*, Cambridge Latin American Studies (Cambridge: Cambridge University Press, 2015).

issue of ecclesial sin. In it I will argue that the church is holy insofar as it is set apart as the means through which God bears witness to himself as reconciler and judge, prefiguring his eschatological reconciliation of the cosmos and judgment of the world.

THE HOLINESS OF THE CHURCH IN LIGHT OF ECCLESIAL SIN

At least since the time of the Protestant Reformation, although perhaps dating back to the Donatist controversy, the church's sinfulness creates a kind of dissonance around this particular *nota ecclesia*. While notions of collective culpability and responsibility are notoriously fraught, the fact of the matter remains that the church is a community of sinners who consistently, collectively, and individually commit heinous acts of sin. What does it mean for the church to be holy when branches disagree on central doctrines or entire communions engage in egregious sin? Two of the more prominent responses to this question are worth engaging briefly: the predication of sin to the church's members and the identification of the church as *simul justus et peccator*.

A HOLY CHURCH WITH SINFUL MEMBERS

One approach to navigating the complex confession of the church's holiness in light of the reality of Christian sin has been to draw a line of demarcation between the church as a whole and the individual members that constitute her body, predicating holiness to the former and sin to the latter.[5] For example, Roch Kereszty wrote, "The church is the spotless bride of Christ and thereby his body itself. The church, insofar as it is the holy bride of Christ, cannot commit a sin. Nevertheless, she accepts solidarity with her sinful members."[6] While much more prominent before the events of Vatican II, on this account the church itself is not complicit or contaminated by ecclesial evil, only the individual persons within her body who commit such acts. Accordingly, the church's holiness remains intact, pure, and undefiled even in spite of the egregious acts of her members. The church is morally pure; her sinful members are not.[7]

---

5. Avery Dulles, *Models of the Church: A Critical Assessment of the Church in All Its Aspects* (New York: Doubleday, 1974), 125.

6. Roch A. Kereszty, *The Church of God in Jesus Christ: A Catholic Ecclesiology* (Washington, DC: Catholic University of America Press, 2019), 142. See also Boris Bobrinskoy, *The Mystery of the Church: A Course in Orthodox Dogmatic Theology*, trans. Michael Breck (Yonkers, NY: St. Vladimir's Seminary Press, 2012), 140–42.

7. Michael Pomazansky, *Orthodox Dogmatic Theology: A Concise Exposition*, trans. Seraphim Rose (Jordanville, NY: Holy Trinity Monastery, 1973), 244.

But this decision to implicate only the members in the sins of the church, ultimately, does not appear to be viable. For one thing, this seems to reduce the body of Christ to a mere aggregate of individuals. As Radner argues, the result is that "'division' and 'sin' are made impossible indicators of any real church. On the one hand, local congregations are not in fact the 'Church as such' but merely aggregates of believers 'on their own way' to a final resting place in the Church; and, on the other, 'division' therefore and its attendant or related vices are matters that touch individual choice, never aggregates of such choices."[8] But surely the church is more than a gathering of individual monads, as Holy Scripture describes it as both an institution (1 Peter 2:4–5, 9) and a living organism (Eph. 4:15–16).[9] Furthermore, what would it mean for a sin to be predicated of all of the church's members but not the body as a whole? As Hans Urs von Balthasar posited, the "Church abstracted from her members is no longer the church. Her destiny is in her members, theirs in her. The sins of the sons and daughters reflect back on the mother."[10] Balthasar's concern is apt. A body, ecclesial or otherwise, disassociated from the members that comprise it ceases to be a body in any meaningful sense of the term.

A JUSTIFIED AND SINFUL COMMUNION

More prominent in the twentieth century has been the attempt to retrieve and apply some form of Luther's insights regarding the Christian's status as *simul justus et peccator*, that is, as simultaneously justified and sinful. For Luther, every Christian exists in this state as they await the return of Christ and their subsequent glorification, an insight he was willing to extend to the church as a whole. "The Church will never be without the impious and the hypocrites, because sins do not cease. . . . The Church is holy, and yet not holy."[11] For those who wish to follow Luther, we might say that the church's holiness is a result of her faith in Christ even while her earthly life

---

8. Radner, *Brutal Unity*, 133.
9. Bavinck wrote, "The gathered company of believers on earth is not only structured charismatically but also institutionally. It is not only itself the possession of Christ but also serves to win others for Christ. It is a gathered company (*coetus*) but also the mother of believers (*mater fidelium*); an organism but also an institution; a goal but also a means to that goal." Herman Bavinck, *Reformed Dogmatics*, trans. John Vriend (Grand Rapids: Baker Academic, 2006), 3:303.
10. Hans Urs von Balthasar, "*Casta Meretrix*," in *Explorations in Theology*, vol. 2, *Spouse of the Word*, trans. A. V. Littledale (San Francisco: Ignatius Press, 1991), 261.
11. "Ecclesia nunquam sit sine impiis et hypocritis quia peccatum non cessat. . . . Ecclesia sit sancta, et tamen non sancta, aliquis sit iustus, et tamen non sit iustus, beatus alius et non beatus" (Martin Luther, *Luthers Werke: Kritische Gesamtausgabe* [Schriften], 73 vols. (Weimar: H. Böhlau, 1883–2009), 39:1, 515). On the ecumenical promise of Luther's application of the *simul* to the church as a whole, see Robert Kress, "*Simul Justus et Peccator*: Ecclesiological and Ecumenical Perspectives," *Horizons* 11, no. 2 (1984): 255–75.

is filled with sin. On this account, the church is truly holy, but it possesses an invisible holiness, one that is only perceivable with the eyes of faith. But lest this holiness be conditioned on account of the church's works, it remains present in spite of her sins. For someone like G. C. Berkouwer, this should not lead us to an inert or tacit acceptance of the church's sinfulness. Rather, it should inspire the church "to a visible intolerance" of the *simul*, ever striving to fulfill the church's commission of walking in the truth.[12]

This approach is not without significant merits, namely, in the way it takes seriously both the church's sin and the promises of the gospel. But it still falls short in that it is unclear how this actually addresses the issue of the church's *holiness*. The question at hand is what does it mean to say that a church whose hands are stained with blood is also holy? To answer that it is so because the church is simultaneously justified and sinful seems to avoid the question altogether. Minimally, the explicit connection between the church's present holiness and its status as justified and sinful requires elucidation. Presumably, one could eschatologize the church's holiness, a move found in the work of John Calvin and Wilhelmus Brakel.[13] Here it might be argued that identifying the church in the saeculum as *simul justus et peccator* anticipates the full realization of the church's holiness in the eschatological kingdom. But in the Apostles' and Nicene Creeds, we claim to *believe* in the Holy Spirit and, subsequently, in the church's holiness. In short, holiness is an object of faith, not an object of hope. As Karl Rahner noted, we cannot relegate the holiness of the church to the realm of anticipation, because Holy Scripture (e.g., 1 Peter 2:9) and, importantly in Rahner's case, church tradition and doctrine decree that the church is a "holy nation" even as it journeys in the saeculum.[14] And if that is the

---

12. Berkouwer, *The Church*, 355–57.

13. Calvin wrote, "The church's holiness is not yet complete. The church is holy, then, in the sense that it is daily advancing and is not yet perfect: it makes progress from day to day but has not yet reached its goal of holiness." John Calvin, *Institutes of the Christian Religion*, 2 vols., ed. John T. McNeill, trans. Ford Lewis Battles, Library of Christian Classics (Philadelphia: Westminster, 1960), 4.1.17. Elsewhere, Calvin commented on Ephesians 5:27, writing, "Paul does not state what has been done, but for what purpose Christ has cleansed his church. . . . We do not deny that the holiness of the church is already begun; but, so long as there is daily progress, there cannot be perfection." John Calvin, *Commentaries on the Epistles of Paul to the Galatians and Ephesians*, trans. William Pringle (Grand Rapids: Eerdmans, 1948), 321–22. Wilhelmus Brakel echoed this sentiment, proposing that confession in the church's holiness does not entail a claim to Christian perfection. Rather, "This is not to suggest that the church is pure and perfect, for all her members have but a small beginning of this holiness and still have much corruption within themselves." Wilhelmus à Brakel, *The Church and Salvation*, vol. 2 of *The Christian's Reasonable Service*, trans. Bartel Elshout (Grand Rapids: Reformation Heritage Books, 1992–95), 2.17. See also Bavinck, *Reformed Dogmatics*, 4:321–22.

14. See Karl Rahner, "The Sinful Church in the Decrees of Vatican II," in *Concerning Vatican Council II*, vol. 6 of *Theological Investigations*, trans. Boniface Kruger (Baltimore: Helicon, 1969), 288–92.

case, there must be some way of articulating how exactly the church *is holy now*. Furthermore, for someone like Calvin, this eschatological trajectory of holiness is evidenced through the daily and progressive advancement of the church in holiness.[15] But this seems almost incredible. With the proliferation of ecclesial division, consistency of religious scandal, and frequency of ecclesial participation in "the works of the flesh" (Gal. 5:19–21), in what meaningful sense can we say that the church is more holy now than it was in the first or thirteenth centuries?

Endemic to both of these approaches is the tendency to view the church's holiness as a kind of moral perfection. And indeed, the scriptural injunction to be holy as God is holy does call for a certain moral correspondence in life and action to the living God (1 Peter 1:15–16). So Bullinger observed in his defense of the Reformation's departure from Rome, "the holy catholic church cleaveth unto her only shepherd Christ, believeth his word, and *liveth holily*."[16] But, as I will argue below, to confess that the church is holy is to say more than that. In expositing the nature and scope of the church's holiness, we must maintain three tensions. First, an articulation of the grammar of our confession in the church's holiness must take seriously the church's active participation and complicity in a world of sin. Even as the church stands before its Lord presented in splendor, "holy and without blemish" (Eph. 5:27), her sins remain an inexorable part of her historical past and present. It is these marks that are cleansed; it is these sins that are the object of the Son's reconciling action and Spirit's perfecting work. Second, this articulation must remember that the third article of the Apostles' Creed correlates a confession of the church's holiness with our faith in the Spirit's action.[17] This seems to indicate that holiness, however it is to be understood, must be tethered to divine action. This commitment rejects any reduction of the church's identity to the mere concrete actions of her members, for the church is not a community like other communities due to the constitutive activity of God and the continued presence of God in her midst. And third, an articulation of the church's holiness must make sense of the fact that the church *is holy now*. Her holiness is something the

---

15. Calvin, *Institutes*, 4.1.17.
16. Henry Bullinger, *The Decades of Henry Bullinger: The Fifth Decade*, ed. Thomas Harding (Cambridge: Cambridge University Press, 1852), 65, emphasis added.
17. As Hans Urs von Balthasar noted, after the first line of the Apostles' Creed's third article, "the acknowledgment of belief in the Father, Son, and Spirit is finished. What still follows is acknowledgment, in belief, of the redemptive work of the three divine Persons. . . . We now acknowledge, in belief in this God, what he has done for us in grace. The first gift is the Church." Hans Urs von Balthasar, *Credo: Meditations on the Apostles' Creed*, trans. David Kipp (San Francisco: Ignatius Press, 1990), 77.

church confesses in faith and is not reducible to the eschatological future. Holiness, then, must in some sense pertain to the church in her present, earthly life, even in spite of her persistent participation in sinful ways of life.

THE HOLINESS OF GOD AND HIS PEOPLE

Holy Scripture declares that the Lord God is holy and that there is none holy like him (1 Sam. 2:2; Rev. 15:4). Far from merely indicating God's transcendence or moral purity, holiness, as John Webster reminded us, "is an indication of the name of God. God's *name* is his enacted identity, God's sheer irreducible particularity as *this One* who is and acts *thus*. God's name is his incomparability, his uniqueness."[18] To declare that the Lord is holy is to make a claim of the very being of the triune God, one revealed and exposited in the incarnation of the beloved Son as he is the instantiation of the holiness of God in creaturely space-time.[19] It is in the face and in the mission of "the Holy One of God" (John 6:69) that we come to see and know the Lord who is "majestic in holiness" (Ex. 15:11; 2 Kings 19:22; Ps. 71:22). The holiness of God, then, refers to the "mode of God's activity of relation to us . . . the manner of his relation to us" as perfecter, reconciler, and judge.[20]

While God is holy by nature, the church's holiness is derivative. As John Owen attested, "God himself is the absolute infinite *fountain*, the supreme efficient *cause*, of all grace and holiness; for he alone is originally and essentially holy, as he only is good, and so the first cause of holiness and goodness to others."[21] It is only in light of the fact that this community,

---

18. John Webster, *Holiness* (Grand Rapids: Eerdmans, 2005), 36, emphasis original. Some, such as Rudolph Otto and, more recently, Mark C. Murphy, have proposed that the holiness of God refers to the effect God's presence has on humanity insofar as experiencing the mysterious and fascinating. Rudolph Otto, *The Idea of the Holy*, 2nd ed. (Oxford: Oxford University Press, 1958); Mark C. Murphy, *Divine Holiness and Divine Action* (Oxford: Oxford University Press, 2021). Yet, as John Goldingay notes, this does not cohere with the majority of the biblical portraits of divine holiness. With the exception of Isaiah 6, the people of Israel "do not regularly speak of God's holiness in that connection. It is God's majesty rather than God's holiness that provokes a reaction of dread and wonder. . . . Only quite late on in the Sinai story does Yhwh declare, 'I am holy' (Lev 19:2), and Yhwh's point there is not that people need to respond with dread and wonder." John Goldingay, *Old Testament Theology: Israel's Faith*, vol. 2 (Downers Grove, IL: IVP Academic, 2006), 23.

19. I am indebted to Kimlyn Bender for this phrasing. Admittedly, the Old Testament has plenty to say about the holy God of Israel, namely, that he is holy (Isa. 6:3), his name is holy (Ps. 145:21), his works are holy (Lev. 10:3), his presence makes things holy (Ex. 3:5), and his people are called to be holy before him (Lev. 20:26). But, as Gordon Wenham notes, the Old Testament also displays surprisingly little interest in providing any kind of positive content when it comes to divine holiness in itself. Gordon Wenham, *Leviticus*, NICOT (Grand Rapids: Eerdmans, 1979), 22.

20. Webster, *Holiness*, 41.

21. John Owen, *The Works of John Owen*, ed. William H. Goold, vol. 3 (repr., Edinburgh: Banner of Truth Trust, 1977), 514–15. Owen's claim has good backing within the rest of the Christian tradition. See Basil of Caesarea, *On the Holy Spirit*, 16.37. Similarly, Cyril of Alexandria averred, "For

this people is "of God" that we might rightly call it holy, that is, "sanctified in Christ Jesus" (1 Cor 1:2).[22] If the church is to be holy, it can only be so in a way that is proper to its nature as a created thing.

So what then does it mean to confess that the church is holy? Paul provided us with resources in his warning to his Corinthian readers: "Do you not know that your body is a temple of the Holy Spirit within you, which you have from God, and that you are not your own? For you were bought with a price" (1 Cor 6:19–20). Three things about ecclesial holiness might be gleaned from this text. First, the church is holy even as she is mired by grievous sin and doctrinal error. Throughout the epistle, Paul highlighted a series of issues that plagued the Corinthian congregation, including sexual misconduct (5:1–2), idolatry (10:14), division (3:1–4; 11:17–22), and skepticism regarding matters of apostolic testimony and doctrinal import (15:12–19). This church's life stands out, not for its moral purity, but for pride and arrogance displayed in spite of the fact that their way of life was so abhorrent that it was "not tolerated even among pagans" (5:1 ESV).[23] Yet even in the midst of her failures and shortcomings, the church is called holy and identified in relationship to the God who purchased her and dwells within her midst, setting her apart as holy ground.

Second, the church is holy in that it belongs to God. Bought with a price, the church exists as "God's own people" (1 Peter 2:9), that is, the people created by him, who belong to him, and who exist in a particular relationship to him. Paul did not exposit the metaphor, explaining to whom the payment (τιμῆς) was directed. Rather, the focus here is on the costly action of God in Christ and the subsequent relationship that results that constitutes the church as such, transforming disparate individuals into a people, that is, from "no-people" to "God's people" (1 Peter 2:10; Eph. 2:15, 19).[24] This people, this body and its members, are not their own but together belong to God. And this relationship endures. The church is

---

truly One only is holy—holy, that is, by nature; yet we also are holy, not, indeed, by nature, but by participation, training and prayer" (Cyril of Alexandria, *Mystagogical Lectures* 5.19). More recently Will Bankston has written, "Holiness must be understood as a reality that primarily applies to God and, only be derivation, to humanity. While God *is* holy, humans must *become* so." Will Bankston, "'You Shall Be Actualized, for I Am Pure Actuality': Holiness and the Perfecting Relation of Grace," *International Journal of Systematic Theology* 23, no. 2 (2021): 156–57.

22. As many readers will no doubt know, the verb "to sanctify" in Holy Scripture is a translation of the Greek word ἁγιάζω. This is the verbal form of the noun ἅγια, a noun normally translated as "holy."

23. Garland notes a rhetorical connection to the prophetic critiques of Amos 1–2 where Israel's sin is decried as being worse than that of the surrounding nations. Similarly, the behavior that was tolerated in the Corinthian church was considered unacceptable in their surrounding context. David E. Garland, *1 Corinthians*, BECNT (Grand Rapids: Baker Academic, 2003), 157.

24. Ephraim Radner, *Church* (Eugene, OR: Cascade Books, 2017), 70, 82–87.

holy, then, because it is created by God and belongs to God, built on the Living Stone (1 Peter 2:4–6, 9–10), rooted and grounded in Jesus Christ, the Holy One.[25] And insofar as the church is created by God and belongs to God, the church is holy ground.

Yet the church's holiness is not merely a claim made retrospectively, looking back toward its creation at Pentecost or its origin in the eternal plan of God. The church is also holy, third, because God has promised to dwell here, that is, to be present to and with them, and to act in and through this community. The church is "a temple (ναός) of the Holy Spirit," language that indicates not the temple precincts in general but "the actual sanctuary, the place of a deity's dwelling."[26] The church is set apart as the place where the all-consuming fire condescends to dwell (1 Cor. 3:16; Eph. 2:22).[27] The omnipresent, holy God is somehow uniquely present here, among his people. But God's promise to dwell with this community, contains an attendant promise to act. In fact, as James Arcadi has observed, this may be one of the primary points of emphasis in descriptions of divine presence throughout the canon.[28] Minimally, divine presence connotes divine action. God confronts the church with himself in the reading and preaching of the Word, presenting himself to this people as "the Alpha and the Omega . . . the Lord God, who is and who was and who is to come, the Almighty" (Rev. 1:8). Of course, God is free to do so elsewhere and otherwise. And we dare not conflate the actions of the *ecclesia* with the actions of her Lord.

---

25. Brakel, *Church and Salvation*, 2.17. As Christoph Schwöbel observed, "To talk about the holy Church can only refer . . . to the fact that it is constituted as the creature of the Word of God and not to any characteristic which the Church possesses independently of its divine constitution." Christoph Schwöbel, "Creature of the Word," in *On Being Church: Essays on the Christian Community*, ed. Colin Gunton (London: T&T Clark, 1989), 129.

26. Gordon D. Fee, *God's Empowering Presence: The Holy Spirit in the Letters of Paul* (Grand Rapids: Baker Academic, 2011), 114.

27. Richard Hays also notes the relationship between holiness and Israel's cultus, commenting on 1 Corinthians 1:2, "They are called to be *hagioi*, 'saints.' . . . all the members of the community are gathered up into this calling. To be 'sanctified' means to be set apart for the service of God, like Israel's priests or the vessels used in the Temple." Richard B. Hays, *First Corinthians*, Interpretation (Louisville: Westminster John Knox, 1997), 16.

28. James Arcadi writes, "The process is such that God will act at a location, *l*, entails God will be present at *l*, and this presence consecrates *l*, such that, ultimately, *l* becomes holy." James Arcadi, "God Is Where God Acts: Reconceiving Divine Omnipresence," *Topoi* 36 (2017): 637. A parallel here can be found in 1 Kings 8:27 where Solomon marveled, "But will God indeed dwell on the earth? Even heaven and the highest heaven cannot contain you, much less this house that I have built!" Solomon recognizes that God is omnipresent and simultaneously acknowledges that God is somehow "uniquely present" in the temple. Solomon then goes on to ask the Lord to hear, forgive, and attend to his people when they come to the temple. The implication is that discussions of divine presence and absence, specifically with reference to the church, indicate, minimally, divine action. For the omnipresent God to be present in a place refers to his commitment to communicating the blessings of redemption. For the omnipresent God to be absent from a place minimally refers to his execution of judgment upon that specific locale.

But God has promised to be and to act here, in the gathering of his people as church (Matt. 28:20).[29] And insofar as God is actively dwelling in her midst, confronting her with his Word, and attesting to himself, the church is holy ground.

THE ALL-CONSUMING FIRE: RECONCILER AND JUDGE

Our confession of faith in the holiness of the church indicates the divine activity and relationship that constitutes her as a creature of the Word, with the attendant promise that God will manifest himself in, with, through, and to her.[30] Notice that this description of the holy, omnipresent God uniquely dwelling and speaking in the church primarily indicates the activity *God* promises to bring about in and through the church. As I have written in another place, "The church is the means through which God communicates his word to his creatures."[31] Reflection on the holiness of the church should focus primarily on divine, *communicative* action. That is, the church is holy insofar as God promises to bear witness to himself in *this place*, through *this people*, declaring himself to be both judge and reconciler. And it is this promise of presence and self-attestation that provides us with the resources to engage the issue of ecclesial sin and the holiness of the church.

FORESHADOWING OF DIVINE RECONCILIATION

First, God has set apart the church as a unique recipient of his benefits and his redeeming love, establishing it as a witness to and foreshadow of the cosmic reconciliation of all things in Christ.[32] On the one hand, God does this in virtue of establishing the church as a foretaste of a coming renewal. The ecclesial community is born of the "word of truth," and exists as the "first fruits of his creatures" (James 1:18).[33] The language of

---

29. John Colwell writes, "While the Spirit may mediate God's presence and action through the means of any aspect of material creation, God has not promised to do so. . . . God has promised to speak and act through the church." John Colwell, *Promise and Presence: An Exploration in Sacramental Theology* (Eugene, OR: Wipf & Stock, 2005), 111.
30. Oliver O'Donovan, *Entering into Rest*, vol. 3 of *Ethics as Theology* (Grand Rapids: Eerdmans, 2017), 72.
31. Daniel Lee Hill, *Gathered on the Road to Zion: Toward a Free Church Ecclesio-Anthropology* (Eugene, OR: Pickwick, 2021), 166.
32. Radner writes, "The election of the Church discloses the divine destiny of the world, and it is of the *world* in all her peopled fullness that the church functions as the firstfruits, not of something else" (Radner, *Church*, 85).
33. Commenting on this verse, Dibelius and Greeven noted the soteriological and cosmological implications. "Ja[me]s calls [Jewish-Christians and other Christians] all first-fruits, and in doing so he expresses the hope that the others also will yet come to salvation, namely, all other people

first fruits carries with it both eschatological and cultic notions, as the term throughout the LXX frequently refers to "anything that is the first of an acquisition or is a thing of value," ranging from gold and silver (Ex. 35:5) to firstborn sons (Gen 49:3; Deut. 21:17).[34] As John Painter observes, "God's purpose . . . in the divine begetting is that humans should be the harbinger (*aparchē*) of the new creation."[35] Notice, however, that it is divine action that establishes this community as a precursor of a still future renewal. It is a result of God's act that the future restoration of all things breaks into the present as the church exists as evidence of "the full redemption that the rest of creation still awaits."[36] In other words, the Spirit's work of rebirth of the ecclesial community signifies a final renewal that extends beyond the church to incorporate "the whole creation in the renewal of life."[37] Even the church's praxis orbits around the concept of bearing witness to the future renewal of all things. Baptism heralds our resurrection (Rom. 6:4). The Eucharist portends our feasting with the risen Lamb in the fullness of his kingdom (Matt. 26:29).[38]

Yet at the same time, while God announces himself as reconciler of the cosmos in virtue of the church's very existence, he also comes to his people and repeatedly announces and reaffirms his commitment to bring about "the renewal of all things" (Matt. 19:28). The Lord is present in the gathering of his church, and this presence can be understood as a kind of *communicative presence*. He appropriates the proclamation of the church and, as I have argued elsewhere, the elements of the Supper as vehicles of self-communication.[39] As Nicholas Wolterstorff has argued, Christian worship seems to presuppose "that, by way of the reading aloud of Scripture,

---

and—since he obviously uses the expression κτίσματα deliberately—all God's creatures in general." Martin Dibelius and Heinrich Greeven, *James: A Commentary on the Epistle of James*, Hermeneia (Philadelphia: Fortress, 1976), 106. Similarly, Bloomberg and Kamell write, "Believers form the first harvest that God is reaping from all that he fashioned, prior to the eventual re-creation of the entire cosmos." Craig L. Bloomberg and Mariam J. Kamell, *James*, ZECNT (Grand Rapids: Zondervan, 2008), 75.

34. Dan G. McCartney, *James*, BECNT (Grand Rapids: Baker Academic, 2009), 110.

35. John Painter, "James" in *James and Jude*, Paideia (Grand Rapids: Baker Academic, 2012), 75. He goes on to note, "The purpose of the generous gift-giving God is the renewal and completion of the whole creation, a work begun with reborn humans, who are the sign and guarantee (*aparchē*) of the renewed creation" (76).

36. McCartney, *James*, 111.

37. Richard Bauckham, *James: Wisdom of James, Disciple of Jesus the Sage*, New Testament Readings (London: Routledge, 1999), 179.

38. See J. Todd Billings, *Remembrance, Communion, and Hope: Rediscovering the Gospel at the Lord's Table* (Grand Rapids: Eerdmans, 2018), 169–70. This is not intended to suggest that either of these ecclesial acts is reducible to the mere signification of future events, merely that whatever else it might accomplish, it *also* serves as a visible word, as a sign of the renewal of the world.

39. Daniel Lee Hill, "Tokens of Presence: Second-Personal Presence and Baptistic Accounts of the Eucharist," *Pro Ecclesia* 31, no. 1 (2022): 69.

God speaks anew, here and now to the congregants."[40] And it is then fitting and appropriate for the church to offer the response "Thanks be to God" when Holy Scripture is read.[41] It is here in the church that God repeatedly makes himself known. He declares in and through this body that the rebirth and regeneration of the world is coming and that he will bring it about. It is here, in the church, that God promises to bear witness to the regeneration of the world and reiterates his vow to liberate it from futility and decay, to make "all things new" (2 Cor. 5:17; Rev. 21:5). The church is holy because she is uniquely created by the God who promises to come into her midst, bearing witness to himself through her in the world.[42] Within the church, God prefigures the eschatological renewal of the cosmos and declares himself to be the reconciler of all things.

THE SIGN OF DIVINE JUDGMENT

Yet if the church is holy insofar as God has committed to bear witness to his work in Christ in and through her, how does this relate to the issue of ecclesial sin? The answer lies in the fact that the church is not only set apart as the means through which God announces the still future reconciliation of all things, but also the means through which God has promised to declare his impending judgment on the destructiveness of human sin. Insofar as the church is held up to the light of the Word and the judgment of God breaks in upon this community, it exists as something of a byword and warning among the peoples (Deut. 28:37). In short, the church is elected not only as the place where God declares his redeeming and reconciling love, but it is also the place where God unmasks the heinousness of sin and foreshadows his judgment of the world as the life of the church is held up against the backdrop of the Word.

THE CHURCH IN THE LIGHT OF THE WORD

First, insofar as God bears witness to himself in the preaching of his Word, the church is held up against the light of that self-same Word and God reveals the nature of sin in her midst. The church experiences a unique intimacy and proximity to the Righteous One in virtue of her union with him. But this closeness also exposes the failures of the church to live in

40. Nicholas Wolterstorff, *Acting Liturgically: Philosophical Reflections on Religious Practice* (Oxford: Oxford University Press, 2018), 219.

41. Wolterstorff, 218.

42. Eberhard Jüngel, "The Church as Sacrament?," in *Theological Essays*, trans. John Webster (repr., London: T&T Clark, 2014), 205.

accordance with his call, highlighting, in the words of Richard Baxter, the uncleanliness, hypocrisy, and carnal worship of the ecclesial community.[43] As Jüngel averred, the church ought to see herself as the *peccatrix maxima* in virtue of her nearness to her sinless and holy Lord. "It is precisely through the church's understanding of itself as *peccatrix maxima* that the intimate relation between the church and Jesus Christ is expressed. . . . [Christ's] holiness . . . makes him the *peccator peccatorum* (sinner of sinners); the holiness of the church, on the other hand, leads it to recognize itself as *peccatrix maxima*."[44] It is in the light of the Lord who presents himself to her, a Lord whose goodness, faithfulness, and lovingkindness know no bounds, that the church is shown again and again to be a community of the unfaithful, a community of sinners in desperate need of their Savior, a community who falls woefully short of his glory and excellence.

Accordingly, it is here, in the church and in the light of redemption, that God exposes the sins of the world for what they truly are: as that which he judges and forgives (Eph. 2:3–7). As Karl Barth noted, "For only as we realise that the divine grace is offered us can we understand the fact and nature of our sin, and the self-contradiction in which we are involved."[45] It is only in the light of Christ that human sin is revealed and the depth of human sinfulness is disclosed.[46] Gathered around the Word, it is in the church that we hear anew "that God is light and in him there is no darkness at all" (1 John 1:5). And it is as the light of this God who shines in our midst that we not only see light (Ps. 36:9), but also hear God's judgment on the darkness in our lives. In hearing and proclaiming the perfection of Christ, the corruption and impurity of the church's life is consistently set over against the sinlessness, holiness, and righteousness of her Lord. But the church's sins *just are* a sharing in, a fellowship with the sins of the world. So when the blemishes of the church are held up against and exposed in the light of God in Christ, so, too, are the sins of the world.

---

43. Richard Baxter, *The Practical Works of the Rev. Richard Baxter*, vol. 13 (London: James Duncan, 1830), 141–42.

44. Eberhard Jüngel, "Church as Sacrament?," 211.

45. Karl Barth, *Church Dogmatics*, ed. G. W. Bromiley and T. F. Torrance, trans. G. W. Bromiley, G. T. Thomson, et al., 4 vols. in 13 pts. (Edinburgh: T&T Clark, 1936–77), III/2, 32. The logic here is worth unpacking briefly. If sin is defined theologically, it can be minimally understood as that which God judges and that which God forgives. And if that is the case, then it is only in the light of the judgment and forgiveness of God as instantiated in the person of Christ, that is, the light of redemption, that we are able to see sin for what it truly is: as something that is fundamentally against God.

46. Barth, *CD*, IV/1, 399–400.

THE CHURCH AS THE FORESHADOWING OF DIVINE JUDGMENT

Yet not only does God's self-attestation in the church highlight the depth of the church's sinfulness as he holds its life up to the light of the Word, but this self-attestation also involves a denunciation of the church's sin. The church *is* a community of sinners who cling to the promise of forgiveness, and attendant to that promise is the realization that sin warrants and demands divine judgment. And it is on account of this sin that God continually promises to reprove, correct, and discipline this community (1 Cor. 11:27), coming against it in judgment (Rev. 3:3). The Lord warns his church, "Repent and do the works you did at first. If not, I will come to you and remove your lampstand from its place, unless you repent" (Rev. 2:5), a statement that has strong resonances with the prophetic warnings to Israel.[47] And insofar as this is the case, as T. F. Torrance argued, the church is that place where the Lord of hosts comes "into [its] midst always as the Lord whose awful presence among [his people] opposes and judges their impurity and sin."[48]

Yet again it is important to note that God's announcement of judgment on the sin of the church is a judgment on the impurity and corruption that the church *shares with the world* (Col. 3:5; 2 Peter 1:4). As such, God's pronouncement of judgment upon the church and her sin is a foreshadowing of the judgment that is coming. As William Cavanaugh puts it, "The church is visibly holy not because it is pure, but precisely because it shows to the world what sin looks like."[49] Cavanaugh's statement focuses on how human actions, namely, repentance, allow the holiness of the church to become visible in and to the surrounding world. Yet if the church's holiness refers to God's commitment to bear witness to himself as judge and reconciler through her, as I have argued above, we can perhaps extend Cavanaugh's point in another direction. In the church, God bears witness to the world of the gravity of human sin and the reality of divine judgment because it is precisely her "friendship with the world" in its sinfulness that he comes to judge (James 4:4). This, too, is reflected in ecclesial praxis. As Amy Peeler avers, speaking specifically about the Lord's Table in 1 Corinthians 11:27, "When one is responsible for mishandling the body and the blood,

47. G. K. Beale writes, "If they will not exercise their call to be a lamp of witness, then their lamp will be removed, as with Israel in the OT." G. K. Beale, *The Book of Revelation: A Commentary on the Greek Text*, NIGTC (Grand Rapids: Eerdmans, 1999), 231.

48. Thomas F. Torrance, *The Trinitarian Faith: The Evangelical Theology of the Ancient Catholic Church*, Cornerstones, 2nd ed. (London: T&T Clark, 2016), 281.

49. William T. Cavanaugh, "The Sinfulness and Visibility of the Church," in *Migrations of the Holy: God, State, and the Political Meaning of the Church* (Grand Rapids: Eerdmans, 2011), 165.

judgment results. . . . Mishandling the body of the Lord results in judgment on one's own body."[50] The same holds true for baptism, which proclaims that crucifixion of the "old self" and all its ways must die (Rom. 6:6).

The church, then, is the place where the divine "No" to the sin of the world is proclaimed as she is confronted with the presence of the God who judges sin and, accordingly, places her beneath the judgment of the Word. Here we must take seriously the images that litter Israel's history throughout the prophetic literature of God abandoning the temple in light of Israel's violation of the covenant (e.g., Ezek. 10). Of course, it must be said that the sin of the church will not have the final word, as both Torrance and Cavanaugh make clear. Cavanaugh writes, "The church . . . plays out the tragedy of sin while living in the hope that, in the end, the drama is in reality a comedy and not a tragedy. . . . The sin of the church is manifest, but it is incorporated into a larger drama of salvation."[51] Indeed, even in God's judgment, he "gives all the more grace" to this body (James 4:6). Yet even the focal point here is on divine action: for it is God who will deal thusly with his church, removing her transgressions from her "as far as the east is from the west" (Ps. 103:12).

IN PLACE OF A CONCLUSION

In this essay, I have argued that the Christian confession of the church's holiness is first and foremost a claim that describes God's promise to present himself in and to this gathered community as reconciler and judge. It is here, in the church, that the Lord of hosts bears witness of his judgment on sin and prefigures the eschatological renewal of all things. In so doing, I have not attempted to render the sin of the church reasonable and rational, for sin defies both reason and rationality. If the sin of Adam and Eve in the garden is the great impossible possibility, how much more so is this the case for the sin of the church, the body and bride of Christ in whom the Spirit dwells? The question that naturally follows, then, is not how can it be possible that the church sins, for she plainly does. Rather, the question as

---

50. Amy Peeler, "The Supper of the Lord: Goodness and Grace in 1 Corinthians 11:17–34," in *Come, Let Us Eat Together: Sacraments and Christian Unity*, ed. George Kalantzis and Marc Cortez (Downers Grove, IL: IVP Academic, 2018), 19. Peeler goes on to note that this judgment is different from eternal condemnation (20). Ian Boxall echoes a similar sentiment, albeit when focusing on the judgment warnings in the opening chapters of Revelation. He writes, "The coming of Christ, whether on the last day or in the Eucharist, can be experienced as either salvation (as at 3:11) or judgement." Ian Boxall, *The Revelation of Saint John*, Black's New Testament Commentary (London: Continuum, 2006), 50.
51. Cavanaugh, "Sinfulness and Visibility of the Church," 162.

it pertains to the holiness of the church should focus on what God is doing in the presence of this sinning, sinful community and, subsequently, how the community ought to live in response to this promised presence. Indeed, as some like William Cavanaugh, Ephraim Radner, Lauren Winner, and John Webster have noted, the church ought to respond by embracing the path of penitence, repentance, and gratitude.[52] This is well and good. The church has received good gifts from its covenant Lord for its upbuilding (Eph. 4:11–12), for which the church should rejoice and be grateful. But the church also needs to repent continually of the many ways she has often and invariably used these gifts to maim, wound, and break her members. As Lauren Winner writes, "Eucharist, baptism, and prayer are perfect in kind, and are given by a flawless giver. But any gift given by a Giver like that to a recipient like us will be damaged."[53] Repentance, as Winner goes on to note, is an appropriate response to this reality, especially in light of the fact that only God can undo much of the damage we have wrought.[54] And so it may also be the case that ecclesiology in particular must be undertaken in the mode of lament, "[pouring out our hearts] like water before the presence of the Lord" even as we hopefully and joyously cling to the promise of the gospel (Lam. 2:19). And so I will end with these words from the epistle of James: "Adulterers! Do you not know that friendship with the world is enmity with God? . . . Lament and mourn and weep. Let your laughter be turned into mourning and your joy into dejection. Humble yourselves before the Lord, and he will exalt you" (James 4:4, 9–10).

---

52. Webster, *Holiness*, 73; Ephraim Radner, *The End of the Church: A Pneumatology of Christian Division in the West* (Grand Rapids: Eerdmans, 1998), 352; Cavanaugh, "Sinfulness and Visibility of the Church," 167.

53. Lauren F. Winner, *The Dangers of Christian Practice: On Wayward Gifts, Characteristic Damage, and Sin* (New Haven, CT: Yale University Press, 2018), 155.

54. Winner, 156–57.

CHAPTER 11

GOD'S STORY FOR THE CHURCH

The Will of God and Ecclesial Persistence

STEPHEN T. DAVIS AND ERIC T. YANG

I

The church founded by Jesus Christ has existed for around two thousand years.[1] If we say this, then by "church" we cannot be referring to a particular building or a particular local community (e.g., the church in Philippi during the ministry of the apostle Paul) since no such building and no specific local community has lasted that long.[2] Rather, we are talking about the entire ecclesiastical body that was founded by Christ through his apostles. This seems to be the intended meaning in the Nicene Creed, when it states that we believe in the "one, holy, catholic and apostolic church."

The continued existence of a particular society or group of people may not be complicated to determine if that society or group has not been around for a long time or if there have been no substantive changes to it. However, the Christian church has been around long enough to undergo some significant events—such as the so-called Great Schism of 1054 (between Roman Catholicism and Eastern Orthodoxy) or the Protestant Reformation that began in the sixteenth century—thereby making it more complex to ascertain whether later bodies of Christians should be counted as members of one

---

1. Restorationists, and perhaps others, may believe that the church's lifespan is much shorter, especially if there was a large period in which the church went out of existence only to be revived later.

2. For different meanings or referents of the term *church*, see William J. Abraham, "Church," in *The Cambridge Companion to Christian Philosophical Theology*, ed. Charles Taliaferro and Chad Meister (Cambridge: Cambridge University Press, 2010), 171.

and the same church that began with the apostles of Jesus. There is now a bewildering variety of Christian denominations, movements, and sects. Do the plethora of different Protestant groups such as Presbyterians, Methodists, Southern Baptists, and the like count as part of the one, holy, catholic, and apostolic church? The question is not whether such groups are genuinely Christian but whether they are the same church (or part of the same church) as the one that began with Jesus' apostles. Without surprise, some Roman Catholic and Eastern Orthodox theologians have averred that their own respective group has sole claim to being the true church. But evaluating these claims depends on what the conditions are for the church to persist, that is, for a body of believers at one time to be the same church as a body of believers at another time.[3] An initially promising answer relies on the satisfaction of certain kinds of continuity relations between particular bodies of believers.

In this chapter, we take this initial answer as a starting point, though we raise a serious concern for it. We believe that there is a way of solving this worry, which is by adding another condition for ecclesial persistence, one that posits a role for the will of God to play. We show that a position that includes divine volitions avoids these problems and offers a viable account of ecclesial persistence. We also provide some considerations for expanding the divine volition theory into a divine narrative theory, especially as it relates to the identity conditions of the church. An upshot of this view is that there may be multiple branches within the church, and hence claims that only a single branch can count as the true church are rendered less plausible. We believe that God may have a story to tell, one that includes a church that involves separated streams—yet all being the one, holy, catholic, and apostolic church.

II

Given that the church is in some ways like other human groups and human societies, it may be expected that the conditions for what makes the church the same over time would be the same or at least very similar as it is for other groups and societies. What should we expect the persistence

---

3. To be clear, we are not addressing the question of whether a particular church counts as being a genuine Christian church. That question may be answered in the following way: just in case there is a bishop, just in case the word is proclaimed and the sacraments administered, and so on. While that question may be intertwined with our question, they are not exactly the same, and it is only the question stated in the body of the paper with which we will be concerned. Moreover, we are not asking about the synchronic unity of the church or the ontology of a spatially scattered group, which for more, see Joshua Cockayne, "Analytic Ecclesiology: The Social Ontology of the Church," *Journal of Analytic Theology* 7 (2019): 100–123.

conditions for human societies to be? When considering the persistence of ordinary objects, the usual approaches typically appeal to similarity or continuity relations (where continuity is construed as overlapping chains of similarity) or appealing to some further fact over and above these types of relations.[4] The former is an initially plausible way of answering the persistence question for societies. And the relevant kind of similarity or continuity for societies is with respect to the aims and the organization of that group.[5] A society or group can persist over time even if it undergoes some changes, provided that the changes are gradual. Over a long period of time, the same society might appear drastically different, but it will be the same society provided that the stages of the society maintain sufficient similarity at contiguous stages.

What the organization and aim of a society are depends on the kind of society being considered. With regard to the church, similarity (or continuity) of aims is tantamount to similarity (or continuity) of doctrine.[6] Doctrine will determine the content and manner of worship as well as provide an interpretation of the original revelation upon which the church was founded. Later ecclesial bodies that have adopted doctrines that significantly deviate from the teachings of the early Christian bodies will not be the same church as the original church.[7] Similarity (or continuity) of organization, on the other hand, will be

> a matter of admission procedures (e.g., baptism), kinds of worship (e.g., the eucharist), who conducts the worship (e.g., episcopally ordained priests), how officers are appointed (e.g., elected by the congregation, or appointed by the Pope), and how they are installed (whether bishops are consecrated by bishops, or elected by congregations), and how interpretations of doctrine are worked out and proclaimed.[8]

Any organizational change will have to be authorized by a previous ecclesial body. Additionally, similarity and continuity will be a matter of degree, and as long as sufficient similarity and continuity are maintained, the church persists.

---

4. Another option would be to deny that there are any criteria of identity over time (e.g., Trenton Merricks, "There Are No Criteria of Identity over Time," *Nous* 32 [1998]: 106–24).

5. For a view like this, see Richard Swinburne, *Revelation: From Metaphor to Analogy*, 2nd ed. (Oxford: Oxford University Press, 2007), 174–80.

6. Swinburne, 180.

7. Swinburne, 181.

8. Swinburne, 182.

Now, similar to the issue of personal identity, cases of fission or duplication may occur for ecclesial persistence given that there may be a plurality of successor church bodies, each of which bears some similarity or continuity with the original church. Indeed, such cases are not merely theoretical (as in the case of personal identity) but are in fact historical, as the history of the Christian church involves various episodes of church division, where the successor church bodies are similar in doctrine and organization to a church body immediately prior to the split. These successor ecclesial bodies have often incorporated and taught the same doctrine, typically centered on the books that comprise Scripture, and maintained a similar structure around Sunday worship, the sacraments (baptism, Communion), the presence of church leaders and ministers, and so on. In some cases, one ecclesial body may satisfy the similarity and continuity criteria better than the others, and so it will be regarded as the same church. For example, while the Montanist church in the second century was similar to the apostolic church in several respects, the mainline church better satisfied the criteria. Therefore, the Montanist church is ruled out as being the same church as the apostolic church. In cases of church division, it appears that the best candidate is to be regarded as the same church.

But what about instances in which there is no best candidate? In cases of personal identity, this is problematic since it would entail violating the transitivity of identity or admitting of a contradiction. That is, two distinct successors, A and B, may be continuous with some person such that they should both be regarded as identical to the original person, and so by transitivity would be identical to each other. Thus, A and B would be identical and not identical to each other. Yet this problem does not arise for ecclesial persistence since it may be possible for there to be a plurality of successors without denying the transitivity of identity or admitting of a contradiction. This is possible given that it seems possible for the church to exist as a multilocated or a spatially scattered object (unlike ordinary human persons).[9]

While the worry of division that besets personal identity does not threaten ecclesial persistence, the main problem that we find with the view that grounds ecclesial persistence in the similarity and continuity of doctrine and organization is that continuity admits of degrees, thereby leaving open

---

9. Being a multilocated or spatially scattered object seems less worrisome for societies than it does for persons or other material objects such as baseballs. For even those who claim that there is a single successor, such as some Roman Catholic or Eastern Orthodox thinkers, must account for their local congregations that are spatially scattered.

(metaphysical) indeterminacy with regard to ecclesial persistence. How much similarity or overlapping chains of similarity is required in order for a church to count as the same as another? A criterion based on similarity and continuity allows for there being no determinate answer in some cases.[10]

While there are philosophical arguments against the indeterminacy of identity or persistence,[11] indeterminacy in ecclesial persistence is even more worrisome because there should be a clear demarcation for those who are the bride of Christ. Either a particular church body will be wedded to Christ or not, and so it cannot be an indeterminate matter. The church also is a group that is subject to praise or blame (as the apostle Paul seems to assume with, *inter alia*, the church of Philippi and the church of Galatia), and there are some problems of harmonizing ascriptions of responsibility with such indeterminacy.[12] This is troubling since such indeterminacy would threaten the possibility of morally appraising the church.

III

The worry over the indeterminacy of ecclesial persistence may be resolved in several ways.[13] However, we will propose a solution that has already been applied to worries raised in personal identity. In fact, one of us has defended an account of personal identity that (partially) grounds our persistence on the will of God. Prior to applying this approach to ecclesial persistence, we seek to motivate this approach based on God's relation to the world and on the way it resolves worries for personal identity.[14]

It is a crucial part of Christian doctrine that God is the creator of all (contingent) things. But God also sustains or conserves in existence the world and all of the objects in it. Objects in the world have no ability on

---

10. Additionally, William Abraham worries that the continuity-based account such as Swinburne's leaves open the possibility that no later body satisfies the criteria of continuity of aim and organization with the apostolic church, and if so, the church that Christ founded would no longer be in existence. Swinburne, 177.

11. For some notable examples, see Nathan Salmon, *Reference and Essence* (Princeton, NJ: Princeton University Press, 1981); and Gareth Evans "Can There Be Vague Objects?," *Analysis* 48 (1978): 130–44.

12. Ryan Wasserman, "Personal Identity, Indeterminacy, and Obligation," in *Personal Identity: Complex or Simple?*, ed. Georg Gasser and Matthias Stefan (Cambridge: Cambridge University Press, 2012), 66.

13. For example, one may endorse epistemicism and so reject any genuine metaphysical indeterminacy. See Timothy Williamson, *Vagueness* (London: Routledge, 1994).

14. For further defense of the points made in this section, see Stephen T. Davis, "Resurrection, Personal Identity, and the Will of God," *Personal Identity and Resurrection*, ed. Georg Gasser (London: Ashgate, 2010); Davis, *Risen Indeed* (Grand Rapids: Eerdmans, 1993); and Eric T. Yang and Stephen T. Davis, "Composition and the Will of God," *Paradise Understood: New Philosophical Essays about Heaven*, ed. T. Ryan Byerly and Eric Silverman (Oxford: Oxford University Press, 2017).

their own to persist over time—that is, objects lack existential inertia. God's providential care and concern for the world, as we take it, is also meticulous. God cares for the birds and the lilies, as well as every quark and electron and every star and galaxy. These objects would cease to exist were it not for God willing that they continue to exist (as well as willing that they have the attributes and powers that they in fact have). Accordingly, the world of created things would be radically Heraclitean apart from the divine intention that it be stable and enduring. Metaphorically stated, the will of God is the glue that holds things together in the world.

God's involvement in the existence and characteristics of the world and the objects in it provides some motivation for supposing that the grounds for the persistence of things requires God's will. For example, consider the case of personal identity. What conditions must be satisfied in order for one person at a time to be identical to a person at another time? Some may answer this question by stating that there needs to be the same body over time, whereas others may opt for some kind of memory or psychological continuity (e.g., some later person remembers the experiences of an earlier person).[15] However, these relations allow for cases of duplication, which would involve a contradiction or a violation of the law of transitivity. Moreover, these relations also allow for genuine indeterminacy where it is undecidable whether the person persists or not. But such a view not only has philosophical problems but also specific problems for Christians, especially as it relates to the question of the survival after death and the doctrine of the resurrection. It is an essential part of Christian thought that we will be present in the afterlife; otherwise it would make no sense for God to reward or punish people in the life to come.

The possibility of duplication and indeterminacy, however, is eliminated if one of the grounds for personal persistence is that God wills that the later person be identical to the earlier person. The will of God, then, is a necessary condition for personal persistence.[16] Nor is positing divine volitions an *ad hoc* addition, as we noted above that the doctrine of conservation motivates a role for God's will to play in the continued existence of objects in the world.

God's will may not only be a kind of glue that sticks things together

_____

15. These approaches are of course not exhaustive.
16. The will of God is not the only factor, as God's willing that Steve is identical to Julius Caesar or the Washington Monument would not make it so. However, even if all of the typical continuity relations are satisfied by the person we call "Stephen T. Davis" in 2023 and the person we call "Stephen T. Davis" in 2024, if God does not also will that they be the same person, then the person in 2024 would not be identical to Stephen T. Davis in 2023.

diachronically but may also do so synchronically. That is, the world might have been an array of fundamental particles were it not for the divine will purposefully joining some of these particles to form a composite whole. Positing God's will as a condition for the composition of material objects also avoids various problems for theories of restricted composition for material objects (such that God may will a plurality of objects compose some further object). And we have argued elsewhere that such a view mitigates some of the worries for resurrection by reassembly, which is a theory of resurrection that was defended by several patristic theologians.[17]

IV

Theological considerations incline us to take the will of God as (partially) grounding the continued existence and structure of the world, including the diachronic identity of persons and the composition of material objects. Addressing the persistence of the church, an account that employs divine volitions offers a uniform way of resolving several quandaries. Bringing in the will of God seems especially fitting with regard to the identity of the church given the unique relation that God has with the church in comparison to other objects, events, or societies in the world. As Veli-Matti Kärkkäinen avers, the church "is anchored in this same God, whom it reflects, albeit incompletely and often in a broken manner."[18] Indeed, some traditions make the reliance upon God more explicit than others.[19]

Taking God's involvement in the nature and continued existence of the world seriously, the role of divine volitions resolves several philosophical and theological problems. Accordingly, we posit the will of God theory of ecclesial persistence, which can be formulated as follows:

Ecclesial body x at some time is the same church as another ecclesial body y at some other time if and only if (1) y is similar to x or is in a chain of

---

17. An objection to appealing to divine volitions in personal identity and material composition is that it makes persistence and composition partly an extrinsic matter. However, we believe taking seriously the doctrine of divine conservation and God's intimate relation with the world should make us not be surprised that they are not intrinsic but rather depend (at least in part) on God.

18. Veli-Matti Kärkkäinen, *An Introduction to Ecclesiology: Historical, Global, and Interreligious Perspectives* (Downers Grove, IL: IVP Academic, 2021), 12.

19. For example, within Eastern Orthodoxy, some claim that the unity of the church "is a fact, resting on the unity of the Triune Godhead." Andrew Louth, "The Eastern Orthodox Tradition," *The Oxford Handbook of Ecclesiology*, ed. Paul Avis (Oxford: Oxford University Press, 2018), 189, quoting from Alexy Khomiakov, The Church Is One (1863; repr., London: Fellowship of St. Alban and St. Sergius, 1968).

overlapping similarity to x with respect to doctrine and organization, and (2) God wills that y be the same church as x.

The will of God theory of ecclesial persistence is a further fact approach, one that goes beyond mere continuity relations. On this account, indeterminacy is avoided because God's willing that a local ecclesial body be the same church as another body is not a matter of degree. Either God so wills or does not so will. God's will is not alone sufficient for ecclesial persistence. Hence, God's willing that the apostolic church be the same church as the Los Angeles Dodgers baseball team does not make them the same since the two societies fail to satisfy the criteria of similarity or continuity with respect to doctrine and organization.

In cases of personal identity, God cannot will that both successors be identical to the original person since doing so would be contradictory, and God cannot bring about a contradiction (which we do not take to be a limitation to God's power).[20] In ecclesial persistence, there need be no contradiction if God wills that a plurality of successors be the same church as the original church. If so, then by the will of God theory of ecclesial persistence, it is possible that churches that spawned from divisions may be the same church as the original church. We therefore reject claims that the church must exist undivided for its continued existence, and we deny that in cases of church splits there can be only one true successor. Some Christian churches claim that their stream is the only true church; whereas other Christian churches are distinct from the one that began with the apostles and was founded by Christ. However, the will of God theory of ecclesial persistence allows for multiple streams, and therefore churches from different denominations can be the same church as the original. To no surprise, our account is a Protestant-friendly view of ecclesial persistence, rejecting the need for single successors but allowing the true church to be one that involves several branches.

V

An obvious worry arises for the will of God theory of ecclesial persistence: it appears that we are epistemically left in the dark in knowing which (if any) of the successors in a church split counts as the same church given that we

---

20. For more on this, see Stephen T. Davis, "Cartesian Omnipotence," Philosophia Christi 19 (2017): 455–61.

may not know what God wills with respect to this particular issue. Short of God's special revelation, we may be in the same epistemic situation as the mere continuity approach since it is difficult to ascertain whether the condition concerning divine volitions is satisfied or not. A quick response would be to state that the will of God theory is not being offered to answer the epistemic question but rather seeks only to answer the metaphysical question of what makes the church the same over time, and our theory has the added advantage that indeterminacy will be ruled out (whereas the mere continuity approach cannot rule out the possibility of indeterminacy). Yet we maintain that this epistemic worry can be mitigated by expanding the will of God theory into a divine narrative theory of ecclesial persistence.

A divine narrative would be the story that God is either telling or has told (or would tell), whether in some special way, such as in the story of salvation history in Scripture, or in a more general way, such as in the story of the world. Authors in the story must make decisions about what counts as part of the story or not. An author may write a page, and later remove that page, decreeing that the removed page is no longer part of the same story. Suppose Tolkien had such a page that was meant to be in *The Lord of the Rings* that concerned Frodo. Once Tolkien removed that page, the Frodo mentioned in that page may not be the same as the Frodo in the accepted pages. The identity and persistence of characters in the story, then, depend on the will of the author concerning what is in the story and how the characters and objects in the story are related to each other. Now God, being perfect and omniscient, will not write a page (so to speak) and later decree that it is not part of the story. God is the perfect storyteller. But God's volitions make a difference as to what is what in the story, and the kind of narrative that God wants to tell will also influence God's choices and volitions in the story.

One motivation for expanding to a divine narrative approach is the recent uptick in attention to narrative theories in various fields, such as psychology, philosophy, and theology. Additionally, there are theological motivations for appealing to divine narratives. First, the central mode of revelation from God, that is, Scripture, has been given primarily through narratives, from the story of Israel to the story of Christ and the early years of the church. Second, God is not merely a spectator of the world but is also its author. The doctrine of divine conservation and providence highlight the intimate ways in which God is related to the world and its unfolding. Moreover, the central protagonists in Scripture are not the (merely) human characters in it; rather, the hero of the story is God. While many narratives can be offered, the perspectives of the protagonist and the author should be regarded as privileged.

With respect to the epistemological question, the knowledge needed to answer this may be gleaned by examination of the stories. We can learn quite a lot about the characters in the story, and even about the narrator or the author, from careful reflection on the story. Indeed, Eleonore Stump has advanced the acquisition of a form of knowledge different than third-person, propositional knowledge, that is, knowledge of persons or second-personal knowledge. To defend this claim, Stump employs the following story:

> Imagine then that Mary in her imprisonment has had access to any and all information about the world as long as that information is *only* in the form of third-person accounts giving her knowledge *that*. . . . She knows that there are other people in the world. . . . But she has never had any personal interactions of an unmediated and direct sort with another person. She has read descriptions of human faces, for example, but she has never been face-to-face with another conscious person. . . . In short, Mary has been kept from anything that could count as a second-person experience, in which one can say "you" to another person. And then suppose that Mary is finally rescued from her imprisonment and united for the first time with her mother, who loves her deeply. When Mary is first united with her mother, it seems indisputable that Mary will know things she did not know before, even if she knew everything about her mother that could be made available to her in a non-narrative propositional form. . . . Mary is learning something she did not know before the personal interaction.[21]

The kind of knowledge acquired from second-person experiences is not limited only to those who have had such experiences; they can also be acquired by unpacking a second-person account, which often is presented in narrative form. Since God is both a character and the author of Scripture, examination of the biblical narrative can yield second-person knowledge of God, knowledge that goes beyond a list of information.[22] Moreover, acquiring such knowledge yields additional insights into that person's

---

21. Eleanore Stump, *Wandering in Darkness: Narrative and the Problem of Suffering* (Oxford: Oxford University Press, 2010), 52–53. This thought experiment was explicitly borrowed from Frank Jackson's (1982) famous case in defense of qualia.

22. For more on this, see Eleanore Stump, "Revelation and the Veridicality of Narratives," *European Journal for Philosophy of Religion* 13 (2021): 27–43.

character and perspective. By knowing God more in this way, one may come to know or form reasonable beliefs concerning what God would or would not will.

Appealing to narratives may also impose some aesthetic constraints on the kind of narrative that we should expect given that God is the author. There seem to be some moral constraints on what we expect of God (whether those moral constraints are externally imposed or whether they come from God's own good nature). We do not expect God to lie or to be unjust. Similarly, there may be aesthetic constraints on the kind of story that God is writing for the world (whether those aesthetic constraints are externally imposed or whether they come from God's own beautiful nature). We do not expect God to make an ugly or incoherent story, but rather we expect God to design a story that is beautiful and sublime, even if narratively complex.

The divine narrative theory of ecclesial persistence does not give us a direct answer of whether one ecclesial body is willed by God to be the same church as an earlier ecclesial body. However, we can make justifiable assertions concerning divine volitions based on the evidence available, especially the evidence concerning God's character as well as aesthetic constraints for a well-authored story.[23] A particular ecclesial body may also ask itself whether it can coherently fit within the larger narrative of Scripture and church history (especially in those narrative sequences where it is evident that there is a persisting church). A particular ecclesial body's lack of narrative fit may serve as evidence that God would not will that body to be the same church as the apostolic church.

VI

A divine narrative theory of ecclesial persistence also provides some reason not to be surprised at branching or the plurality of ecclesial successors. Narrative examples of this are common, especially in television shows or movies that end up with several spin-offs. Sometimes spin-offs occur sequentially, but other times they occur simultaneously. For example, *Star Trek: Picard* and *Star Trek: Discovery* are both in the same story as the original *Star Trek* series since both narratives can be traced back to the story that

---

23. This is similar to what dualists may say regarding the persistence of a human person. We do not have direct access to whether the soul in another human person is the same soul over time, but we can make reasonable inferences based on the evidence from psychological and physical continuity.

began with Kirk and Spock. And a viewer of one of these successor shows may not realize that both of these shows are part of the same overarching story, but they can learn that they are so by discovering more about the history of the series as well as the intentions of the creators and producers of the show.[24] A creative author, then, may have reasons for having branching stories since it allows for creative outlets and important narrative plots to be developed. Similarly, God may author a narrative of the church that involves various branches that serve God's aim for the church and that further expand its reach in the world. Accordingly, the divine narrative theory of ecclesial persistence will be Protestant (and denomination) friendly because God can will and author a story in a way that yields a plurality of ecclesial bodies, each of which is the same church as the apostolic church.

One objection to this account may be that it violates the Nicene Creed's claim that the church is *one*. How can there be genuine unity if there are so many branches? However, a plurality of ecclesial branches can be regarded as one in the way that distinct branches of a narrative can be one when there is an overarching franchise that organizes the multiple series. For an extant example, the Marvel Cinematic Universe involves phases that organize the various movies. A particular movie and its sequels (such as *Iron Man* and its direct sequels) may be regarded as its own branch, and yet it is in the same story as another branch (such as *Captain America* and its direct sequels) given the overarching organizational structure within the Marvel Cinematic Universe. And this structure has had many creative benefits. Similarly, the story involving John Knox and the Presbyterians may seem like a different narrative than the story involving John Wesley and the Methodists, yet the overarching organization laid out by God may by creatively weaving these such that they are part of the same story, that is, the narrative of Christ's church.

Another objection to the divine narrative theory may be that the allowance of branching will foster continued division and will oppose visible unity in the church. Under the divine narrative theory, different denominations or ecclesial bodies are the same church, even if they do not recognize themselves as the same church or even if they regard other churches as distinct from themselves. However, this may be due to lack of awareness

---

24. Or consider movies with sequels, some of which are regarded as part of the original story and others as not (e.g., the *Terminator* franchise). There have been multiple sequels, some of which have been deemed later as not being a genuine part of the original story (based on decisions made by producers and directors). Human writers, directors, and producers can change their mind about what belongs and what does not. However, God is not so fickle.

of the author's grand narratives or of the history and relationship among these churches. Furthermore, it may be part of the grand story that the different branches be brought together to enhance the aesthetic features of the story arc, similar to the way the Marvel Cinematic Universe creates finales that involve the gathering and cooperation of many different protagonists from different stories into the same film. Concerning the church, we do not know what God, the writer and director of the church's story, has planned for the church. We do know that God is composing a beautiful and intricate narrative, one in which God has acknowledged the importance of unity, as Jesus stated that "all people will know that you are my disciples, if you have love for one another" (John 13:35 ESV). Though divided now, different branches of the church should be encouraged to strive for unity, cooperation, and mutual love—being open to the ways in which the divine author will usher in a climactic finale where "at the name of Jesus every knee should bow, in heaven and on earth and under the earth, and every tongue confess that Jesus Christ is Lord, to the glory of God the Father" (Phil. 2:10–11 ESV).

VII

Ecclesial persistence requires similarity and continuity of doctrine and organization, but we have offered an approach that makes the will of God crucial, and we have argued that a theory of ecclesial persistence that employs the concept of divine volitions avoids a serious problem to mere similarity-and-continuity approaches. While there may be only one true successor of the apostolic church, we believe that a good story can and probably does involve many different extant branches of Christianity today, thereby making each the same church as the one founded by Christ and the apostles. Many of these churches locate themselves in the story of Christ's church, and we take such narrative fit (as well as the continuity of doctrine and organization) as good evidence that they are the same church. While God's story for the church has involved division, we should expect the divine author to have a climactic ending that will be sublimely awesome.[25]

---

25. We are grateful to Oliver Crisp, Jesse Gentile, John Baptist Santa Ana, Steven Nemes, Beau Branson, and David Frederick for helpful comments.

CHAPTER 12

THE TRIUNE GOD AND THE MARKS OF THE CHURCH

Karl Barth on the One, Holy, Catholic, and Apostolic Church

MARGUERITE KAPPELHOFF

ACROSS THE GLOBE CHRISTIANS confess a shared belief in the one, holy, catholic, and apostolic church as outlined in the Nicene Creed. While these four "marks" have a long-standing history, within the contemporary church an obvious tension exists between their stated aspirational intent and their demonstrated empirical evidence.

A brief historical retrace outlines that what were first presented cohesively in the fourth century as descriptors of the church and statements to be made in faith and self-examination did not remain this way. Rather, the marks began to be utilised as individual elements that could be prioritised and employed to support any single group's claim to understand the nature and mission of the church. This treatment of the marks has persisted until the present day, where in the twenty-first century the engagement with and treatment of the marks varies vastly among the ecclesial pool. For instance, while creedal churches engage with the marks, the marks are still defined along preferred denominational and institutional lines marked with differentiation concerning their understanding and application. In non-creedal churches, engagement with the marks is questionable, varying from institution to institution. Although the marks are meant to be indicative of the entire church, this lack of engagement by some or denominational preference by others ensures that literacy concerning the marks has been reduced and has created an impasse on dialogue that churches seem unable to transcend.[1] Taken together, this further outlines the concern that there has been a loss of critical theological functioning concerning the marks that is affecting ecclesial self-understanding and praxis.

The aim of this chapter is to explore the theological function of the marks by doing a case study on Barth's contribution, in which he locates "one, holy, catholic, and apostolic" within the nature and being of the triune God.[2] This understanding has profound significance for ecclesiology, because it would suggest that the marks are not authored and initiated at the institutional level but rather transcend it. It also suggests something about how the marks are sustained. That is, being *from* God and *of* God, their source is therefore necessarily *in* God, and not in the church, even if they are to be appropriated at this level. This means that the marks have a validity that goes beyond being a human construct and are instead a divine initiative to which the church must respond. However, noting that because ecclesial correspondence follows christological correspondence, this identifies the need to understand how Christ models the marks for the church.[3]

In what follows, I briefly outline Barth's foundational understanding of the church followed by his discussion on each of the "marks" in an effort to reveal their theological function. This is followed with a discussion on "correspondence," determining that the significance of the marks' being located in Jesus and empowered by the Holy Spirit is directly related to God's loving action of "seeking and creating fellowship" with humanity.[4] Specifically, that as the church corresponds to Christ in its demonstration of being "one, holy, catholic, and apostolic," it demonstrates its desire to "seek and create fellowship" as a "community of Christ" who "loves in freedom." In this way, it corresponds to the divine initiative of the triune

---

1. The World Council of Churches' ten-year study concluded that despite the ecumenical nature of the marks, there were insufficient grounds for reaching full consensus on how to define them (e.g., the denominational differentiation on "apostolic," §241, including following commentary, pp. 77–78). World Council of Churches, *Confessing the One Faith: An Ecumenical Explication of the Apostolic Faith as It Is Confessed in the Nicene-Constantinopolitan Creed (381)*, Faith and Order Paper no. 153, rev. ed. (Geneva: World Council of Churches, 2010).

2. See Karl Barth, *Church Dogmatics*, 4 vols., ed. Geoffrey W. Bromiley and Thomas F. Torrance (Edinburgh: T&T Clark, 1936–75), IV/1.62, *The Holy Spirit and the Gathering of the Christian Community*, specifically his section "The Being of the Community," in which his discussion on the marks of the church is located. All references to this work hereafter: *CD* followed by the volume/part, section, and page number(s) (e.g., *CD*, IV/1.62, 661).

3. Kimlyn J. Bender, *Karl Barth's Christological Ecclesiology* (Aldershot, UK: Ashgate, 2005), 7.

4. See Barth, *CD*, II/1.28, *The Being of God as the One Who Loves in Freedom.*

God and thereby reclaims theological functioning of the marks within its own self-understanding and ecclesial praxis.

THE MARKS IN RELATION TO JESUS AND MEDIATED BY THE HOLY SPIRIT

Barth's discussion on the church is located in section 62, *The Holy Spirit and the Gathering of the Christian Community*. In his opening statement, Barth immediately placed the church under the headship of Christ as mediated by the Holy Spirit: "The Holy Spirit is the awakening power in which Jesus Christ has formed and continually renews His body, i.e. His own earthly-historical form of existence, the only holy catholic and apostolic Church."[5] Barth clearly outlined that it is a confession of faith in Jesus that is at the "centre" of this "Christian community" that exists "only as it is gathered and lets itself be gathered and gathers itself by the living Jesus Christ through the Holy Spirit."[6] Further, Jesus is the one who "constitutes and organizes and guarantees the community of His body."[7] In Barth's conception, this is because the church is the "earthly-historical form of existence of Jesus Christ Himself," that is, "His body, created and continually renewed by the awakening power of the Holy Spirit."[8]

This has significance. First, because Barth described the church simultaneously as the "earthly-historical form" of Jesus himself and as the "one, holy, catholic, and apostolic Church."[9] Second, because this community does not belong to itself or for its own purposes. Rather, "it lives with Him as His people, His fellowship, His community," and, further, it "can only follow the movement of His life" and thus "in that way attest in its own activity" through "His activity."[10] Consequently, this means that the marks are understood not only as residing in Jesus but any further "movement" of them (i.e., moments of action, when they occur) will follow after Jesus' own. Therefore, any discussion concerning the marks of the church must be viewed through this conception of Christ as the head of the church, who embodies the marks within his being and actions, thereby modeling them to the church and directing any further instances of them. With this foundational significance established, a review of the marks follows.

---

5. Barth, *CD*, IV/1.62, 643.
6. Barth, *CD*, IV/1.62, 645, 651.
7. Barth, *CD*, IV/1.62, 662.
8. Barth, *CD*, IV/1.62, 661.
9. Barth, *CD*, IV/1.62, 643.
10. Barth, *CD*, IV/1.62, 662.

BARTH'S UNDERSTANDING OF "ONE, HOLY, CATHOLIC, AND APOSTOLIC"

ONENESS

Barth summed up the basis of his understanding of "oneness" of the church in his opening statement, immediately locating the unity of the church within the three persons of the Trinity:

> The Christian believes—and there is—only one Church. This means that it belongs to the being of the community to be a unity in the plurality of its members, i.e., of the individual believers assembled in it, and to be a simple unity, not having a second or third unity of the same kind side by side with it. The statement follows necessarily from all that we have seen concerning it. In all the riches of His divine being the God who reconciled the world with Himself in Jesus Christ is One. Jesus Christ, elected the Head of all men and as such their Representation who includes them all in Himself in His risen and crucified body is One. The Holy Spirit in the fullness and diversity of His gifts is One. In the same way his community as the gathering of the men who know and confess Him can only be one.[11]

Further, this oneness remains even though the church has two natures: "visible" ("an earthly-historical fellowship") and "invisible" ("a supernaturally spiritual fellowship"), which cannot be "separated" since "both in their unity are the body," that is the "earthly-historical form of existence of the one living Lord Jesus Christ."[12]

Barth explained that even within the universal church among the multiplicity of churches there is unity, because Jesus is in the midst of every community ruling the church and churches as the "basis and guarantee" of this "unity."[13] Any other form of church would mean a "plurality," or a "co-existence of Churches which are genuinely divided" representing a "conflict with both Ephesians 4 and the *credo unam ecclesiam*."[14] Barth concluded that there is no "legitimate" basis ("theological, spiritual or

---

11. Barth, *CD*, IV/1.62, 668–69.
12. Barth, *CD*, IV/1.62, 669.
13. Barth, *CD*, IV/1.62, 675.
14. Barth, *CD*, IV/1.62, 675; *credo unam ecclesiam* ("I believe one church"). The fact that Barth chose to retain the original Latin *credo* ("I believe") and not *credamus* ("we believe") likely had more to do with his desire to remain faithful to the original text than it being a statement of rejection to the corporate idea.

biblical") upon which churches can be genuinely separated, since "a plurality of Churches in this sense means a plurality of lords, a plurality of spirits and a plurality of gods."[15]

In Barth's theology, church division can be possible only where sin is present since, ontologically, it is impossible to rend the community as it is the body of Christ.[16] Barth reasoned that this disunity is a "scandal" and "the matter demands always, and in all circumstances, *unam ecclesiam.*"[17] Further, when an individual or group of individuals withdraws for whatever reason from all other churches, this is to "abandon" the "hope of the community," because "we are either in the *communio sanctorum* or we are not *sancti.*"[18] Therefore to act in disunity not only reveals the sinfulness of the community but also its lack of holiness.

Further, a lack of unity reveals a lack of "lordship" in the church evidenced as division "right down to its invisible being, its relationship to God and Jesus and the Holy Spirit."[19] This lack of lordship in the church results in an "external division" that can be overcome only by "a healing of both its visible and invisible hurt."[20] Barth outlined that what is required is for the church to first be healed of its invisible hurt by turning to its Lord, and then it needs to be healed of its visible hurt by turning to other churches and finding true unity through Jesus Christ. The ordering of this is important, because "what is demanded is the unity of the Church of Jesus Christ, not the externally satisfying co-existence and co-operation of different religious societies."[21] Once again, Barth made it obvious that the unity of the church is located and founded in Jesus Christ and therefore the hope of sustained unity among the churches must start here. For when this takes place, the church can abandon any "claim to be identical with the one Church in contrast to the others" because this "claim has been dashed out of its hand by the One who is the unity of Church."[22]

One final point to note in Barth's understanding of church unity is the necessary requirement of faith. This faith needs to be "strong and certain and genuinely critical" in order to see the "unity of the Church of Jesus Christ in its disunity."[23] To have faith in the unity of the church "can

---

15. Barth, *CD*, IV/1.62, 675–76.
16. Barth, *CD*, IV/1.62, 677.
17. Barth, *CD*, IV/1.62, 677.
18. Barth, *CD*, IV/1.62, 678; *communio sanctorum* ("communion of saints"); *sancti* ("holy").
19. Barth, *CD*, IV/1.62, 678.
20. Barth, *CD*, IV/1.62, 678.
21. Barth, *CD*, IV/1.62, 678, 679.
22. Barth, *CD*, IV/1.62, 678, 684.
23. Barth, *CD*, IV/1.62, 678, 679.

never be the work of a feeble or uncertain or uncritical faith."[24] Linking faith to unity that is based on the lordship of Jesus Christ, Barth closed the section with a positive appeal: "And, above all, we must not cease to move further along this way—which means, that we must not be afraid to enter the way of the *credo unam ecclesiam* at its very beginning, at the acknowledged centre of every Christian community, and therefore at the lordship of the One to whom the Church belongs, whose body it is, who is Himself its true unity."[25]

HOLINESS

Barth returned to his foundational understanding that the marks are to be found within the triune God, noting that any holiness that the church can claim to possess is not initiated in and of itself, but rather is ascribed to it:

> We cannot believe in the Church—the holy Church—as we believe in God the Father, Son and the Holy Spirit. According to the third article we can believe only in God the Holy Spirit, and as we know and confess His work we can also believe the existence of the holy Church. . . . If it is seriously true and can be known in faith, the holiness of the Church is not that of the Holy Spirit but that which is created by Him and ascribed to the Church. It is He who marks it off and separates it. It is He who differentiates it and singles it out. It is He who gives it its peculiar being and law of life. It is holy as it receives it from Him to be holy.[26]

Having first pointed to God and the Holy Spirit as the source and location of the church's existence and its holiness, Barth continued the argument and included the person of Jesus as the source of the church's holiness: "What else can the holiness of the Church be but the reflection of the holiness of Jesus Christ as its heavenly Head, falling upon it as He enters into and remains in fellowship with it by His Holy Spirit?"[27]

This polemic prepares the pathway through which Barth could continue to outline that this holiness is the resulting work of the relationship that exists among the three persons of the Godhead. As such, the church can be certain of its holiness because the source from which it is obtained ensures that its holiness is characteristically "indestructible" and

24. Barth, *CD*, IV/1.62, 678, 679.
25. Barth, *CD*, IV/1.62, 685.
26. Barth, *CD*, IV/1.62, 686.
27. Barth, *CD*, IV/1.62, 687.

"infallible."[28] Further, the church can have confidence because this ascribed holiness is "final" with a "categorical definitiveness, inviolably and unalterably."[29] This discussion (that the holiness of the church is indestructible, infallible, and final) follows Barth's previous point, arguing that the church cannot lose its holiness any more than it can lose its identity and cease to be the church because it is "from Jesus" as "His Body" that it gains its identity and calling.[30] Neither of these can be "set aside" or "taken from it."[31]

Barth was not naive in the shortcomings of the visible institution. He noted that the church "may deny its Lord and fall from Him" and that it "may degenerate."[32] It may also be "sick or wounded."[33] Further still, "it has always needed, and it always will need, self-examination and self-correction."[34] Yet, despite all of this, "as the body of this Head it cannot die," since the "authority and power of God are behind it . . . it will never fail."[35] In fact, so bound is the church's holiness to Christ that Barth warned that no one should criticise the church because, in doing so, they maybe be criticising Christ himself.[36]

Barth made two final interrelated points in regard to the church's holiness—that of its passivity in receiving it and its required action of obedience to it.[37] Reiterating that the church can never "be holy of itself," but rather gains its holiness through the presence of the Holy Spirit and through Christ because "He is always the Subject, the Lord, the Giver of the holiness" in regard to the church.[38] Nevertheless the church should understand this holiness as "the imperative and standard of its own human activity" and be "summoned to a very definite expectation and movement."[39] Therefore, when it comes to the "question of holiness," it is answered by a "question of obedience" as the church "cannot answer this question of its holiness by any answer of its own," nor can it "make itself holy by its human Church work."[40] The church's holiness then, not only resides in Christ its head, but the church can only respond by allowing its actions to follows his movement.

---

28. Barth, *CD*, IV/1.62, 689.
29. Barth, *CD*, IV/1.62, 686.
30. Barth, *CD*, IV/1.62, 689.
31. Barth, *CD*, IV/1.62, 689.
32. Barth, *CD*, IV/1.62, 689.
33. Barth, *CD*, IV/1.62, 691.
34. Barth, *CD*, IV/1.62, 690.
35. Barth, *CD*, IV/1.62, 691.
36. Barth, *CD*, IV/1.62, 693.
37. Barth directly quoted Luther: *"Christiana sanctitas non est active, sed passive sanctitas"* ("Christian holiness is not active, but passive holiness"). Barth, *CD*, IV/1.62, 693.
38. Barth, *CD*, IV/1.62, 693–94.
39. Barth, *CD*, IV/1.62, 701.
40. Barth, *CD*, IV/1.62, 701.

CATHOLICITY

Barth's understanding of catholicity refers to an "identity" and a "continuity" that are "maintained" in "all differences."[41] As it is applied to the church, catholicity refers to a character that remains the same in all places, is "recognisable in this sameness," and carries an "essence" that "never has altered and never can or will alter."[42] Despite being "surrounded by a continually changing landscape" in which its form "is itself continually subject to change," the catholic church "can never become anything other than itself."[43] This is because it is "obliged and summoned always to be the same and continually to maintain itself as the same in forms which are always new."[44] In other words, despite changes in context, culture, and times in history in which the church must live and navigate, there is a "character of this sameness" that "exists and shows itself to be the true Church, the Church of Jesus Christ."[45] Barth was quick to point out that what "makes the Church the true Church" has nothing to do with any "historical" or "modern" forms of church.[46] Instead, it has an "abiding possession" that is "superior to every yesterday and to-day and is therefore the criterion of its catholicity."[47] Before naming this "abiding possession" that ensures this characteristic "catholicity" within the church, Barth clarified that "just as without faith we cannot see unity or holiness, so without faith we cannot see its catholicity."[48] Further, any church that believes that it can see and maintain its own catholicity acts in arrogance, because the catholicity of the church resembles its "unity and holiness" in that "the Church has no control over it."[49] The church is "catholic" because it is the "earthly-historical form" of the "man who maintains His sovereign identity both here and there, yesterday and to-day."[50] Further, this catholicity results not from its own "labor," but in him alone, "the Son of God who gathers and protects and maintains it, His work and His Spirit."[51] Jesus is thus identified as the "source and norm" for the church's catholicity that establishes it as the "true Church" in contrast to the "false" church.[52] Therefore, because the

---

41. Barth, *CD*, IV/1.62, 701.
42. Barth, *CD*, IV/1.62, 702.
43. Barth, *CD*, IV/1.62, 704.
44. Barth, *CD*, IV/1.62, 704.
45. Barth, *CD*, IV/1.62, 702.
46. Barth, *CD*, IV/1.62, 705.
47. Barth, *CD*, IV/1.62, 705.
48. Barth, *CD*, IV/1.62, 708.
49. Barth, *CD*, IV/1.62, 708, 710.
50. Barth, *CD*, IV/1.62, 708, 710.
51. Barth, *CD*, IV/1.62, 711.
52. Barth, *CD*, IV/1.62, 712; *veritas catholica* ("catholic truth").

church has been ascribed this catholicity as a gift, it is now the task of the church to participate in the maintaining of this identity through faith and obedience. First the "true Church" is "humbly content to be thrown back entirely upon faith in respect of its truth" as it "confidently" exists "in this faith as the true community of Jesus Christ."[53] Second, through obedience the church participates in its tasks of service, holding Christ at the centre of its existence and witness.[54] Barth unreservedly concluded that when it comes to the catholicity of the church, this "mark" is executed through faith in which, "as He makes it one and holy, so He makes it universal. And therefore faith in Him, which can never cease to be a busy faith, is the only effective and not really passive but supremely active realization of the *credo catholicam ecclesiam*."[55]

APOSTOLICITY

Barth's opening discussion on "apostolic" summarises his understanding on this mark along with its position and relationship to the other three marks:

> It is excellent that in the creed of 381 after *una, sancta, catholica* there appeared for the first time a fourth predicate. . . . All four predicates describe the one being of the Christian community. But we can and should read and understand them as mounting to a climax. *Una* describes its singularity. *Sancta* describes the particularity which underlies this singularity. *Catholica* describes the essence in which it manifests and maintains itself in this particularity and singularity. And finally *apostolica* does not say anything new, in relation to these three definitions, but describes with remarkable precision the concrete spiritual criterion which enables us to answer the question whether and to what extent in this or that case we have or have not to do with the one holy catholic Church. The criterion is not sociological or juridical or psychological, but spiritual. The word *credo* is still in front, and must not be forgotten. Even the criterion that the Church is apostolic, with all that that involves, can be known only in faith, and cannot be seen except in faith.[56]

Here Barth highlighted his two foundational points concerning the mark of "apostolic" from which his discussion builds. The first point he made

---

53. Barth, *CD*, IV/1.62, 708.
54. Barth, *CD*, IV/1.62, 712.
55. Barth, *CD*, IV/1.62, 712; *credo catholicam ecclesiam* ("I believe the catholic church").
56. Barth, *CD*, IV/1.62, 712; *una* ("one"), *sancta* ("holy"), *catholica* ("catholic"), *apostolica* ("apostolic").

is that the four marks are linked to one another and that together they "describe the one being" of the church. The second point he made is in regard to the nature of this mark (apostolic) having both a "spiritual" and a "concrete" criterion. Highlighting the distinction, Barth stated, "In attempting to fill out the first three terms we could point only to Jesus Christ as the Head of the community which is His body, and therefore to the work of the Holy Spirit."[57] However, he noted that "apostolic" is also a "concrete criterion."[58] Apart from assisting in locating the "true Church" (as opposed to the false) in the midst of many churches, this concrete criterion also provides a "standard" as a means of self-examination.[59]

As a concrete criterion then, Barth was highlighting the concept of "task." In this way, he understood the apostolicity of the church as being linked to the "instruction" and "direction" of the apostles, in which there is a "listening to them" and an "accepting of their message."[60] Further recognising that apostolicity "describes the being of the community as an event" that concretely witnesses to Jesus as the "community of Jesus Christ."[61] Yet this is not to suggest that apostolic is only a concrete criterion. Rather, Barth quickly pointed out that understanding apostolic as a concrete criterion is only "truly helpful" when it is not "deprived" of its "character as a spiritual criterion" that recognises the "work of the Holy Spirit."[62]

Apostolicity can be expressed in a community concretely (as a task), but it is also received in faith (as a gift) as the community is empowered by the Holy Spirit and governed by Jesus Christ. Barth's concern was that any institution or human-made ritual would seek to lay claim to this mark as if it were its own possession and thus seek the apostolicity of the church solely on "historical or juridical grounds."[63] Here Barth was directly challenging the notion of apostolic succession. He noted that "one or many exalted members of the community" (e.g., some forms of the institutionalised church) have attempted to do with "legality and ritual" what can be accomplished only through the work of the Holy Spirit and Jesus Christ.[64] Here again, Barth was pointing out the spiritual criterion of apostolicity, thereby locating it within the being and action of the divine Godhead. Further, Barth made

---

57. Barth, *CD*, IV/1.62, 712.
58. Barth, *CD*, IV/1.62, 713.
59. Barth, *CD*, IV/1.62, 714.
60. Barth, *CD*, IV/1.62, 714.
61. Barth, *CD*, IV/1.62, 714–15.
62. Barth, *CD*, IV/1.62, 714–15.
63. Barth, *CD*, IV/1.62, 714–15.
64. Barth, *CD*, IV/1.62, 717.

it very clear that when it comes to apostolicity, both the Holy Spirit and Jesus participate, and this action is done in freedom.[65]

Having turned the focus toward Jesus, Barth continued in his discussion, weaving back and forth between the concrete criterion and the spiritual criterion in discussing various aspects of apostolicity as it relates to the church. In sum, the church is apostolic when it is (1) obedient in witness;[66] (2) empowered by the Holy Spirit;[67] (3) grounded in Scripture;[68] and (4) looking toward the living Jesus.[69]

Barth concluded, highlighting that the apostles were obedient in service as they were sent out to preach the gospel, but that it was a message that pointed beyond them. In this way, the church emulates the apostles in being "sent" in an "outward movement" pointing beyond itself.[70]

To summarise this section, from Barth's theology it can be affirmed that the marks are to be received in faith as an indicative gift for the whole church because they are grounded in Christ and empowered by the Holy Spirit, and belong to the nature and being of the triune God.[71] More so, if Jesus within his being and nature bears the essence of "one, holy, catholic, and apostolic," then so will his church. Yet it is not simply that the church will *contain* these characteristics, but that the church will *exhibit* these characteristics. This understanding is often expressed in the concept of "gift and task," in which the church through its corresponding nature is to emulate the gift it has been given through its ecclesial task.[72] However, if the church does already *possess* the marks as a gift, how is this task to be expressed? What, then, is the significance of Jesus' bearing within his nature and being, the essence of the marks? These questions are directly related to the concept of correspondence.

Kimlyn Bender argues that correspondence is first and foremost a "Christological notion," and that it refers "to the manner in which Christ's

---

65. See Barth, *CD*, II/1.28: God is listed as the one who loves in freedom. See also *CD*, II/1.31, *The Perfections of Divine Freedom*.

66. Barth, *CD*, IV/1.62, 720.

67. Barth, *CD*, IV/1.62, 720.

68. Barth, *CD*, IV/1.62, 722.

69. Barth, *CD*, IV/1.62, 723.

70. Barth, *CD*, IV/1.62, 724–25.

71. "None of these terms can be applied to anything but the divine operation which takes place in the church." Barth, *CD*, IV/2.67, *The Holy Spirit and the Upbuilding of the Christian Community*, 617.

72. Elsewhere I have presented the marks as a "gift-task paradigm" constructed as a communicative, analytical, and theological tool offering the contemporary church a way of engaging with and understanding their significance. See Marguerite Kappelhoff, "The Marks of the Church: A Paradigm for the Twenty-First-Century Church," in *Hope in the Ecumenical Future: Pathways for Ecumenical and Interreligious Dialogue*, ed. Mark D. Chapman (Cham, Switzerland: Palgrave Macmillan, 2017).

life mirrors and indeed represents the divine life of God in its own proper sphere of being and activity."[73] Furthermore, this christological correspondence is followed by an ecclesiological one in which the church is to bear within its life an imitation and representation of what has been modeled.[74] Regarding the correspondence of Christ, the understanding is that Jesus within his actions demonstrates what he sees the Father doing (John 5:19). The question that then arises is, *what is it that the Father does that Jesus demonstrates?* Barth, in his treatment of the doctrine of God, suggested that God is the "being who loves in freedom" and in doing so "seeks and creates fellowship" with humanity.[75] Engaging this concept of correspondence as foundational, the remainder of this chapter focuses on developing the argument that God's loving action of "seeking and creating fellowship" reveals an understanding of what it means to be "one, holy, catholic, and apostolic," to which Christ and the church correspond.

THE GOD WHO SEEKS AND CREATES FELLOWSHIP[76]

When Barth presented God as the being "who loves in freedom," his discussion focused on the "essence" of God, or that which "makes God God," as foundational.[77] Barth noted that God's essence can be seen in his "revealed name," "being," and "act as Father, Son, and Holy Spirit."[78] Purposely and as a self-motivated act, God, "without having to do so, seeks and creates fellowship between Himself and us."[79] It is this statement of "seeking and creating fellowship" that becomes a predominant theme through which God is revealed as the "being who loves in freedom." God already exists in fellowship as part of the Trinity, but out of an "overflow of His essence," God "turns to us" and seeks to create fellowship with humanity despite our distinctive otherness.[80] This is the "conduct" of God's action, that it

establishes and embraces the antithesis between the Creator and His creatures. It establishes and embraces necessarily, too, God's anger and

---

73. Bender, *Karl Barth's Christological Ecclesiology*, 6–7.
74. Bender, 6–7.
75. See Barth's work in *CD*, II/1.28.
76. This section draws from Barth's work in *CD*, II/1.28, *The Being of God as the One Who Loves in Freedom*.
77. Barth, *CD*, II.1.28, 273.
78. Barth, *CD*, II.1.28, 273.
79. Barth, *CD*, II.1.28, 273.
80. Barth, *CD*, II.1.28, 273–74.

struggle against sin, God's separation from sinners, God's judgment hanging over them and consummated on them. There is death and hell and eternal damnation in the scope of this relationship of His. But His attitude and action is always that He seeks and creates fellowship between Himself and us.[81]

In other words, God not only "seeks" fellowship, but God also "creates" the necessary conditions to ensure that fellowship can occur. It was in this "primal decision" that "God did not remain satisfied with His own being in Himself" and instead "reached out to something beyond" himself.[82] As properly understood of God, "He wills to be ours, and He wills that we should be His," therefore he "leans toward this unity with our life."[83]

Following on then, "seeking and creating fellowship" is an act initiated by God as an overflow of God's essence, but it is an action that will find its fulfillment in and through Jesus Christ as it's "crown and final confirmation."[84] This, then, is the link between the "essence of God" and the outworking and establishing of that fellowship with humanity—starting with God who reveals himself as the God of fellowship who will "seek and create" ways in which to establish that fellowship, and then continuing in that process through the election of Jesus for humanity. Therefore, what Jesus sees the Father doing is "seeking and creating fellowship." As related to the marks of the church, I would argue that God's "love" is catholic; that God's act of "seeking" is apostolic; that to "create" fellowship requires holiness; and that "fellowship" is about unity.

The *love of God* has shown itself to be *catholic* in that it is inclusive of the distinctive "other." God's love is such that it does not require the object of God's love to be "worthy" of that love, because God's love in and of itself is more than enough. Additionally, this love is "eternal," "everlasting"; stretching across time with a "continuity" that is "maintained" in "all differences," referring to the character that never changes.[85] In this way, God's love can be trusted as the everlasting and eternal source that reaches out to all and excludes none.

God's *seeking* can be likened to *apostolic*, for in God's seeking, God sends Godself in an outward movement beyond Godself, searching for the

---

81. Barth, *CD*, II.1.28, 274.
82. Barth, *CD*, II/2.33, "The Election of Jesus Christ," 168.
83. Barth, *CD*, II/1.28, 274.
84. Barth, *CD*, II/1.28, 274.
85. Barth, *CD*, IV/1.62, 701, 710.

"other" in order to bring God's message of love and create fellowship.[86] God wills to be *for* humanity, and this self-motivated movement comes from God's desire to be "with us" and "not without us."[87] *Apostolic* in this sense is understood as "seeking" or "sending" not as "in line" with or subject to the apostles, but rather in terms of its root meaning of "sent," "messenger." God in this action is the Sender, the Sent and the Sending.[88]

Creating is about holiness, with God ensuring and establishing all the necessary conditions for fellowship to exist. This includes making the "other" holy in order that she or he might be taken up into God's fellowship. God's action of "throwing a bridge across a crevasse" includes "election," where the "other" is reconciled, justified, and made holy.[89] Despite being distinct from this "other," "alien," "hostile" one, God "seeks" this "other" and then makes it holy for the purposes of fellowship offered through God's eternal and everlasting love.

Unity is about *fellowship*. True unity of the church is about the "other" being taken up into the fellowship of the triune God. There is a "singularity" despite the "plurality" that exists.[90] Further, this fellowship is at a depth that humanity cannot create or sustain on its own. Nor can the church create or sustain unity, because true unity only exists within the triune God.

In summary and in support of the argument at hand, God is revealed as the one who is so concerned with seeking and creating fellowship with humanity that God establishes and creates the conditions by which God can be in fellowship with the distinctive other. God wills so desperately to be *for* and *with* humanity that God will not allow God's transcendence to get in the way of God's immanence, but instead ensures that this action is continued in the sending of Jesus. It is that "seeking and creating fellowship" that Jesus then emulates in a corresponding action to the Father's action and, in doing so, draws from his own nature and being those characteristics found in the marks—not simply in correspondence to the Father but further as an example for the church to follow in corresponding action.

---

86. For more on this, see Barth, CD, IV/1.59, *The Obedience of the Son of God*, 157: "the way of the Son of God into the far off country."

87. Barth, *CD*, II/1.28, 274.

88. See also David J. Bosch, *Transforming Mission: Paradigm Shifts in Theology of Mission* (Maryknoll, NY: Orbis Books, 1991); John G. Flett, *The Witness of God: The Trinity, Missio Dei, Karl Barth, and the Nature of Christian Community* (Grand Rapids: Eerdmans, 2010), 194; and Timothy C. Tennent, *Invitation to World Missions: A Trinitarian Missiology for the Twenty-First Century* (Grand Rapids: Kregel, 2010).

89. Barth, *CD*, II/1.28, 278.

90. Barth, *CD*, IV/1.62, 675.

THE CORRESPONDENCE OF CHRIST AND THE CHURCH

Barth's understanding of Jesus' correspondence to God is located in his discussion on "The Royal Man," which examines the "kingly office" of Jesus Christ.[91] Specifically, Barth "considers what it means that the royal man is a reflection of God in correspondence with his purpose and work."[92] To be sure, "The royal man of the New Testament tradition is created 'after God' (κατὰ θεόν). This means that as a man, He exists analogously to the mode of existence of God. In what He thinks and wills and does, in His attitude, there is a correspondence, a parallel in the creaturely world, to the plan and purpose and work and attitude of God."[93] Barth highlighted the understanding that "we know God in Jesus Christ alone" because "He reflects God."[94] Barth continued, "In Him the will of God is done on earth as it is in heaven. . . . He does that which is demanded and expected in the covenant as the act of human faithfulness corresponding to the faithfulness of God."[95] Therefore, Jesus is God in action. Jesus can be seen doing what God does because he is concerned with and for the concerns of God. This being the case, when Jesus is represented as "one, holy, catholic, and apostolic," it then naturally suggests that God also must first be represented in this same way. Nevertheless, if God in God's love is "concerned with seeking and creating fellowship," then Jesus' action must in some way represent this same concern, and the church in corresponding action follows.

Bender argues that, for Barth, "the true church exists only as a unity of event and historical manifestation in dialectical relation—the historical and enduring existence of the church exists insofar, paradoxically, as it is an ever-new event."[96] He says that "the first without the second would be a platonic conception of an invisible church that is disembodied, and thus not incarnate" and that "the second without the first leads to a loss of the church's very essence and can only be seen as an empty shell, a visible though dead and false church."[97] The presenting concern is the danger of a church's life not corresponding to Christ. The end result is that "the unity of

---

91. See Barth, *CD*, IV/2.64, *The Exaltation of the Son of Man*.
92. G. W. Bromiley, *An Introduction to the Theology of Karl Barth* (Edinburgh: T&T Clark, 1979), 201.
93. Barth, *CD*, IV/2.64, 166.
94. Barth, *CD*, II/1.28, 318; and IV/2.64, 167.
95. Barth, *CD*, IV/2.64, 167.
96. Bender, *Karl Barth's Christological Ecclesiology*, 156.
97. Bender, 157.

the church with her Lord ceases" and "the church is no longer addressed by her Lord and renewed by his Spirit."[98] Even if the "outer, visible, historical and institutional form of the church" exists, "this church is no longer the true church"; it is "instead a "nominal church," an ecclesiastical shell from which the life has fled."[99]

The church is therefore "an event and a history" that needs to be renewed by being in relationship with God (event) and by hearing the voice of Jesus; otherwise the institution (its place in history) will fail to exist as a true church.[100] So there is a danger for the church that does not act in a way corresponding to Christ, its head: it can lose its way.[101] This means that the church needs to concern itself with the things that concern Christ and not concern itself with the things that do not concern Christ. What is Christ's concern? To correspond to the Father. What is the Father's concern? God's love is concerned with "seeking and creating fellowship" with humanity. Jesus' actions correspond to that of the Father, as demonstrated with his concern for "one, holy, catholic, and apostolic" originating in an effort to emulate God's action of "seeking and creating fellowship."

This loving that is concerned with "seeking and creating fellowship" has much to say to ecclesiology in terms of its orthodoxy and its practices. However, it is important to remember that the church already possesses the marks as an ascribed gift and as a continual source of renewal that comes through being part of the nature and being of the triune God. Meaning that this act of the divine being who "chooses," "wills," and "desires" to be "with us and not to be without us" offers to the church a way to exist and be sustained in its efforts to be the "one, holy, catholic, and apostolic" community.[102] Barth noted,

> God can allow this other which is so utterly distinct from Himself to live and move and have its being within Himself. He can grant and leave it its own special being distinct from His own, and yet even in this way, and therefore in this its creaturely freedom, sustain, uphold and govern it by His own divine being, thus being its beginning, centre and end. God can in fact be nearer to it than it is to itself. He can understand it better

---

98. Bender, 155. See also the discussion in Karl Barth, "The Threat to the Church," in *God Here and Now*, trans. Paul M. van Buren (New York: Harper and Row, 1964), 83–92.

99. Bender, *Karl Barth's Christological Ecclesiology*, 155–56. See also Barth's discussion on the "apparent Church" in Barth, *God Here and Now*, 91ff.

100. Bender, *Karl Barth's Christological Ecclesiology*, 155.

101. Barth, *God Here and Now*, 76.

102. Barth, *CD*, II/1.28, 274.

than it understands itself. He can inspire and guide it at a deeper level than it knows how to do itself—infinitely nearer, better, more deeply, yet not in dissolution but in confirmation of His own divine singularity and again not in dissolution but in confirmation of the singularity of the creature. The fact that God can do this is His freedom in immanence.[103]

It has already been well established that God's love is concerned with seeking and creating fellowship, yet as is highlighted in this quote, God's desire for fellowship goes beyond the initial seeking and creating and extends itself to "sustain," "uphold," "govern," "inspire," and "guide" at a "deeper level" than the other "knows how to do itself."[104] It stands to reason therefore that God will be interested in any fellowship that concerns God, because God is the author, creator, initiator, and sustainer of true fellowship. God does not and will not leave God's church alone in its efforts to seek and create fellowship, but rather, remains present in its midst. Therefore, because it is God's desire to seek and create fellowship, and because God has set up all the conditions necessary to establish and maintain fellowship, it stands to reason that in this God has provided the basis of what it means for the church to be one, holy, catholic, and apostolic. If God is the one who seeks and creates fellowship first and foremost, then any attempts on the part of the church can only be in correspondence to the divine action and in correspondence to Christ. Indeed, Barth located the divine immanence as outworked in Jesus, the head of the church, who is the "crown of all relationship and fellowship between God and the world."[105]

Therefore, relationship and fellowship created and sustained in Jesus becomes the way forward and the test by which every relationship is measured. If, as I have already argued, "one, holy, catholic, and apostolic" is about "seeking and creating fellowship" between God and humanity (among the churches and with the "other"), then the test for that fellowship is found in the church's ability to be recognised as a "community of Christ," with Jesus as its centre and its sole basis for unity, holiness, catholicity, and apostolicity.

By way of conclusion to this discussion on correspondence, Jesus does not do anything but that which he sees his Father doing. It was the Father's love, concerned with seeking and creating fellowship, that sent Jesus. Jesus, filled with the same concern, sends his church empowered by the Holy

---

103. Barth, *CD*, II/1.28, 314.
104. Barth, *CD*, II/1.28, 314.
105. Barth, *CD*, II/1.28, 318.

Spirit to be "one, holy, catholic, and apostolic." As the church corresponds to Christ in its efforts to express the gift and task of the marks within its own nature and mission, it corresponds to the loving action of God who desires to "seek and create fellowship."

CONCLUDING COMMENTS

In this chapter, I have argued that one of the tensions within the contemporary church is that the marks have been relegated to an institutional handling of them and have, as a result, lost their critical theological functioning. Reviewing Barth's engagement of the marks revealed that the marks are found first and foremost within the nature and being of the triune God. This understanding informs ecclesiology and its practices because it locates the origin of the marks of the church outside the institution of the church and further indicates something of how the marks are sustained. That is, being *from* God and *of* God, their source is therefore necessarily *in* God and not in the church, even if they are to be appropriated at this level. The institutional church therefore can only respond in a corresponding manner to the example it has been given regarding the marks. This chapter argues that it is God who "seeks and creates fellowship" with and among humanity; it is Christ as the head of the church who within his actions demonstrates what he sees the Father doing (continues the mission); and it is the church empowered by the Holy Spirit that responds in corresponding action as it engages the task of being one, holy, catholic, and apostolic. In this way, it goes out beyond itself to find the "other," leaning toward them in an effort to develop relationship. From a missional perspective, this is the self-evident task of evangelism. However, from an ecumenical perspective, it highlights that any efforts to approach the marks through denominational "basic affirmations" is too limiting a position that robs them of their theological function. Instead, any appeal made to the marks on an institutional level must be measured against the theological criterion of "true" unity as only found in Christ. Where there is a lack of unity, efforts need to be made to correct this. Churches need to find ways to seek and create fellowship among the body of Christ, as it were. Churches need to overcome any division by "healing" any visible/invisible hurt. Then this "community of Christ" can be "gathered," finding "continual renewal" as it lives as his body, his community, his fellowship. This is theologically significant for ecclesiological orthodoxy and praxis because "the gathering of this community" is the "provisional representation of the whole world of humanity justified in Him."[106] Understanding that the church's claim to be "one, holy, catholic, and apostolic" can only be founded in him who is within his nature and being "one, holy, catholic, and apostolic." Accepting this is a "gift" that is ascribed to the whole church, even as it is a "task" that the church must engage as it corresponds to its head through the power of the Spirit, in its effort to reflect God's desire and loving action "to seek and create fellowship."

106. Barth, *CD*, vol. IV, bk. 1, §62, p. 643.

CHAPTER 13

BOND OF PEACE

Ecclesial Unity as Participation in the Son and Spirit

STEVEN J. DUBY

INTRODUCTION

"We believe in one, holy, catholic, apostolic church." Such has been the confession of Christian believers around the world for centuries. And it is the privilege of dogmatic theology to ponder what Scripture presses the church to confess and to take Christian believers further into its inner logic and spiritual depth. In the case of the church's confession about itself, dogmatic theology has the task of reminding the church that it is not self-sufficient or self-sustaining but rather lives and moves within the triune life of God, whose gracious work determines what the church is and what it is for.

Connecting any of the four creedal attributes of the church (unity, holiness, catholicity, apostolicity) back to the being and works of God would be a worthwhile endeavor, but this essay focuses on the unity of the church, particularly how the unity of the church is rooted in Christians' participation in the persons of God the Son and God the Holy Spirit. The importance of ecclesial unity and the call to promote that unity are set forth in a variety of places in Holy Scripture, but perhaps John 17 and Ephesians 4 bear mentioning from the outset. In the prayer of Jesus in John 17, the Lord asks those who will believe in him to be one even as the Father and Jesus are one (17:20–22). Astonishingly, one of the results of this unity is that the world will know that the Father has loved Jesus' disciples even as the Father has loved Jesus himself (17:23). In Ephesians 4, when Paul urged his readers to live worthily of their Christian calling, he exhorted them "to maintain the unity of the Spirit in the bond of peace" (4:3). This exhortation discloses that believers' actions follow on a more fundamental reality—the fact that there already *is* a unity of the Spirit and bond of peace.

In light of these and some other relevant texts, this essay will suggest that underlying and empowering institutional, visible ecclesial unity is the saints' conformity to the sonship of the Son and to the Spirit's relationship to the Father and Son. The description offered here will unfold in three movements. First, it will require discussing the way in which the processions and personal properties of the Son and Spirit are manifested in their missions in the world. Second, it will require discussing the way in which the mission of the Son secures the saints' union with the Son and conforms the saints to the Son's sonship. Finally, it will require discussing the way in which the mission of the Spirit, who is the bond of love between the Father and Son, enables us to participate in the Spirit's relationship to the Father and Son and is fittingly said to establish the church's unity and bond of peace.

PROCESSIONS, MISSIONS, AND THE MANIFESTATION OF THE PERSONS

In biblical Trinitarianism, the three divine persons do not merely coexist. One of them (the Son) exists and comes from another person (the Father), and one of them (the Holy Spirit) exists and comes from two other persons (the Father and Son). In the very name "Son," there is reference to a Father from whom the Son is or by whom he is begotten. As Cyril of Alexandria put it, "No one ever learns what a father is unless he acknowledges in his mind a son subsisting and being begotten; but nor does anyone ever learn what a son is unless he acknowledges that a father begets."[1] That the eternal Son is from the Father and receives from the Father the divine nature is corroborated in a number of biblical texts. He is the Son who receives from the Father "life in himself" (John 5:26). He is the Son "from the Father" in a manner that gives him perfect knowledge of the Father (Matt. 11:27; John 6:46; 7:28–29). He is Son, heir, and the radiating forth of the Father's glory who bears the "imprint" of the Father's substance (Heb. 1:2–3). In

---

1. Cyril of Alexandria, *Oratio ad Theodosium*, in Eduard Schwartz, ed., *Acta Conciliorum Oecumenicorum*, vol. 1.1.1 (Berlin: de Gruyter 1927), 7, 13 (50–51). Cf. Cyril of Alexandria, *In divi Ioannis Evangelium*, 3 vols., ed. P. E. Pusey (Oxford: Clarendon, 1872), 11.12.1010A (3:14). In earlier works that include numbering for chapters, sections, and the like, the page numbers from the edition used in this essay appear afterward in parentheses.

short, he is the one begotten of God and thus at the same time true God and Son of God (1 John 5:18–20).[2]

Although the Bible is more discreet about the Spirit's procession, a number of texts bear witness to his being and going forth from both Father and Son and, in so doing, receiving from them the divine nature (e.g., John 16:12–15; 1 Cor. 2:10–12). While the terms *holy* and *spirit* can signify that which is common to all three divine persons, *Spirit* or *Holy Spirit* is also a proper name signifying a particular person. And that proper name can have reference back to a principle spirating or breathing forth.[3] Echoing God's transformation of the valley of dry bones by his Spirit in Ezekiel 37, the risen Christ breathes on his disciples and tells them, "Receive the Holy Spirit" (John 20:22). This event, often called the *insufflatio* ("in-breathing"), tells us something about the meaning of the Spirit's name and thus the identity of the Spirit: the Spirit is one spirated by another and coming forth from another with divine power. According to Cyril, this event shows that "the Holy Spirit is not alien to the Son, but of the same substance with him and through him going forth from the Father."[4]

That the Spirit—the "eternal Spirit" (Heb. 9:14)—comes forth from another (or two others) not merely in time but even eternally is corroborated elsewhere in Scripture. According to Jesus in John 16:12–15, for instance, the reason the Spirit does not operate "from himself" in the world is that the Spirit receives from Jesus, who shares all that belongs to the Father. If the Spirit is true God, he cannot receive knowledge, power, authority, and the like at a particular point in time (e.g., Pentecost). One who is true God cannot be a newcomer to divine attributes or divine efficacy. The receiving that the Spirit does, therefore, is an eternal receiving from the Son that is then expressed outwardly and at various times in the economy. And as John 16:15 indicates, this receiving takes place from the Son because the Son shares whatever belongs to the Father, including, evidently, the spiration of the Spirit and the attendant communication of divine perfection and

---

2. One could add other indicators of the Son's eternal generation, including the Son being the "image" of the Father (see Col. 1:15, 19; 2:9; cf. Gen. 5:3) and even the complementary name "Logos." For in the designation "Logos," there is reference back to a principle (the Father) whose Logos (concept, expression) he is (cf., e.g., Gregory Nazianzen, *Discours 27–31 [Discours Théologiques]*, SC 250 (Paris: Cerf, 1978), 30.20 (266–70); John of Damascus, *Expositio fidei*, in vol. 2 of *Die Schriften des Johannes von Damaskos*, ed. P. Bonifatius Kotter (Berlin: de Gruyter, 1973), 1.13 (41); Nicolaus of Lyra, *Postilla super Evangelium Ioannis*, in *Biblia Sacra cum Glossa Ordinaria*, vol. 5 (Venice: 1603), 1017–18).

3. Cf. Ambrose, *De Spiritu Sancto libri tres*, in *Sancti Ambrosii opera, pars VIIII*, ed. Otto Faller, CSEL 79 (Vienna: Hölder-Pichler-Tempsky, 1964), 1.3, 44 (32–33).

4. Cyril of Alexandria, *In Ioann.*, 12.1.1095A (3:131).

operation to the Spirit.[5] Thus, as the Son is and is called true God and Son of God, the Spirit is and is called YHWH and Spirit of YHWH (2 Cor. 3:17). Furthermore, the Spirit is and is called the Spirit of God the Father in particular and also the Spirit of the Son or Spirit of Christ in particular (Acts 16:7; Rom. 8:9–11; 1 Cor. 6:11; Gal. 4:6; Phil. 1:19; 1 Peter 1:11). The former manner of speaking in a place like 2 Corinthians 3:17 leaves unexpressed the distinction between the Father and Son as two persons who together are one principle of the Spirit; the latter manner of speaking explicitly distinguishes the Father and Son within their shared principial relation to the Spirit.

The processions of the Son and Spirit, often condensed for heuristic purposes in the personal properties of filiation and passive spiration, are manifested in their missions in the world. As the Son is begotten of the Father, so he is said to be sent from the Father (e.g., Mark 9:37; 12:6; Luke 4:18, 43; John 3:17; 20:21; Gal. 4:4). As the Spirit proceeds from the Father and Son, so he is said to be sent from the Father and Son (e.g., John 14:26; 15:26; 16:7; Gal. 4:6). A few things ought to be highlighted here to set out the meaning of mission in Trinitarian doctrine.

The first component in the concept of mission is the sent one's relation to the one from whom he comes, his origin and principle and thus his sender. The emissary's relation to his origin and principle has a distinct import in divinity. As true God, who eternally knows all things and is King of kings and Lord of lords (Isa. 46:9–10; 1 Tim. 6:15), a divine emissary cannot begin to exist or receive new knowledge or dominion at the time of sending (cf. Mark 12:35–37; Heb. 1:10–12; Rev. 17:14; 19:16).[6] Sending in divinity implies no inferiority or recent equipment of the emissary (cf., e.g., John 3:8; 5:21; 8:58). Rather, when a divine person is said to be "sent," the reason behind that language is that the divine person who comes to be present in the world in a particular way is one of the divine persons who is and acts from another and so comes from another. Because he is and does whatever he does *ab alio*, he comes into the world *ab alio* and so is aptly called "sent."[7] It follows that in divine sending, there is no new act of origination or new communication of perfection to the person sent. Instead, there is

---

5. On which, see, e.g., Augustine, *De trinitate libri XVI*, 2 vols., ed. W. J. Mountain, CCSL 50–50A (Turnhout, Belgium: Brepols, 1968), 4.20.29 (1:200); Cyril of Alexandria, *In Ioann.*, 11.2.930A–931A (2:637–39).

6. Cf. also Philippians 2:9–11 applying the name YHWH to Jesus and alluding to Isaiah 45:23, where, in context, YHWH proclaims his unique divine knowledge over against the ignorance of false gods.

7. See Augustine, *De trinitate*, 4.19–20.27 (1:194–96); Thomas Aquinas, *Summa contra Gentiles*, vols. 13–15 of *Opera omnia*, ed. Leonine (Rome: Typis Ricardi Garroni, 1918–30), 4.23 (15:86).

just the extension of the eternal act of origination to an outward effect in the economy to which the emissary has a new connection.

Second, then, there is the sent person's new connection to the outward effect whereby he takes up a new mode of presence in the world and is newly manifested or communicated in the world. There is, for example, the Son's new relation to the flesh that he assumes or the Spirit's new (and temporary) relation to the tongues of fire at Pentecost. As Augustine pointed out, a mission of the Son, for example, is not to be equated with the Son's eternal generation. For there is the necessary element of the emissary's new manifestation or communication in the world: "The Son is not called 'sent' from the fact that he is born of the Father, but either from the fact that he has appeared to this world . . . or from the fact that in time he is perceived by someone's mind."[8]

Third, to round out the meaning of mission in Trinitarian doctrine, it can be noted that when the sent person comes into the world, he carries with him and manifests or communicates his eternal relation to the person (or persons) from whom he exists. The manifestation of this eternal relation takes place in several ways. For instance, the sent person always acts from the person(s) from whom he proceeds and is sent. So Jesus: "When you lift up the Son of Man, then you will know that I am, and from myself I do nothing" (John 8:28). In addition, the sent person's teaching (whether it be the Son's proclamation or the Spirit's inward illumination) refers back to and discloses the one from whom he has come (Matt. 11:27; John 1:14, 18; 8:28; 14:6–11, 26; 15:26; 16:12–15; 17:6–8, 25–26; 1 Cor 2:10–12; Eph. 1:17–23; Heb. 1:1–3). All of this is rooted in the fact that the identity of the person sent remains the same in the mission. His personally constitutive relation to the mission's principle (i.e., the one from whom he proceeds) is not changed. His act of coming forth is not changed or supplemented but only extended outward. And the sent person's identity is not changed by his relation to the mission's *terminus ad quem* (i.e., the created effect whereby he manifests himself or to which he communicates himself). He still is who he is by virtue of his eternal relation to the one from whom he proceeds. That the person sent enables us to participate in this relation or personal property is the subject of the next section dealing with God the Son. The following section will then deal with participation in God the Holy Spirit.

---

8. Augustine, *De trinitate*, 4.20.28 (1:198). Augustine's statements here are foundational to subsequent discussion of the distinction between "visible" and "invisible" missions (see Peter Lombard, *Sententiae in IV libris distinctae*, Spicilegium Bonaventurianum 4B (Rome: Editiones Collegii S. Bonaventurae ad Claras Aquas, 1971), 1.15.7 (135–36).

MISSIONS AND CHRISTIAN PARTICIPATION IN THE SON

Thus far the argument may seem distant from the topic of ecclesial unity, but this section will hopefully begin to show how the procession and mission of the Son matter for the oneness of the church. To that end, I will offer four main points.

1. The mission of a divine person involves the giving of a divine person in order to bring created things or persons into union with the divine person.[9] In the case of God the Son, the Father visibly gives the Son in the Son's assumption of human flesh and subsequent crucifixion (John 3:16; 6:32–33; Rom. 8:32).[10] But this visible giving of the Son is ultimately ordered toward an invisible giving: the Father gives the Son when the Son comes into spiritual union with the adopted children of God (John 1:9–13; Eph. 1:22–23; cf. Rom. 8:9–11; 1 Cor. 12:12; Gal. 3:26–27; Col. 1:27). In the case of the Holy Spirit, there are visible missions of the Spirit that outwardly manifest a grace or empowerment inwardly given to someone (so Matt. 3:17; Acts 2:1–4). But much more frequent in Scripture is the invisible sending or invisible giving of the Spirit—his coming to indwell, transform, and empower someone (Luke 11:13; John 3:34; 4:14; 7:39; 14:16; Acts 2:38; 5:32; 8:18–20; 10:45; 11:17; 15:8; Rom. 5:5; 1 Cor. 1:22; 5:5; Gal. 4:6; Eph 1:17; 1 Thess. 4:8; 1 John 3:24; 4:13; cf. Acts 1:4, 8; Gal. 3:14).[11]

2. If the invisible giving of a divine person entails the union of the Christian with that divine person, there are at least two things about this union that need mentioning. First, the new union wrought between the Son or Spirit and the Christian is not the first moment in which God or this particular divine person is present in the believer. For God already fills heaven and earth, and in him we live and move and have our being (Jer. 23:23–24; Acts 17:28). Second, then, the novelty of the union between

---

9. By the giving of a divine person is meant that, according to a free choice of God, a created thing or person comes to possess (or to be possessed by) a divine person in a new way. It may be worth clarifying here that a divine mission is not the only scenario in which the giving of a divine person can take place. For the Father proceeds from no one and is never "sent," but the Father can still be said to give himself to us. In this connection, the act of giving does not require a distinction between giver and gift but only between giver and receiver (i.e., one can give oneself). But whenever a divine mission does occur, it will involve some sort of divine giving.

10. It is, of course, not the divine operation itself that is visible but the created effect (i.e., the flesh or the crucifixion). In various places the Son also gives or gives up himself (Mark 10:45; John 6:51; Gal. 1:4; 2:20; Eph. 5:2, 25; 1 Tim. 2:6; Titus 2:14). With respect to the hypostatic principle from whom the Son proceeds and comes into the world in a new manner, only the Father gives the Son. But with respect to the operation itself of the divine giving, the Son always acts together with the Father and Spirit and thus gives himself.

11. See also the "outpouring" of the Spirit in Joel 2:28; Acts 2:18, 33.

the Son or Spirit and the Christian does not rest on bare presence but on the performance of a new divine action that takes effect in the believer, particularly an action that brings about an effect that in some way conforms the believer to the divine person.

This second comment requires some elaboration. Among other things, it has to be noted that the whole Trinity is the efficient cause of the new spiritual union. Indeed, the whole Trinity is the efficient cause of a range of salvific effects that are now resident in the Christian (e.g., John 14:23; Rom. 8:9–11; 1 John 3:24), though this efficient causality is often appropriated to the Holy Spirit who is said to dwell in us (e.g., Acts 2:33, 38; Rom. 8:15–16; 1 Cor. 2:6–16; 3:16–17; Gal. 4:6).[12] The salvific effects that might be considered are diverse. Justification, for instance, is distinctly forensic and grants the believer the legal standing of Christ (Rom. 5:12–21; 1 Tim. 3:16). Other gifts or effects pertain to godly virtue and assimilate the believer to the divine nature common to the three divine persons (2 Peter 1:4). And yet, as the passages cited in the previous point suggest, it is still fitting to speak of an invisible reception of the Son or the Spirit that effects something in the believer that assimilates the believer to the proper character of the Son or the Spirit. For even given the undivided efficacy of the Trinity and the believer's union with all three divine persons, there can still be a distinct union with one divine person in the sense that a certain effect in the believer may have one divine person as an exemplar or prototype.[13]

3. It is to this exemplar causality that I want to appeal in order to maintain that the invisible missions of the Son and Spirit unite us to the Son

---

12. In my judgment, the appropriation of indwelling and sanctification may have a twofold basis: (1) the conferring of gifts especially resonates with the manner of the Spirit's procession as love or gift (on which, see the next section); (2) the application of the benefits of Christ after the meritorious work of Christ especially resonates with the Spirit being the final person in the order of the divine persons (see further, Augustine, *De trinitate*, 15.17.29 (2:503–4); 15.19.33–6 (2:508–13); Thomas Aquinas, *Super Evangelium s. Matthaei lectura*, 5th ed., ed. R. Cai (Rome: Marietti, 1951), 1.4.112 (17); *Summa theologiae*, in vols. 4–12 of *Opera omnia*, Leonine ed. (Rome: ex Typographia Polyglotta, 1888–1906), 1.38 (4:392–94) (hereafter *ST*); 3.32.1 (11:333–34); John Owen, *Pneumatologia*, in *Works of John Owen*, ed. William H. Goold, vol. 3 (Edinburgh: Banner of Truth Trust, 1965), 1.1 (20); 2.3 (161–62); 3.1 (209); Herman Witsius, *Exercitationes in symbolum*, 4th ed. (Herborn, Germany: Iohannes Nicolaus Andreas, 1712), 6.3 (66); Witsius, *De oeconomia foederum Dei cum hominibus*, 2nd ed. (Leeuwarden, Netherlands: Jacob Hagenaar, 1685), 3.12.48 (352).

13. An exemplar cause is an example or model after which something is made. It is distinct from a formal cause in particular in that an exemplar cause is extrinsic to the subject made and not necessarily of the same kind as the subject made, whereas a formal cause is intrinsic to the subject made and constitutive of the subject's own essence. Along with rooting our adoption in the Son's sonship as exemplar cause, a number of theologians point out that it can also be rooted in regeneration (we are born of God by grace) and the nuptial imagery in which the church is the bride of the Son and thus the daughter-in-law, as it were, of God the Father. See Witsius, *De oeconomia*, 3.10.9–14 (319–21); Wilhelmus à Brakel, *The Christian's Reasonable Service*, vol. 2, ed. Joel R. Beeke, trans. Bartel Elshout (Grand Rapids: Reformation Heritage, 1993), 419–20.

and Spirit by conforming us to them. In particular, the invisible mission or reception of the Son conforms us to the sonship of the Son. As the prologue of John's gospel teaches us, to receive the Logos and Μονογενής of the Father grants one the right to become a child of God (John 1:12). Or, as Paul told us, our predestination in Christ is a predestination to be conformed to Christ, so that he may be firstborn among many brothers and sisters (Rom. 8:29; Eph. 1:3–6). Indeed, according to Paul, to put on Christ the Son by baptism and through faith makes us sons of God (Gal. 3:26–27). Why does receiving or putting on Christ by baptism make us sons of God? Because, as discussed in the previous section, the divine person sent or received carries in himself and communicates to us his relation to his principle. In the case of the Son, he carries in himself and communicates to us his filial relation to the Father. We then come to participate in the Son's sonship or personal property as the exemplar cause of our own sonship.[14] That this is only a participation—a possessing in a derivative,

---

14. Additional texts that instruct us about union with Christ and conformity to the sonship of Christ include Romans 8:14–17, 23 and Hebrews 2:11–13. It may be that in these texts (and others) we are conformed to Christ as man and as our federal representative. Does this mean that we are conformed to only a distinctly *human* sonship of Christ? There are at least three things worth bearing in mind here. First, earlier theologians caution against positing two "filiations" of Christ, for sonship properly pertains to the person, who is one. Sonship pertains at most indirectly to the human nature in virtue of the person. See Bonaventure, *Commentaria in quatuor libros Sententiarum*, 4 vols., in vols. 1–4 of *Doctoris seraphici s. Bonaventurae opera omnia* (Florence: ex Typographia Collegii S. Bonaventurae, 1882–89), 3.8.2.2 (3:193–95); Thomas Aquinas, *Quaestiones de quolibet*, in vol. 25/1 of *Opera omnia*, Leonine ed. (Rome: Commissio Leonina, 1996), 9.2.3; Aquinas, *Compendium theologiae*, in vol. 42 of *Opera omnia*, Leonine ed. (Rome: Editori di San Tommaso, 1979), 1.212 (165–66). The Son himself is indeed born of Mary and is truly her Son, but because he was already born of the Father and eternally constituted a person, the birth from Mary does not introduce a new, personally constitutive sonship in him. Second, it is still possible to say that just as Christ's one existence and filial mode of being are applied to his human nature so that he now has a "twofold way of subsisting" (so Thomas Aquinas, *Quaestio disputata de unione Verbi incarnati*, in vol. 2 of *Quaestiones disputatae*, 10th ed., ed. P. Bazzi et al. [Rome-Turin: Marietti, 1965], q. un., a. 3 ad 11 [431]; William Ames, *Medulla theologica*, 2nd ed. [Amsterdam, Ianssonius, 1659], 1.18.16 [77]), so he now has a "twofold way" of sonship. Third, however, there are reasons to conclude that even if we are conformed to the sonship of Christ as applied to his humanity, we are still also conformed to the divine sonship of Christ. For there are texts like John 1:12 and Galatians 3:26–27; 4:4–7 that imply that our conformity to the sonship of Christ is not limited to the sonship as applied to his humanity. For according to John 1:14, 18, Christ is the Μονογενής from the Father who shares the divine glory, grace, and truth and who is eternally in the bosom of the Father. And according to Paul in Galatians, Christ is not a mere man (1:1) and is the Son who (together with the Father) is the principle of the Holy Spirit (4:6). Furthermore, even when we are conformed to the sonship of Christ as applied to his humanity, that is, ultimately, still a conformity to Christ's divine sonship. For the human nature and actions of Christ are determined and characterized by the communication of Christ's prevenient ὑπόστασις and filial mode of subsisting to his human nature, making him as man and mediator fit to be heir of all things and making Christ's divine sonship at least the original or mediate exemplar of our own sonship. On another note, in certain passages (esp. Rom. 8:14–17; Gal. 4:6–7), our adoption is secured by the Holy Spirit. In these passages, it remains that our sonship has the Son's sonship as its exemplar cause, but because the Spirit is the Spirit of the Son and the third person of the Trinity, indwelling, sanctification, and the sealing of sonship are fittingly appropriated to the Spirit. Cf. Aquinas, *ST*, 3.3.5 ad 2 (11:63); 3.23.2 ad 3 (11:265–66).

partial way that which someone else has originally and entirely—indicates that it does not override our creaturely status or jeopardize the uniqueness of the eternal Son.[15] At the same time, that it is a participation in the very sonship of the eternal Son indicates something of the profundity of the church's unity, which is a claim that may be filled out by revisiting John 17 and Galatians 3.

4. In John 17, Jesus asked that his disciples would have a unity reflective of the unity between him and the Father (vv. 20–21). While Jesus envisions this to be a unity in which we are in him and in the Father (cf. 14:23), he adds that he gives us glory and that he in particular will be in us and the Father in him (vv. 22–23a), which seems to be a special reference to the Son's mediatorial office and to our union and participation in the Son in particular.[16] The unity of the disciples will lead to the world knowing that the Father has sent the Son and has loved the disciples just as he has loved the Son (17:23b). In this regard, the unity of the church is a sign to the world of a deeper reality, namely, that the Father has directed his love toward us just as he has always directed it toward his Son. The Father loved his Son before the foundation of the world according to 17:24, and it is that very same love that is extended to us and present in us according to 17:26, where Jesus said to the Father, "I made your name known to them, and I will make it known, so that the love with which you have loved me may be in them and I in them." Augustine asked, then, "In what way is the love with which the Father has loved the Son also in us, except that we are his members, and in him we are loved, because he himself—the whole—is

---

15. It can be added here that our participation in Christ's sonship does not erase or compromise the spiritual status of female Christians. That Christian women are brought into spiritual union with Christ and assimilated to his sonship means not that they must be somehow treated as male but that they also are born of God by grace and made coheirs of the kingdom of God. Cf., e.g., Douglas J. Moo, *Galatians*, BECNT (Grand Rapids: Baker, 2013), 250.

16. Cf. Augustine, *In Iohannis Evangelium tractatus CXXIV*, CCSL 36 (Turnhout: Brepols, 1954), 110.4 (624); Nicolaus of Lyra, *Super Ioann.*, 1291; John Calvin, *Commentarius in Evangelium Ioannis*, in vol. 47 of *Ioannis Calvini opera quae supersunt omnia*, ed. Guilielmus Baum et al. (Brunswick, Germany: Schwetschke, 1892), 388. Note also Christ giving us the Father's name, thereby enabling us to know and address God as Father, and dwelling in us in John 17:26, which again implies participation in Christ's sonship. Calvin insisted that John 17 does not invite us to "bare speculation of [Christ's] divinity." That is, Christ's unity with the Father here does not pertain *simpliciter* or *praecise* (absolutely or in the abstract) to Christ's divinity. For that would be "unfruitful" or "useless" for us. Instead, without omitting all reference to his divinity, Christ is speaking about himself "in the person of the mediator, and as he is our head." Thus, we are unified with Christ "not because he transfuses his own substance into us but because by virtue of his own Spirit he shares with us his own life and whatever goods he receives from the Father" (*In Ioann.*, 387). My sense is that, although Calvin did not need to downplay the role of the essential unity of Christ and the Father here (a move taken further in Herman Ridderbos, *The Gospel of John: A Theological Commentary*, trans John Vriend [Grand Rapids: Eerdmans, 1997], 560–61), Calvin's emphasis on Christ's mediatorial office also does not have to negate that in our union with Christ we are conformed ultimately to Christ's divine sonship (see n. 14 above).

loved, that is, head and body?"[17] Thus, in the order of being, ecclesial unity flows from and is grounded in the saints' participation in Christ's sonship, wherein the saints have become objects or even one composite object of the Father's singular delight in his consubstantial Son who is our head.

More briefly, Galatians 3 also connects our participation in Christ's sonship to the unity of the church. For, according to Paul, putting on Christ in baptism and becoming sons of God relativizes (without eradicating) typical human differences: "There is neither Jew nor Greek, neither slave nor free, there is no male and female, for you are all one in Christ Jesus" (v. 28). Indeed, those who belong to Christ are Abraham's seed and heirs of the Abrahamic promises (v. 29). As participants in sonship and fellow heirs, we are a spiritual family, a "household of faith," to which especially we must continue doing good (Gal. 6:10). Thus, the assimilation of Christians to the sonship of Christ is constitutive of our identity and unity, an established unity that both supports and necessitates outward expressions of unity in Christian behavior.

BOND OF LOVE AND BOND OF PEACE: CHRISTIAN PARTICIPATION IN THE HOLY SPIRIT

This final main section now has to show the way in which the invisible mission of the Spirit, who is the bond of love between the Father and Son, enables us to participate in the Spirit's relationship to the Father and Son and is fittingly said to establish the church's unity and bond of peace. To that end, I will offer three main points.

1. It will be necessary to say a word about whether it is right to identify the Spirit as the bond of love between the Father and the Son (*vinculum amoris, vinculum caritatis*). The doctrine of the Spirit as the bond of love has been propounded in various ways. The teaching of 1 John 4, where there is a love that is God and is from God and in us, has played a role, not least in Augustine's description of the Spirit as the bond of love.[18] There are also

---

17. Augustine, *In Iohann.*, 111.6 (632). Cf. Calvin, *In Ioann.*, 391. Of course, the Father loves the Son, the head of the church, above all his members. This is due to the Son's deity and then derivatively to his perfect humanity and redemptive work, so the Father's delight in the Son is already fulfilled without reference to us. The Father's paternal delight is then just extended to us. His paternal delight terminates necessarily in the eternal Son and then freely (with an original liberty of contrariety) in us on account of the eternal Son who is our head and exemplar. For similar clarifications, see John Chrysostom, *Homiliae LXXXVIII in Joannem*, in PG 59 (Paris: J.-P. Migne, 1862), 82.2 (444); Augustine, *In Iohann.*, 110.5 (625–26); Cyril of Alexandria, *In Ioann.*, 11.12.1003A (3:5); Calvin, *In Ioann.*, 388.
18. Augustine, *De trinitate*, 15.17.31 (2:505–7).

different theological reasons, linked in varying degrees to a psychological analogy for the Trinity, that have been put forward regarding the Spirit as the bond of love.[19] Such lines of thinking often found a somewhat cool reception among the early Reformed authors, who were concerned not to overestimate what pilgrims in this life can know about the manner of the divine processions.[20]

It seems to me that one can affirm that the Spirit is the bond of love between the Father and Son without slipping into conjecture or laborious reasoning. Within the life of the Trinity, the Spirit is the person who proceeds from both the Father and the Son. The Father and Son are united in essence, but they are also united in the act of spirating the Spirit. And that which unites two in common action toward a common *terminus* is love— mutual complacency in one another in virtue of which they undertake something together.[21] Thus, the Spirit's mode of proceeding from two who act together is specially characterized by love. In that regard, the Spirit is rightly identified as the union of the Father and Son and the bond of love. For his mode of procession is distinctly expressive of union and love. This point is corroborated by Romans 5:5 where Paul wrote that it is by giving us the Spirit that God has poured out his love into our hearts, implying that something about the Spirit renders him particularly fit to confirm and communicate the love of God to us. It is also corroborated by other texts in which the Spirit is identified as the gift of God or is said (by appropriation) to confer salvific gifts of God to us (Luke 11:13; John 4:14; 7:39; Acts 1:4–5; 2:38; 5:32; 8:18–20; 10:45; 11:17; 15:8; Rom. 5:5; 1 Cor. 12:4–11; 2 Cor. 1:22; 5:5; Gal. 3:14; 1 Thess. 4:8; 1 John 3:24; 4:13). For love is the reason for freely giving something to another.[22] In light of all this, the Spirit is the hypostatic prototype of unity and love.

---

19. See, e.g., Augustine, *De trinitate*, 15.17.27–32 (2:501–8); Lombard, *Sent.*, 1.10 (110–14); Richard of St. Victor, *La Trinité*, trans. Gaston Salet, SC 63 (Paris: Cerf, 1999), 5.23 (358–62); 6.6, 14 (386–88, 412–16); Bonaventure, *In Sent.*, 1.10.1 (1:194–200); Thomas Aquinas, *Scriptum super libros Sententiarum*, vol. 1, 2nd ed., ed. R. P. Mandonnet (Paris: P. Lethielleux, 1929), 1.10.1.1 (261–64); *ST*, 1.27 (4:305–6, 309–11, 313–16); 1.37 (4:387–90). For a study of the use of psychological analogies in the medieval period, see Russell L. Friedman, *Intellectual Traditions at the Medieval University: The Use of Philosophical Psychology in Trinitarian Theology among the Franciscans and Dominicans, 1250–1350*, 2 vols (Leiden: Brill, 2012).

20. One notable exception is Bartholmäus Keckermann, *Systema s.s. theologiae*, in vol. 2 of *Operum omnium quae extant* (Geneva: Petrus Aubertus, 1614), 1.3 (72–76). For common reservations, see Amandus Polanus, *Syntagma theologiae christianae* (Hanover, Germany: Johannes Aubrius, 1615), 2.2 (173); Francis Turretin, *Institutio theologiae elencticae*, 3 vols., 2nd ed. (Geneva: Samuel de Tournes, 1688), 3.29.31 (1:332); 3.31.3 (1:339).

21. See Lombard, *Sent.*, 1.10.2 (113); Aquinas, *Super Sent.*, 1.10.1.3 (266).

22. So Aquinas, *Super Sent.*, 1.18.1.2–3. Accordingly, in the order of being, the Spirit as the bond of love is the reason that the giving of salvific gifts is appropriated to the Spirit, while, in the order of knowing, the appropriation of the giving of salvific gifts to the Spirit reinforces our understanding

2. In accordance with the Spirit being the hypostatic prototype of unity, Paul instructed the Ephesians to "keep the unity of the Spirit in the bond of peace" (4:3). It is fitting here to offer a few comments on the words and grammar of this text in connection with its broader theological aspects. First, the instruction to "keep" (τηρεῖν) something implies that it is already there.[23] This coheres with Paul's forthcoming statements that ground ecclesial unity not in human effort but in God and the works of God in verses 4–6. Second, what must be kept is ἡ ἑνότης τοῦ πνεύματος. The πνεῦμα in view is not a human spirit or the collective spirit of a human community per se but rather the Holy Spirit himself. For Paul spoke not of a "πνεῦμα of unity" but of a "unity of the πνεῦμα" and clearly invoked the distinct divine persons in verses 4–6.[24] Third, τοῦ πνεύματος is a genitive of source, signifying that the unity of the church comes from the Holy Spirit and thus that the divine work of unifying the church is appropriated to the Holy Spirit. Fourth, the unity of the Spirit is kept ἐν τῷ συνδέσμῳ τῆς εἰρήνης, in the sphere of the bond that is peace (taking τῆς εἰρήνης to be a genitive of apposition). Of course, in Ephesians 2:11–22 it is Christ who secures the peace of the church by his atoning death that brings us to God and breaks down ethnic barriers. Indeed, in 2:14 Christ himself "is our peace," a statement whose meaning is filled out by Paul calling Christ "the one who makes both [Jews and gentiles] one and destroys the dividing wall, the enmity, in his flesh."

That Christ effects the unity of the church in Ephesians 2:14 while the Spirit does so in Ephesians 4:3 prompts some clarification relative to the argument of this essay. On the one hand, it is Christ's mediatorial work that procures the unity of the people of God. And in that mediatorial and reconciling work, the Father and Spirit also are active (cf. 2 Cor. 5:19; Col. 1:19–20; Heb. 9:14). On the other hand, the common activity of the Father, Son, and Spirit in unifying the church does not contradict the claim that the Spirit is the hypostatic prototype of this unity. The work of unifying

---

that the Spirit is the bond of love. The names "love" and "gift" are proper to the Spirit, while the giving of gifts, the efficient causality of which belongs to all three persons, is just appropriated to the Spirit due to his mode of procession.

23. Cf., e.g., Lynn H. Cohick, *The Letter to the Ephesians*, NICNT (Grand Rapids: Eerdmans, 2020), 247–48.

24. *Pace* the readings of Thomas Aquinas, *Super epistolam ad Ephesios lectura*, in vol. 2 of *Super epistolas s. Pauli lectura*, 8th ed., ed. R. Cai (Turin-Rome: Marietti, 1953), 4.1; and John Calvin, *Commentarius in epistolam Pauli ad Ephesios*, in vol. 51 of *Ioannis Calvini opera quae supersunt omnia*, ed. Guilielmus Baum et al. (Brunswick: Schwetschke, 1895), 4.3 (190), but with, e.g., John Chrysostom, *Homiliae XXIV in epistolam ad Ephesios*, in PG 62 (Paris: J.-P. Migne, 1862), 4.9.3 (72); Nicolaus of Lyra, *Postilla super epistolam Pauli ad Ephesios*, in *Biblia Sacra cum Glossa Ordinaria*, vol. 6 (Venice: 1611), 548. See also Ernest Best, *Ephesians*, ICC (Edinburgh: T&T Clark, 1998), 365; Cohick, *Ephesians*, 248.

may be appropriated to the Son in one place for a certain reason (i.e., he alone has the flesh by which he has reconciled us to God and each other) and then to the Spirit in another place for another reason (i.e., his coming forth from two). Yet the hypostatic exemplarity of union itself is not merely appropriated but proper to the Holy Spirit.[25] Expressions of ecclesial unity, then, can enrich our understanding of the Spirit. Believers' enactments of the church's oneness can visibly set forth something of what the Spirit is like. In the reverse, the exemplarity of the Spirit can enrich our understanding of ecclesial unity: such unity is not merely a matter of keeping unpleasant conflict at bay but also a matter of communicating in the sight of all creation the truth about the very Spirit of God.

3. The Spirit as the hypostatic prototype of love also should be considered in relation to ecclesial unity. In Ephesians 4:1–3, Paul's first instruction is for Christians to "walk worthily" of their calling. The meaning of the instruction is developed with prepositional phrases (e.g., "with all humility") and then two participial clauses: "bearing with one another in love, being eager to keep the unity of the Spirit in the bond of peace" (4:2–3). There is a parallel between "bearing with one another *in love*" and "being eager to keep the unity of the Spirit *in the bond of peace*."[26] The sphere in which we bear with one another is love, and the sphere in which we keep the unity of the Spirit is the bond of peace.[27] The parallel suggests that love is further described as a bond of peace, that which holds Christian believers together in a state of harmony: *caritas est coniunctio animorum* ("love is the union of souls") (cf. Col. 3:14).[28] Love, then, is integral to the preservation and actualization of the church's unity. And since the Spirit is the hypostatic exemplar of love, our participation in and reflection of the Spirit as love is integral to that preservation and actualization of church unity.

Regarding our participation in the Spirit as love for the sake of ecclesial unity, let me add three brief comments. First, if the love that is required is a participation in the Spirit, then, happily, it is not something that must begin from our own strength. For the Spirit, the exemplar in whom we must participate, is sent and given to us. He is not a Platonic abstraction

---

25. Cf. Aquinas, *ST*, 1.39.8 corp. (4:409), who discusses Augustine's appropriation of *unitas* to the Father, *aequalitas* to the Son, and *unio* to the Holy Spirit. In the Trinity, only the Spirit is the hypostatic bond between two persons.

26. So Best, *Ephesians*, 364–65; Cohick, *Ephesians*, 245.

27. If the prepositional phrase "in love" is indicative of the sphere in which something happens, that need not entail that love is passive. It is a sphere of activity in which believers actively seek the good of one another.

28. Aquinas, *Super Eph.*, 4.1.

but a sovereign Lord who actively comes from the Father and Son in time to transform our hearts.[29] Second, while the Spirit sovereignly moves us to love one another, his invisible mission does not eliminate human subjectivity or agency in so doing. Instead, the invisible mission involves the production and residence of a created habit of love in the soul that the Christian believer exercises (cf. Gal. 5:22–23; 2 Peter 1:3–7). In this way, we truly do participate in the Spirit and are conformed to him.[30] Thus, Richard of St. Victor:

> So what is the giving or the mission of the Holy Spirit except the infu-sion of indebted love? Therefore, the Holy Spirit is then divinely given to man, when the indebted love of the deity is breathed into the human mind. For when this Holy Spirit enters a [human] rational spirit, he inflames its affection with divine ardor and transforms it to the similitude of his own property so that it should present the love which it owes to its author. For what is the Spirit except divine fire? For every love is fire—but spiritual fire.[31]

Third, then, the acts of love that conserve ecclesial unity can enrich our understanding of the Spirit, for these acts of love display something of what the Spirit is like. In the reverse, the exemplarity of the Spirit as love can enrich our understanding of the love that conserves ecclesial unity: such love is not only for alleviating the trials of other Christians in this life but is also for conveying to the world the truth about the very character of God's Spirit.

CONCLUSION

This essay has sought to ground ecclesial unity in the saints' participation in the persons of God the Son and God the Holy Spirit, particularly the sonship of the Son and the Spirit's relation to the Father and Son, whereby he is the hypostatic exemplar of union and love. This required first discussing

---

29. It is true that the work of the invisible mission or giving of the Spirit is the conformity of the Christian to the Spirit, but the fact that it is called a divine mission or giving still signals that it is God who sovereignly does the conforming, initially implanting a new habit of love reflective of the proper character of the Spirit and subsequently working in us to increase the habit of love and its various acts.

30. This second point is linked to the discussion in Lombard's *Sentences*, 1.17.2–4 (142–43) about the Spirit himself being the love by which we love one another. See the clarifications in Bonaventure, *In Sent.*, 1.17.1.1 (1:294–96); Aquinas, *Super Sent.*, 1.17.1.1.

31. Richard of St. Victor, *La Trinité*, 6.14 (412–14).

the way in which the mission of a divine person manifests or communicates his personal property. The next section discussed the way in which the mission, especially the invisible mission, of a divine person involves the giving of a divine person in order to bring created persons into union with that divine person. In the case of the invisible giving of the Son, this giving entails conforming created persons to the Son's sonship, which then grounds the unity of the church in that the saints share the eternal love of God the Father and a common inheritance. In the case of the invisible giving of the Spirit, this giving entails conforming the saints to the Spirit as exemplar of union and love, which then grounds the unity of the church in that the saints are empowered to promote the harmony and well-being of the church.

To be fair, ecclesial unity is not grounded exclusively in the saints' participation in the Son and Spirit. There are other factors at work or at a minimum various means of participation, including the one Christian baptism into the triune name and the one bread and cup of which we all partake (1 Cor. 10:16–17; Eph. 4:5). But recognizing that ecclesial unity is grounded at least in part in our participation in the Son and Spirit has some salutary implications. Among other things, it clarifies that ecclesial unity is a gift, and one that ultimately cannot be lost. For it is anchored in God himself. Perhaps this might bring poise to situations in which external unity is hastily sought at the expense of doctrinal fidelity or frank discussion. And, equally, it might bring energy to situations in which there is indifference to ecclesial unity. For knowing that the momentum and outcome of the task lie in the hands of the Lord frees us up to play our small part in the time that he gives us.

SCRIPTURE INDEX

Scripture Index

SUBJECT INDEX

sin
   definition of, 195n45
   of the church, 185–89, 194–95
Sixtus IV, Pope, 162
Skobtsova, Mother Maria, 96
solus Christus, 78
Stang, Dorothy, 97
subjectivism, 136
suffering
   as displacement, 168, 179
   faithful, 181
   as mark of apostolicity, 19, 161,
      165–73, 176–78, 179, 180, 183
   purposes of, 180
   as sign of salvation, 173, 175
   unity of Christ with the church in,
      76–78
totus Christus, 69–70, 72n13
transitivity of identity, 202, 204
unity
   faith as requirement for in the
      church, 216–17, 219
   and fellowship of the triune God, 225
   of the church as a sign of God's
      love, 20, 232, 239–40, 240n17
   of the church through participation

in God the Son and God the
      Holy Spirit, 231, 236–44
   of the church through shared
      commitment to Jesus, 18, 147,
      148, 153–57, 211, 214, 215–17,
      228, 229
   of the church with Jesus, 17, 66–80,
      67n4, 72n13
universalism, 108–11, 108n24, 109n27,
      111n36
Vaudois, the, 166, 176
via moderna, 162
vine, the
   ecclesiology of model of, 119,
      125–28
   metaphor of, 121–22
   as model of indwelling spirit, 119,
      122–23
   theological implications of model
      of, 119, 123–25
Waldensians, the, 166, 174n65, 175, 176
William of Ockham, 162–63
witness, manifold, 119, 127–28
women, preaching of, 175
worldliness, 93–94
Wyclif, John, 161, 162, 165

AUTHOR INDEX